Leeds Studies in English

New Series XLVI

© *Leeds Studies in English* 2017
School of English
University of Leeds
Leeds, England

ISSN 0075-8566
ISBN 978-1-84549-707-1

Copyright

All rights reserved. No part of this publication may be reproduced in any material form (including photocopying or storing it in any medium by electronic means, and whether or not transiently or incidentally to some other use of this publication) without the written permission of the copyright owner, except in accordance with the provisions of the Copyright, Designs and Patents Act 1988, or under terms of a licence issued by the Copyright Licensing Agency Ltd, 33-34, Alfred Place, London WC1E 7DP, UK. Applications for the copyright owner's permission to reproduce part of this publication should be addressed to the Publishers.

Printed in the UK

Publishing Office
Abramis Academic
ASK House
Northgate Avenue
Bury St. Edmunds
Suffolk
IP32 6BB

Tel: +44 (0)1284 700321
Fax: +44 (0)1284 717889
Email: info@abramis.co.uk
Web: www.abramis.co.uk

Leeds Studies in English

New Series XLVI

2015

Edited by

Alaric Hall

Reviews editor
N. Kıvılcım Yavuz

Leeds Studies in English

<www.leeds.ac.uk/lse>
School of English
University of Leeds
2015

Leeds Studies in English

<www.leeds.ac.uk/lse>

Leeds Studies in English is an international, refereed journal based in the School of English, University of Leeds. *Leeds Studies in English* publishes articles on Old and Middle English literature, Old Icelandic language and literature, and the historical study of the English language. After a two-year embargo, past copies are made available, free access; they can be accessed via <http://www.leeds.ac.uk/lse>.

Editorial Board: Catherine Batt, *Chair*
                         Venetia Bridges
                         Marta Cobb
                         Alaric Hall, *Editor*
                         Paul Hammond
                         Oliver Pickering
                         Helen Price
                         Slavica Ranković
                         N. Kıvılcım Yavuz *Reviews Editor*

Notes for Contributors

Contributors are requested to follow the *MHRA Style Guide: A Handbook for Authors, Editors, and Writers of Theses*, 2nd edn (London: Modern Humanities Research Association, 2008), available at <http://www.mhra.org.uk/Publications/Books/StyleGuide/download.shtml>.

Where possible, contributors are encouraged to include the digital object identifiers or, where a complete free access text is available, stable URLs of materials cited (see *Style Guide* §11.2.10.1).

The language of publication is English and translations should normally be supplied for quotations in languages other than English. Each contributor will receive a free copy of the journal, and a PDF of their article for distribution. Please email all contributions to <lse@leeds.ac.uk>.

Reviews

Copies of books for review should be sent to the Editor, *Leeds Studies in English*, School of English, University of Leeds, Leeds LS2 9JT, United Kingdom.

Contents

Kinsmen Before Christ, Part II: The Anglo-Saxon Transmission   1
      P. S. Langeslag   *University of Göttingen*

Saint as Seer: Structure and Style in Ælfric's Life of St Cuthbert   19
      Hiroshi Ogawa   *University of Tokyo*
                                                      (emeritus)

The Virgin's Kiss: Gender, Leprosy, and Romance in the Life of Saint   38
Frideswide
      Gary S. Fuller   *Brigham Young University*

The Terror of the Threshold: Liminality and the Fairies of *Sir Orfeo*   57
      Piotr Spyra   *University of Łódź*

Þjalar-Jóns saga: A Translation and Introduction   73
      Philip Lavender   *University of Copenhagen*

Reviews:

Geraldine Barnes, *The Bookish Riddarasögur: Writing Romance in*   115
Late Mediaeval Iceland. Odense: University Press of Southern
Denmark, 2014
      [Sheryl McDonald Werronen]

Carolyn P. Collette, *Rethinking Chaucer's 'Legend of Good Women'*.   117
York: York Medieval Press, 2014
      [Pelia Werth]

Elizabeth Cox, Liz Herbert McAvoy and Roberta Magnani,   119
Reconsidering Gender, Time and Memory in Medieval Culture.
Cambridge: Brewer, 2015
      [Benjamin Pohl]

Kinsmen Before Christ, Part II

The Anglo-Saxon Transmission

P. S. Langeslag

The first of this pair of articles defined the core of the homiletic motif 'no aid to kin'[1] as '(1) one kinsman being unable or unwilling to help another in (2) an eschatological setting referenced by way of (3) a deictic word or phrase [such as] the locative adverb *þær*'.[2] Using a stemmatic model of motif derivation based on the traditional text-critical method, it proposed that the motif reached Germanic authors by the routes visualised in Figure 1. This second part of the series turns to the motif's dissemination in Anglo-Saxon England, seeking to establish further its routes of transmission and put the model of local stemmatics to the test within the narrower textual confines of Old English homiletics. It concludes with a stemmatic visualisation of the arguments of both articles, and appendices providing a full list of attestations of the motif and an index to the English homilies (including alternative titles to the *Dictionary of Old English* short titles used in the body of this article).

Anglo-Saxon attestations

In a narrower reading of the above definition, the motif is found in eight distinct Old English texts, all homilies, across fourteen manuscripts. I have provided translations of the first two (*HomU 55* (traditionally referred to as the 'Macarius Homily') and *HomM 8*), but in view of the large number of close variants presented in this section, English attestations will not be translated from this point onwards. Readers unable to make out the subtleties of language in these variants are advised to keep these initial translations of the motifs in mind as the argument unfolds.

---

[1] See Patrizia Lendinara, '"frater non redimit, redimet homo...": A Homiletic Motif and its Variants in Old English', in *Early Medieval English Texts and Interpretations: Studies Presented to Donald G. Scragg*, ed. by Elaine Treharne and Susan Rosser (Tempe, AZ: ACMRS, 2002), pp. 67–80.

[2] P. S. Langeslag, 'Kinsmen Before Christ, Part I: The Latin Transmission', *Leeds Studies in England*, 45 (2014), 34–48 (p. 35).

Ne mæg þær þonne gefultmian se fæder þæm suna, ne se suna þæm fæder, ac sceal þonne anra gehwilc æfter his agenum gewyrhtum beon demed. (*HomU 55*, ll. 27–29)[3]

('A father will then not be able to help his son there, nor a son his father, but each will then be judged according to his own works.')

Eala, man þe þis gehyrst þæt ic ðe secge, þæt on þære stowe þe fæder ne gehelpð his suna, ne him to nane gode beon ne mæg, ne suna þam fæder, ne moder þæra dohter, ne nan oðer freond ne mæg to nane helpe, ne þær naht elles nis gehyred butan wanung and granung and gristbitung of toþe. (*HomM 8*, ll. 58–62)[4]

('O you man who hears this that I am telling you, that in that place a father does not help his son, nor may he be of any use to him, nor a son to his father, nor a mother to her daughter, nor may any other friend [be] of any help, nor is anything heard there but wailing, groans, and the gnashing of teeth.')

Þær se broðor ne mæg þam oðrum helpan ne se fæder þam suna, ne þa neahmagas ne ða maðmgestreon ne þysse woruldæhta ænigne man þær gescyldan magon. Ac Drihten gyldeð anra gehwylcum menn æfter his sylfes gewyrhtum. (*HomS 44*, ll. 98–101)[5]

Þær ne ongyt se fæder þone sunu ne se sunu þone fæder ne wyrðað, ne seo dohtor þa modor ne lufað ne seo modor þære dehter ne miltsað. Ac anra gehwilc hys sylfes yrmða wepað and heofað. (*HomS 44*, ll. 115–18)

Þer se broþer þam oþrum ne mæg gehelpan, ne se fæder þam suna, ne þa neahmagas ne þa madmgestreon. Ne þysse worulde æhta ænigne man þer gescyldan ne mæg oþrum. Ac Drihten gyldeþ anra gehwylcum men æfter his sylfes gewyrhtum. (*HomS 33*, 134.22–26)[6]

Ðer ne ongit se feder þone sunu; ne se sunu þone fæder ne wurðaþ; ne seo dohter þa modor ne lufað; ne seo moder þa dohter ne miltsað. Ac anra gehwylc his sylfes yrmþa heofað. (*HomS 33*, 135.15–18)[7]

Þær þonne ne mæg se fæder helpan þam suna, ne [se] sunu þam fæder, ne nan mæg oðrum. Ac anra gehwylcum men sceal beon demed æfter his agenum gewyrhtum. (*HomU 9* (Vercelli), ll. 69–71)[8]

---

[3] 'Der Text der ae. Macarius-Homilie (Hs. A)', ed. by Hans Sauer, in *Theodulfi Capitula in England: Die altenglischen Übersetzungen, zusammen mit dem lateinischen Text*, Münchener Universitäts-Schriften: Texte und Untersuchungen zur englischen Philologie, 8 (Munich: Fink, 1978), pp. 411–16.

[4] 'Sermone di Agostino', in *Nuove omelie anglosassoni della rinascenza benedettina*, ed. and trans. by A. M. Luiselli Fadda (Florence: Felice le Monnier, 1977), pp. 139–57.

[5] 'Homily 3', ed. by Joyce Bazire and James E. Cross, in *Eleven Old English Rogationtide Homilies* (Toronto: University of Toronto Press, 1982), pp. 40–55.

[6] 'Bittwochen-Predigt aus Hatton 116', ed. by Max Förster, in 'Der Vercelli-Codex CXVII nebst Abdruck einiger altenglischer Homilien der Handschrift', in *Festschrift für Lorenz Morsbach*, ed. by F. Holthausen and H. Spies, Studien zur englischen Philologie, 50 (Halle: Niemeyer, 1913; repr. as a book, 1913), pp. 20–189 (pp. 128–37). For this text, and in all other citations lacking the specification page, line, or column, referencing is by page and line number.

[7] The unstressed syllable in both occurrences of *dohtor* is the editor's expansion and thus tells us nothing about source or dialect.

[8] 'Homily IV', ed. by Donald G. Scragg, in *The Vercelli Homilies and Related Texts*, Early English Text Society, 300 (Oxford: Oxford University Press, 1992), pp. 90–107. The second nominative use of *se* is not in the manuscript.

> Þær þonne ne mæg se fæder gefultumian þam suna ne se sunu ðam fæder ne dohtor þære meder ne nan mæg oðrum ac anra gehwylcum men scal beon demed æfter his agenum gewyrhtum. (*HomU 9* (CCCC 41), p. 262)[9]

> Ðær þonne ne mæg ænig man oðres gehelpan, se fæder þam suna ne se sunu þam fæder, ne seo modor þære dehter ne seo dohtor þære meder, ne nan ne mæg oðrum; ac anra gehwylcum men byð gedemed æfter his agenum gewyrhtum. (*HomU 27*, 149.27–31)[10]

> Þær he mæg nan mann oþran gehelpan, ne se fæder þam sunu, ne se sunu þam fæder, ne nan mann þær ne mæg oþrum gehelpan, ac anra gehwylcum menn þær bið gedemed æfter his agenum gewyrhtum. (*HomS 41*, ll. 25–28)[11]

> Ne byrhð se gesibba þonne gesibban þe ma þe þam fremdan. (*WHom 3*, ll. 54–55)[12]

> Ne byrhð þonne broðor oðrum hwilan ne fæder his bearne ne bearn his agenum fæder ne gesibb gesibban þe ma þe fremdan. (*WHom 5*, ll. 98–100)[13]

The majority of these texts contain all the elements of the motif in its Pseudo-Bedan form:[14] the inability (in Wulfstan's case perhaps unwillingness) of one kinsman to help another, a Judgement Day or last-days setting, and an adverb indicating location or time. Only in *HomM 8* and in the second occurrence of the motif in *HomS 33/44* do we find the infernal setting of the earlier Latin witnesses. A ninth text, the Bodley 340 copy of *HomS 4* (Vercelli Homily 9), uses a more concise implementation of the motif, likewise set in hell:[15]

> ⁊ ne mæg nan oðres gehelpan. (*HomS 4* (Bodley 340), 111.6)[16]

The Vercelli Book copy of *HomS 4* lacks a leaf at this point in the text, so the presence and form of the motif there cannot be ascertained.[17] An approximation of the motif furthermore shows up without the eschatological timeframe in *The Seafarer*,[18] but the likeness is too vague and any connection too remote for this configuration to be included in the stemmatic analysis. Wulfstan in *WHom 5* and *WHom 3* excerpted above situates the motif during the last days. However, he also included it in his *Sermo Lupi ad Anglos*, where the action is set in Wulfstan's own day. The lack of blood loyalty is here intended as evidence that the end-times are at hand:

> Ne bearh nu foroft gesib gesibban þe ma þe fremdan, ne fæder his suna, ne hwilum bearn his agenum fæder, ne broðer oðrum; ne ure ænig his lif ne fadode swa swa he sceolde, ne gehadode regollice, ne læwede lahlice; ne ænig wið oðerne getreowlice ne þohte swa rihte swa he sceolde. (*WHom 20.1*, ll. 56–61)[19]

---

[9] This text is a marginal addition to Cambridge, Corpus Christi College MS 41, running across pp. 254–80. It represents a close textual variant of *HomU 9* (Vercelli).

[10] 'XXX', ed. by A. S. Napier, in *Wulfstan: Sammlung der ihm zugeschriebenen Homilien nebst Untersuchungen über ihre Echtheit*, Sammlung englischer Denkmäler, 4 (Berlin: Weidmann, 1883; repr. with an appendix by K. Ostheeren, 1967), pp. 143–52.

[11] 'Homily 7', ed. by Bazire and Cross, pp. 90–100.

[12] 'Secundum Lucam', ed. by Dorothy Bethurum, in *The Homilies of Wulfstan* (Oxford: Clarendon, 1957), pp. 123–27.

[13] 'Secundum Marcum', ed. by Dorothy Bethurum, pp. 134–41.

[14] For a discussion of this parallel see Langeslag, 'Kinsmen Before Christ, Part I'.

[15] An edition based on the Vercelli witness may be found in Scragg, *Vercelli*, pp. 151–90.

[16] Ed. by Förster, 'Der Vercelli-Codex', pp. 100–16.

[17] See Donald Scragg, 'Napier's "Wulfstan" Homily XXX: Its Sources, Its Relationship to the Vercelli Book and Its Style', *Anglo-Saxon England*, 6 (1977), 197–211 (pp. 203–4).

[18] Lendinara, pp. 74–75.

[19] 'Larspell', ed. by Bethurum, pp. 255–60.

Two further texts excerpt from this work and copy out the same context for the motif.[20] Finally, Stephen Pelle has pointed me to a further modified match in the second homily found in the twelfth-century manuscript British Library, Cotton Vespasian A. xxii (*VespHom* 2):[21]

> Wat sceol se wrecce don. þe bufon iseȝð his hlaford þe he ȝegremed afed. under him helle muð open. abuuten him all folc. him selfe bi sandlice senne beswapen. þer ne mai non frend oðre helpe. ælc had innoh to donne an him selfe. (*VespHom* 2, p. 239)

The language of this text has undergone greater inflectional levelling than the other English texts in question and may be referred to as Middle English. This late attestation follows several of the Old English texts in its use of a Judgement Day setting.

In the four Old English texts that situate the motif exclusively at the last judgement, it was borrowed not in isolation but rather as part of a longer passage. The longest parallels to *HomU 55* are found in *HomU 9*, whose passage 'bion we symle sorgfulle [...]. Lytel is betwyh mannum ⁊ nytenum butan andgite' (58–77) corresponds to *HomU 55* 'symble beo gesorhfulle [...] þa sawle andgyt þæt nafað þæt nyten' (15–33), and *HomU 27*, which shares in the same passage ('hit is ealra wundra mæst [...] æfter his agenum gewyrhtum', 149.11–31). *HomS 41* too contains a substantial echo of this episode ('nis us nan þing selre [...] æfter his agenum gewyrhtum', ll. 16–28). *HomS 33/44* contrasts with these attestations inasmuch as it borrows only the core motif, 'þær se broðor [...] æfter his sylfes gewyrhtum' (*HomS 44* 98–101; cf. *HomS 33* 134.22–26). Its phrasing nevertheless suggests that these two witnesses, *HomS 33* and *HomS 44*, derive the motif from the same vernacular translation that also gave rise to the other attestations. *HomM 8* diverges significantly from the common form: here the adverb has become an adverbial phrase, and the setting is an infernal one, as it is for Pseudo-Augustine and Pseudo-Isidore. These differences warrant the distinct textual history outlined above, and some degree of discussion below in isolation from what will hereafter be referred to as the Macarius group after the traditional editorial name for *HomU 55*.

Situating the texts of the Macarius Group

HomU 55 is a short composite piece on penitence. It is found in between the Latin *Capitula Theodulfi* and their Old English translation in Cambridge, Corpus Christi College MS 201, a manuscript written in Exeter in the mid-eleventh century;[22] the homily has been dated to the early tenth century on lexical grounds.[23] It incorporates material from a Latin version of the vision of Macarius but opens, as was seen in the first part of this series, with a substantial section from *De paenitentia*, including the kinsmen motif,[24] for which it also draws on Pseudo-

---

[20] 'To eallum folce', ed. by Napier, pp. 128–30 (hereafter *HomU 25*); 'Be hæðendome', ed. by Napier, pp. 309–10 (hereafter *HomU 49*). The dependence of *HomU 25* on *WHom 20* is proposed in Richard Becher, *Wulfstans Homilien* (Leipzig: Sturm, 1910), p. 63; Karl Jost, *Wulfstanstudien* (Bern: Francke, 1950), pp. 199–200. For the derivation of *HomU 49* see below.

[21] 'An bispel', ed. by Richard Morris, in *Old English Homilies and Homiletic Treatises of the Twelfth and Thirteenth Centuries*, Early English Text Society, 29, 34, 2 vols (1867–68; repr. in one volume, London: Trübner, 1868), I, 230–41. Morris's text is here reproduced without diacritics.

[22] N. R. Ker, *Catalogue of Manuscripts Containing Anglo-Saxon* (Oxford: Clarendon, 1957), item 50 (pp. 90–91).

[23] Sauer, p. 94 and the literature there cited; Charles D. Wright, 'The Old English "Macarius" Homily, Vercelli Homily IV, and Ephrem Latinus, *De paenitentia*', in *Via Crucis: Essays on Early Medieval Sources and Ideas in Memory of J. E. Cross*, ed. by Thomas N. Hall, Thomas D. Hill, and Charles D. Wright (Morgantown, WV: West Virginia University Press, 2002), pp. 210–34 (pp. 213–14).

[24] Wright, 'Macarius'.

Isidore. Before Wright identified the Ephraemic source, the received view was that *HomU 55* followed a version of *HomU 9* for this material.[25] Wright assumes that this opinion was based on the fact that the account in *HomU 55* is more concise than that in the Vercelli homily, combined with the understanding that compilers working in this genre are expected to abbreviate rather than expand their material,[26] an inversion of the *lectio brevior potior* principle. The *ubi sunt*-motif of lines 61–63, meanwhile, is found not in *HomU 9*, but in comparable forms in *HomU 27* (148.28–149.9), *HomM 8* (ll. 32–43), Pseudo-Augustine (Migne, *PL* 40, col. 1355), and Pseudo-Isidore (Einsiedeln, Stiftsbibliothek MS 199 (638), p. 455; Migne, *PL* 83, col. 1224A).[27]

HomU 9 is best known as the fourth homily in the Vercelli Book,[28] a verse-interspersed homiliary produced in the southeast of England late in the tenth century.[29] Although vernacular sources for *HomU 9* were not identified until quite recently,[30] Scragg in his 1992 edition reasoned that the homiliary as a whole, with the explicit inclusion of *HomU 9*, drew on the same sources as a number of externally attested texts, a recognition that helped him situate its production in a southeastern library, which he suggested was St Augustine's Abbey, Canterbury.[31] *HomU 9*, though not the Vercelli copy itself, has been cited as a source for other homilies, including *HomU 27* and *HomU 55*.[32] As noted, its relationship to the latter was demonstrated to be the reverse in Wright's 2002 essay,[33] a reversal whose ramifications have yet to be incorporated into discussions of the wider textual field.

These ramifications include the place in the transmission history of a variant text of *HomU 9* found in the margins of CCCC 41, pp. 254–80. This witness is a generally faithful copy of all of *HomU 9* as represented by the Vercelli text, containing only minor divergences. Scragg observes that this witness shares with *HomU 55* the peculiarity that the verb *gefultumian* is used, whereas all other Old English attestations of the motif use *(ge)helpan*; he also points out that CCCC 41 contains errors not found in *HomU 55*. Mistakenly assuming that *HomU 55* followed *HomU 9* in the transmission history, Scragg reasoned that the two shared a branch, but that a parent copy of CCCC 41 must have been the source of *HomU 55*.[34] Given the understanding that the Macarius homily in fact precedes Vercelli IV in the chain of transmission, this particular objection to a direct relationship is now lost, and the aforementioned shared use of *gefultumian* between *HomU 55* and the CCCC 41 copy of *HomU 9* in fact suggests that this representation of *HomU 9* is closer to the source than that in the Vercelli Book.

---

[25] *Die Vercelli-Homilien: 1.–8. Homilie*, ed. by Max Förster (1932; repr. Darmstadt: Wissenschaftliche Buchgesellschaft, 1964), pp. 72, n. 1; 75, n. 16; 79, nn. 46–47; Ker, item 50, article 2 (pp. 90–91); Scragg, *Vercelli*, p. 87.

[26] Wright, 'Macarius', pp. 213–14.

[27] *Patrologia cursus completus: Patrologia latina*, ed. by J. P. Migne (Paris: Migne, 1844–64). As in the first part of this study, the abbreviation *PL* will hereafter be used to introduce new texts in this series, whereas the designation 'Migne' will be used when contrasting the *PL* redactions of Pseudo-Augustine and Pseudo-Isidore with manuscript readings.

[28] Vercelli, Biblioteca capitolare MS CXVII, fol. (fols 16ᵛ–24ᵛ).

[29] Scragg, *Vercelli*, xxxvii–lxxix.

[30] Cf. the empty 'sources' column in Milton McC. Gatch, 'Eschatology in the Anonymous Old English Homilies', *Traditio*, 21 (1965), 117–65 (p. 139).

[31] Scragg, *Vercelli*, pp. lxxiv–lxxix; cf. xxxvii–xxxviii.

[32] Scragg, 'Napier XXX'; *Vercelli*, pp. 87–89.

[33] Wright, 'Macarius'.

[34] Scragg, *Vercelli*, p. 87.

CCCC 41 was produced in the first half of the eleventh century, and the homily was added no later than the middle of that century, along with several further marginal texts in the same hand.[35] It thus postdates the composition of the Vercelli Book. In addition to its use of the verb *gefultumian*, CCCC 41 is of interest because it adds the phrase 'ne dohtor þære meder', otherwise found only in *HomU 27* and, with the reverse syntactic relationship, in *HomM 8*.

HomU 27 has received a good deal of attention for its composite nature. Among its proposed sources are *HomU 26*, *HomU 55*, four Vercelli homilies including *HomU 9* and *HomS 4*, the prose *Solomon and Saturn*, *The Rewards of Piety*, various homilies associated with Wulfstan, and possibly *Judgement Day II* in loose paraphrase.[36] Crucially, it echoes several of Wulfstan's last writings, so that it cannot have been written before about 1020.[37] Accordingly, it was put together considerably later than the late tenth-century Vercelli Book,[38] where several of its sources come together.[39] Becher and Whitbread have suggested that *HomU 27* was compiled in Worcester, where its sole surviving copy was written in the third quarter of the eleventh century[40] and where many of the sources were available. While Becher proposes that the Worcester monk Wulfgeat both compiled the text and entered it into MS Hatton 113 about the middle of the eleventh century, Whitbread points out that the text shows no influence from material postdating Wulfstan, and that it was probably composed prior to the time of Wulfgeat's literary productivity, which began in the 1050s.[41] On the other hand, Godden takes issue with the Worcester attribution, instead suggesting mid-eleventh century Winchester as the setting for its compilation, on the grounds that an associated text was available there.[42] It is clear at any rate that *HomU 27* must be placed nearer the end of the motif's Anglo-Saxon transmission history.

The next parallel of this group to the *HomU 55* passage, *HomS 41*, uses, among other things, material from (Pseudo-)Wulfstan and especially Ælfric, including passages from the Lives of Saints.[43] Moreover, Godden has shown that *HomS 41* draws on what seems to have been a version of *HomU 27*, now lost.[44] The manuscript in which *HomS 41* survives, Cambridge, University Library MS Ii. 4. 6, was compiled in mid-eleventh century Winchester at the New Minster.[45] The homily immediately preceding *HomS 41* in the manuscript, Ker item 27,[46] which seems to have been composed by the same individual,[47] was clearly not copied straightforwardly from an exemplar but received its current form as it was being written into the manuscript. On the basis of this evidence, the composition of both homilies seems to

---

[35] Ker, item 32 (pp. 43–45).
[36] Jost, *Wulfstanstudien*, pp. 208–10; L. Whitbread, '"Wulfstan" Homilies XXIX, XXX and Some Related Texts', *Anglia*, 81 (1963), 347–64; Angus Fraser McIntosh, *Wulfstan's Prose*, Proceedings of the British Academy, 34 (London: British Academy, 1949); Scragg, 'Napier XXX'. Scragg makes a strong case against the text's dependence on either *HomU 26* or *The Rewards of Piety* ('Napier XXX', 209–10).
[37] Whitbread, p. 362; Scragg, 'Napier XXX', pp. 205–7.
[38] Ker, item 394 (pp. 460–64); Scragg, *Vercelli*, pp. xxxviii–xlii.
[39] Whitbread, pp. 354–56, 351.
[40] Ker, item 331 (pp. 391–99).
[41] Becher, p. 67; Whitbread, p. 362.
[42] Malcolm Godden, 'Old English Composite Homilies from Winchester', *Anglo-Saxon England*, 4 (1975), 57–65 (pp. 63–64).
[43] Bazire and Cross, pp. 90–93; Godden, esp. pp. 59–62.
[44] Godden, pp. 59–60, and see below.
[45] Ker, item 21 (pp. 31–35); Terence Alan Martyn Bishop, *English Caroline Minuscule*, Oxford Palaeographical Handbooks (Oxford: Clarendon, 1971), p. xv, n. 2; see also Godden, p. 58.
[46] Ker, pp. 39–40.
[47] Godden, p. 62.

have coincided with the compilation of the manuscript itself, at the Winchester New Minster around the middle of the eleventh century.[48]

The text designated *HomS 33* and *HomS 44* occurs in the homiliaries Hatton 116 (s. xii¹)[49] and CCCC 162 (c. 1020). Max Förster dated their composition to the beginning or middle of the tenth century on stylistic grounds.[50] Late eleventh-century additions to the text of Corpus 162 suggest a southeastern connection, while some of its large initials resemble those in a later eleventh-century manuscript produced in Canterbury.[51] The Hatton manuscript is in a twelfth-century West of England hand, and glosses in the tremulous hand of Worcester provide evidence as to its location in the early thirteenth century.[52]

HomS 33/44 makes use of the Latin *Apocalypse of Thomas*[53] and deploys the kinsmen motif twice, both times in isolation from the material surrounding it in other Old English witnesses. The first use of the motif fits in seamlessly with the focus in this part of the homily, which mentions the opening of the book (*HomS 44*, ll. 96–98) and the souls' bringing forth of their works (ll. 102–9). The second occurrence, just a few lines down, differs considerably in expression and configuration, and is explicitly set in hell. These differences suggest that they may derive from different sources, one closer to the other texts of this group than the other. This question will be considered in greater detail below.

Interrelations within the Macarius Group

As will be clear from the previous section, several homilies in this group have already been subjected to a considerable degree of source analysis. Known connections will now be combined with a developmental analysis of the kinsmen motif to come to a more detailed understanding of its dissemination.

The composite homily *HomS 41* has been shown to depend on a version of *HomU 27* for the kinsmen motif and the surrounding text, while that passage in turn relies on a version of *HomU 9*.[54] Crucially, however, Godden remarks that the *HomU 27* redaction used by the compiler of *HomS 41* must have differed from the surviving text, because *HomS 41* is in places closer to the antecedent source, *HomU 9*. Indeed, part of his evidence relies on the transmission of the kinsmen motif, as he observes that the words in *HomU 27* 'ne seo modor þære dehter ne seo dohtor þære meder' (149.28–29) are absent from the sequence in both *HomS 41* and *HomU 9*, at least in the Vercelli copy.[55] It may be observed, however, that the CCCC 41 redaction of *HomU 9* does contain this element, but in the abbreviated form 'ne dohtor þære meder', lacking the reciprocity which characterises this part of the motif in *HomU 27* and which is found in at least the father-and-son element in *HomU 9* (both witnesses), *HomU 55*, *HomU 27*, *HomS 41*, and *HomM 8*, but not in *HomS 4* or *HomS 33/44*. A straightforward explanation for this distribution of female agents is that CCCC 41 and

---

[48] Ibid., p. 63.
[49] Ker, item 333 (pp. 403–6).
[50] Max Förster, 'A New Version of the *Apocalypse of Thomas* in Old English', *Anglia*, 73 (1955), 6–36 (pp. 11–13).
[51] Ker., item 38 (pp. 51–56).
[52] Ibid., p. 406.
[53] See the discussion in Förster, 'The Apocalypse of Thomas'; Mary Swan, 'The Apocalypse of Thomas in Old English', *Leeds Studies in English*, n. s. 29 (1998), 333–46.
[54] Godden, pp. 59–60.
[55] Ibid.

HomU 27 share a common ancestor, a redaction of *HomU 9* within the CCCC 41 branch and a sibling to Vercelli. If this specification is kept in mind, Godden's stemma, deriving *HomS 41* from *HomU 9* by way of *HomU 27*, is indeed borne out by the kinsmen motif, as may be seen in its concluding clause:

    HomU 9:   ne nan mæg oðrum
    HomU 27:   ne nan ne mæg oðrum
    HomS 41:   ne nan mann þær ne mæg oþrum gehelpan

The development of this clause seems to have been as follows. The reading found in *HomU 9*, though clearly meaning 'nor [can] any kinsman [help] another [kinsman]' in context, is obscure when read in isolation. Either the compiler of *HomU 27* or the scribe of an intermediate copy mistook the noun *mæg* 'kinsman' for the third-person present singular form of the auxiliary verb *magan* and added the now-required negator *ne* to correct the syntax following the principle of minimal intervention. It would be unlikely for a second copyist working from the same exemplar to make both the same error and the same syntactic modification to the clause. Instead, it must be concluded that a scribe of *HomS 41*, faced with the reading of *HomU 27*, simply filled in the omitted elements of the new construction, yielding the clause quoted above. Thus these two texts are clearly closely related, both deriving from *HomU 9* through what may have been an earlier version of *HomU 27*.

Although the surviving copy of *HomS 33*, in Hatton 116, is about a century later than the CCCC 162 text of *HomS 44*, the two are mostly identical, with spelling accounting for the bulk of the variation. They diverge somewhat towards the end, a sign that a copyist gradually allowed himself to intervene more actively in the text. The text has thematic parallels elsewhere in the Old English corpus, but I have been unable to find verbal parallels, so that divergences cannot be compared against a third witness. However, *HomS 33* contains a few corrupt readings against intact readings in *HomS 44*. Thus for *HomS 44* 'næbbe ic ænig wedd to syllenne buton mine sawle' (95–96), *HomS 33* omits 'sawle' (134.19), and for *HomS 44* 'þær is ece blis and engla sang ungeswyðrod' (125–26), *HomS 33* reads 'ðer is ece bliss ⁊ engla sangum geswiþerod' (135.29). In this second passage, *HomS 33* deviates grammatically as well as conceptually, the dative form *sangum* making no syntactic sense. A derivation of *HomS 33* from *HomS 44* likewise seems warranted when 'þær is dead buton life and þystru butan leohte and hreownys butan wæstmum and sar buton frofre and yrmðu butan ende' (*HomS 44*, ll. 114–15) is shortened, conceivably by homoeoteleuton, to 'þær is dead butan life ⁊ þeostru buton leohte ⁊ hreow buton frofre ⁊ yrmþe buton ende' (*HomS 33* 135.14–15).

The first occurrence of the kinsmen motif in *HomS 33/44* differs substantially from all others, but its conclusion is a genetic match to the Macarius reading. In the core motif, *HomS 33/44* begins with fraternal aid, an element not otherwise found in the vernacular attestations except in Wulfstan, before introducing the father/son couple; in this it follows Pseudo-Ephraem. It follows up with *neahmagas* ('near relations'), resembling *mæg* as found in *HomU 9* and its descendants but not *HomU 55*, but then adds *maþmgestreon* ('treasure') and *woruldæhta* ('worldly possessions'), words found nowhere else in the kinsmen motif proper but strongly reminiscent of the sentiment found just prior to it in Pseudo-Ephraem, and displaced to a little after in *HomU 55*, that gold and silver cannot free one from or help against the torments of hell (*De paenitentia* p. 108;[56] *HomU 55*, ll. 37–40). Finally, the text

---

[56] St Gall, Stiftsbibliothek Cod. Sang. 93, pp. 99–111.

declares that the Lord will repay every man according to his works: 'ac drihten gyldeð anra gehwylcum menn æfter his sylfes gewyrhtum' (*HomS 44*, ll. 100–1; cf. *HomS 33*, 134.25–26). This statement is found in all members of the Macarius group, but only in *HomS 33/44* is the active voice used, while this text furthermore substitutes *gyldan* for *deman* and 'sylfes' for 'agenum'. These differences have all the earmarks of independent translation from the same Latin model, for which Pseudo-Ephraem is the natural candidate. Two problems remain, however, one of greater magnitude than the other. The lesser objection is that the setting of this first occurrence is emphatically Judgement Day, a match with the Macarius group but not the central eschatological image in Pseudo-Ephraem. Since some Judgement Day references do occur in *De paenitentia*, however, it is no great surprise if the *HomS 44* compiler chose to incorporate this motif into his discussion of the event. The greater problem is that *HomS 33/44* substitutes for Ephraem's conclusion to the motif the same sentiment found also in *HomU 55* and its derivatives, turning 'unusquisque stabit in ordine suo' ('everyone will stand in his own place') into an observation that God will repay everyone according to his own works. The wording is fairly close to that of the other Old English texts: the only two elements consistently different in the Macarian witnesses are the use of the active voice and the reliance on an auxiliary *sculan*. This close agreement limits the likelihood of a shared Latin model to one with rather specific Latin wording, adapting the Ephraemic text to accommodate any of the biblical 'reddet unicuique secundum opera eius' ('he will give to each according to his works') passages. However, T. S. Pattie records no such variant reading in the manuscripts of *De paenitentia*, of which he consulted nineteen.[57] Admittedly, a full collation of the 90-odd extant witnesses[58] could yet turn up such a model. However, the sources of *HomS 33/44* may more easily be determined by considering its second implementation of the motif.

The second occurrence of the core motif is found a little further down (*HomS 44*, ll. 115–18; *HomS 33*, 135.15–18), but this time the configuration of elements matches the Macarius group rather than Pseudo-Ephraem, containing as it does chiasmatic pairs of father and son, mother and daughter. The concluding statement in this text is 'ac anra gehwilc hys sylfes yrmða wepað and heofað', echoing the 'anra gehwilc' of *HomU 55*, or its impersonal derivative as found in *HomU 9*, *HomU 27*, and *HomS 41*. The mother-and-daughter pair, meanwhile, occurs not in *HomU 55* but in *HomU 27* (in the reverse order) and in CCCC 41 (without reciprocity). Remarkably, while the first occurrence has more in common with Pseudo-Ephraem but adopts the Judgement Day setting of the Macarius tradition, this second application does the opposite, following the Macarius reading but situating it in hell. A combined analysis of the two versions of the motif in *HomS 33/44* thus suggests that the compiler used both Pseudo-Ephraem and a Macarian source, not just in the creation of his text as a whole but also for each of his two applications of the motif.

The variation of verbs in the second implementation of the motif is interesting in the light of the Pseudo-Augustinian group of witnesses discussed in the companion-piece to this article, whose diction varies more than that of the Germanic attestations ('liberabit [...] fidejubebit; [...] redimat [...] succurrat' (Pseudo-Augustine, col. 1355); 'adiuuat [...] redimat [...] succurrere debeat' (Pseudo-Isidore (Einsiedeln), p. 456); 'adjuvat [...] redimat [...] succurrat' (Pseudo-Isidore (Migne), col. 1224B)). Since none of the Old English verbs accurately translates any of the Latin concepts, however, while the configuration of elements

---

[57] T. S. Pattie, 'Ephraem the Syrian and the Latin Manuscripts of *De paenitentia*', *British Library Journal*, 13 (1987), 1–27 (pp. 13–16).
[58] Ibid., p. 10.

resembles rather the Macarius formula, the Anglo-Saxon compiler probably did not have Pseudo-Augustine in mind. Instead, a connection may exist with certain Latin texts left out of consideration here because they contain more distant analogues to the motif,[59] whose choice of verbs (*diligere, honorare*) does overlap substantially with those found in *HomS 33/44* (specifically *lufian, weorþian*). It is certainly possible that the Anglo-Saxon compiler chose to incorporate the lexical variation of this secondary motif into his adaptation of the tradition here discussed and contained in his primary sources.

With Latin witnesses of the Pseudo-Augustinian group discarded as possible sources, we are left in *HomS 33/44* with echoes of Pseudo-Ephraem (for the core motif of the first implementation and the setting of the second) and the Macarius group (for the conclusion and setting of the first implementation and the configuration of the elements in the second), supplemented perhaps with the associated motif found in Paulinus of Aquileia and others (for the choice of verbs in the second implementation). The author did not follow any one source slavishly but freely allowed lexical and grammatical modifications, making it especially difficult to determine his precise models. Nevertheless, the closest matches to the second implementation are *HomU 27* and CCCC 41. The closest match to the conclusion of the first implementation is *HomU 27*, since it too lacks the auxiliary *sculan*. A reliance of *HomS 33/44* on this branch of the tradition may therefore tentatively be posited, with the understanding that the compiler was either working from memory or deliberately paraphrasing his Macarian source.

Given this reading of the *HomS 33/44* derivation, one issue remains. If *HomS 33* is indeed a copy of *HomS 44*, this raises the question how it came to participate in the variation around the verb *magan* discussed above with reference to *HomU 9*, *HomU 27*, and *HomS 41*:

> *HomS 44*: ne þysse woruldæhta ænigne man þær gescyldan magon
> *HomS 33*: ne þysse worulde æhta ænigne man þer gescyldan ne mæg oþrum

Considered in isolation, it may seem this variation supports the precedence of *HomS 44*, as it provides a grammatical reading while *HomS 33* does not. However, the unexpected element resides in the latter's sequence 'ne mæg oþrum', which is not only grammatically confused but also identical to the tail end of the *HomU 27* reading 'ne nan ne mæg oðrum'. One is left with the impression that the *HomS 33* copyist had separate access to this text alongside his primary exemplar, though there is no need to assume he checked his memory against a manuscript of *HomU 27*.

The abbreviated occurrence of the motif in the Bodley 340 version of *HomS 4* is of some value in reconstructing the theme's transmission. As Scragg points out,[60] the genitive form 'oðres' in '⁊ ne mæg nan oðres gehelpan' is shared between this text and *HomU 27*, though the form of the clause there is 'ðær þonne ne mæg ænig man oðres gehelpan' (149.27). This peculiarity is just striking enough to suggest a genetic connection. *HomU 27*, however, despite being the later of the two, contains a much fuller version of the motif, which could not have been reconstructed on the basis of the Bodley 340 wording alone. The explanation must be one of two. The first is that the copy of *HomS 4* used by the *HomU 27* compiler had a fuller form of the motif also containing 'oðres', which was truncated, but not corrected, in the production of Bodley 340. The second explanation is that the *HomU 27* compiler, who is known to have

---

[59] Paulinus of Aquileia, *Liber exhortationis*, ch. 49, *PL* 99, col. 253B; St Gall, Stiftsbibliothek Cod. Sang. 193, pp. 230–65 (p. 262).
[60] Scragg, 'Napier XXX', pp. 203–4.

worked with a large number of sources, copied the motif from *HomU 9* but turned to *HomS 4* for the genitive object only. This latter scenario is proposed by Scragg, who points out that this method (which he suggests is carried out 'unthinkingly') is employed elsewhere in the homily as well.[61] If this sounds unnecessarily complicated, it should be remembered that the first explanation does not permit us to bypass *HomU 9* either, as *HomU 27* shares with this text the substantial passage that precedes the motif. No matter how we look at it, then, the *HomU 27* compiler made use of *HomU 9* and probably *HomS 4*, but its analogue to the latter does not extend beyond the phrasal level. The most straightforward interpretation is therefore Scragg's, namely that a turn of phrase from *HomS 4* came to the compiler's mind while he was adapting material from *HomU 9*.

HomM 8

HomM 8 assumes a special position in the tradition because it clearly betrays a lineage distinct from that of the main group of Old English attestations. As was seen in the first part of this series, it reveals a close association with both Pseudo-Isidore and Pseudo-Augustine following Migne, but the manuscript evidence for the passage under investigation suggests rather that a redaction of Pseudo-Isidore closer to that in Cod. Sang. 614 was its model. The sole manuscript in which *HomM 8* is found, Cambridge, University Library MS Ii. 1. 33, was compiled late, in the second half of the twelfth century.[62] Nevertheless, Murfin adduces a balanced range of orthographical evidence to suggest that the translation was made before the twelfth century and probably before the Norman Conquest.[63]

With regard to its configuration of the kinsmen motif, *HomM 8*'s most distinctive characteristic resides in its setting. Whereas *Muspilli*, *De contemptu*, and nearly all the Old English homilies discussed above bring the motif into their discussion of Judgement Day, this text situates it in hell. The infernal setting is not surprising in the light of its generally close correspondence to the Pseudo-Augustinian tradition. It does, however, add to the evidence that it acquired the kinsmen motif separately from the other vernacular texts.

A question that remains is how *HomM 8* came to share with *HomU 27* and the CCCC 41 redaction of *HomU 9* the element of mother and daughter. With a number of witnesses it furthermore shares the grammatical confusion noted above regarding the interpretation of the form 'mæg', used as a noun ('kinsman') in *HomU 9* but interpreted as an auxiliary verb ('be able') from *HomU 27* onwards, and with varying degrees of success:

HomU 9: ne nan mæg oðrum (noun, correct)
HomU 27: ne nan ne mæg oðrum (auxiliary, awkward)
HomS 41: ne nan mann þær ne mæg oþrum gehelpan (auxiliary, correct)
HomS 44: ne þysse worulædhta ænigne man þær gescyldan magon (auxiliary, correct)
HomS 33: ne þysse worulde æhta ænigne man þer gescyldan ne mæg oþrum (auxiliary, contaminated?)
HomM 8: ne nan oðer freond ne mæg to nane helpe (auxiliary, main verb lacking)

---

[61] Ibid.
[62] Ker, item 18 (the homily is article 40, p. 26); Kathleen Much Murfin, 'An Unedited Old English Homily in MS. Cambridge, U.L. Ii. I33' (unpublished MA thesis, Rice University, 1971), pp. 3–4.
[63] Murfin, pp. 4–9.

The participation of *HomM 8* in this confusion raises the possibility that the *HomM 8* translator may have had a preexisting Old English Macarian text physically available to him alongside the Latin source. The *HomM 8* clause may then be construed as an attempt to repair the damage done in *HomU 27*, whose reinterpretation of *mæg* as a verb had left it without a subject. *HomM 8* offers *freond* as a subject, and expands the rather too compact 'ne mæg oðrum' into 'ne mæg to nane helpe [beon]', the main verb having been dropped by a subsequent scribe. This derivation also explains the similarity between *HomM 8* and *HomU 27* in the configuration of agents (son and father, mother and daughter). Thus even the *HomM 8* compiler, who demonstrably used Pseudo-Isidore as his main source, had access to the preexisting Macarian translation of this particular passage, in a shape much like *HomU 27*.

There is another Old English exception to the Judgement Day setting of the motif, but here the shift should be understood as a late innovation. The brief attestation found in the Bodley 340 redaction of Vercelli Homily 9 (*HomS 4*) inserts it into a metrical enumeration of infernal sufferings ('þar is wop […] ⁊ micel wroht', 132–35). Given the brevity of this instance of the motif, it is clear that the clause '⁊ ne mæg nan oðres gehelpan' (137) was added to the description of hell because it fits the sentiment. Since the form of the motif in this text places it firmly with the Macarius group, in which the setting is otherwise consistently Judgement Day, it may be assumed that the compiler lifted the clause from a Judgement Day context. Along with the recognition that shifts in setting occurred independently in the transmission between Pseudo-Isidore and Pseudo-Bede as well as between Pseudo-Isidore and *HomU 55*, while Otfrid and the *De virginibus* homilist both foregrounded the last judgement setting that was less prominently present in Pseudo-Ephraem, the shift back to hell in *HomS 4* is further evidence that such a transformation of detail was editorially commonplace.

Wulfstan

The motif occurs in five texts by Wulfstan: *WHom 3, 5, 20* (*Sermo Lupi ad Anglos*), and two extracts from the last of these, *HomU 25* and *49*. With the exception of the last-mentioned text, all survive in multiple manuscripts. The wording across the five versions is fairly uniform and contrasts with that of all other surviving witnesses. Accordingly, it merits consideration as a distinct group.

Since the status of *HomU 25* and *49* as extracts from *Sermo Lupi* is beyond doubt, Wulfstan's three earlier applications of the motif may be considered first:

> Ne byrhð se gesibba þonne gesibban þe ma þe þam fremdan. (*WHom 3*, ll. 54–55)

> Ne byrhð þonne broðor oðrum hwilan ne fæder his bearne ne bearn his agenum fæder ne gesibb gesibban þe ma þe fremdan. (*WHom 5*, ll. 98–100)

> Ne bearh nu foroft gesib gesibban þe ma þe fremdan, ne fæder his suna, ne hwilum bearn his agenum fæder, ne broðer oðrum; ne ure ænig his lif ne fadode swa swa he sceolde, ne gehadode regollice, ne læwede lahlice; ne ænig wið oðerne getreowlice ne þohte swa rihte swa he sceolde. (*WHom 20.1*, ll. 56–61)

With the kinsmen tradition in mind, it may seem obvious that *WHom 5* was not distilled from *WHom 3* but builds on a fuller representative of the tradition. Indeed, it seems natural to draw the conclusion that the form of the motif in *WHom 3* derives from that in *WHom 5*: the new, recombined configuration is identical between the two but more concise in *WHom 3*, which lacks the conventional agents that appear to tie *WHom 5* more firmly to the kinsmen tradition. However, the tenuous but persistent consensus is that *WHom 3* was written before *WHom 5*, an assumption based primarily on the understanding that Wulfstan's later works are more expansive and informed by a richer body of sources.[64] Although a general tendency of this sort does not preclude the later composition of a single less eclectic homily, it will be seen that a reconsideration of Wulfstan's chronology is not necessary to make sense of his sequence of readings.

Making no reference to the kinsmen tradition, Karl Jost in 1932 derived the sequence in *WHom 5* directly from Matthew 10:21:[65]

> Tradet autem frater fratrem in mortem, et pater filium; et insurgent filii in parentes, et morte eos adficient.
>
> ('But a brother will consign his brother to death and a father his son, and sons will rise up against their parents and put them to death.')

Although this is a plausible source by its own strength, a knowledge of the kinsmen tradition renders Jost's derivation doubtful. Pseudo-Ephraem's *non liberare* and especially the phrase *ne gescyldan* ('not shield/protect') in *HomS 33/44* are closer to Wulfstan's *ne beorgan* ('not protect') than Matthew's *tradere* ('hand over, betray'); moreover, the gospel does not offer a model for the pair *gesibba:gesibban* where *HomS 33/44* offers *neahmagas*, making it the likelier source. However, it is noteworthy that the passage from Matthew occurs also in Mark 13:12, the immediate context of the *WHom 5* pericope. In fact, the elements of *WHom 5* not found in *WHom 3* are precisely the elements contained in the gospel passage, and in the same order: brother:brother, father:son, son:father. As Wulfstan was contemplating the pericope for *WHom 5*, this verse would have reminded him of the similar sentiment he had adapted from a version of *HomS 33/44* in *WHom 3*; it seems he copied this in with the addition of the agents found in the gospel. Thus although a derivation of *WHom 3* from *WHom 5* may seem more straightforward, the reverse is equally plausible and is furthermore backed by the current state of Wulfstan scholarship. Finally, when writing his *Sermo Lupi*, as Jost also recognises,[66] Wulfstan based his final form of the motif on the sequence in *WHom 5*.

The two shorter Wulfstanian texts based on *Sermo Lupi* formulate the motif as follows:

> Ne bearh nu foroft gesib þam sibban þe ma þe fremdan, ne fæder his bearne, ne hwilum bearn his agenum fæder, ne broðor oðrum; ne ure ænig his lif ne fadode, swa swa he scolde. (*HomU 25*, 128.10–13)

> Ne byrhð se gesibba hwilan gesibban þe ma þe ðam fremdan, ne broðor his breðer oþre hwile, ne bearn foroft his fæder ne meder. Ne na fela manna ne healt his getrywða swa wel, swa he sceolde, for gode and for worolde. (*HomU 49*, 310.7–9)

Like *Sermo Lupi*, these versions use the motif to examine contemporary signs that the end-days are at hand. Both derive independently from that text, as both copy 'swa (swa) he sceolde' while each follows some phrasing of the antecedent text more closely than the other.

---

[64] Bethurum, pp. 101–3, 290; Milton McC. Gatch, *Preaching and Theology in Anglo-Saxon England: Ælfric and Wulfstan* (Toronto: University of Toronto Press, 1977), pp. 105–16; 'Secundum Lucam', ed. and trans. by Joyce Tally Lionarons, in *Wulfstan's Eschatological Homilies* (2000) <http://webpages.ursinus.edu/jlionarons/wulfstan/> [accessed 1 February 2015], introductory note; *The Homiletic Writings of Archbishop Wulfstan* (Woodbridge: Brewer, 2010), pp. 49–50.

[65] Karl Jost, 'Einige Wulfstantexte und ihre Quellen', *Anglia*, 56 (1932), 265–315 (pp. 302–3, n. 3).

[66] Ibid.

Vespasian Homily 2

The version of the motif contained in *VespHom 2* is brief but unique among its English peers. The context matches neither Pseudo-Ephraem nor the texts of the Macarius group; instead, the core of the motif has been inserted into a dramatic spatial positioning of the sinner at the last judgement, with a vengeful God above, the gaping mouth of hell below, and his fellow humans all around. This content, which is found without the kinsmen motif in a further homily of the same period,[67] has been linked to a similar spatial configuration of God and hell in Anselm of Canterbury's *Meditatio ad concitandum timorem*,[68] which likewise lacks the kinsmen motif.[69] The isolated borrowing of that motif may thus be attributed to the *VespHom 2* compiler.

The second half of the motif in this text departs significantly from the Macarian observation that everyone will be judged according to their own deeds. Though the conclusion in this version of the motif is no less inescapable, its emphasis is on where the individual defendants concentrate their attention rather than on personal responsibility: 'ælc had innoh to donne an him selfe' (*VespHom 2* 239.32–33). This conclusion is strikingly similar to Otfrid's aside 'sie sorgent iro thare' ('they will worry for themselves there', V. 19, l. 48). It is, however, also a common-sense inference. It may be assumed that the two authors reached it independently.

A precise derivation of the sentence in *VespHom 2* is not possible based only on the attestations here collected. Middle English *frend* ('friend; kinsman; in-law') covers equally every type of relationship found in the Latin and Old English versions. The Judgement Day setting brings us no closer to singling out a source, although this scene sets *VespHom 2* a little apart from the attestation in *HomM 8*, which is set in hell. Finally, the conclusion of the motif in the Middle English text has no resemblance to any Old English or Latin counterpart.

The phrasing of the core motif in *VespHom 2* is remarkably close to that found across the Macarius group, yet not so close as to have been copied out verbatim from a text looking very much like any of the surviving versions. Of course, the motif's productive survival into the twelfth century suggests a lost intermediary tradition whose verbal proximity to the surviving text cannot be demonstrated. However, given the short form of the motif in *VespHom 2*, its development of a new and unconnected conclusion, and the precise fit between the motif and its context here, it seems more likely that the compiler while at work transmitting the spatial judgement motif saw fit to copy in an appropriate ancillary motif from memory.

A thematic stemma may now be posited for the kinsmen motif, for which see Figure 2.

Conclusions

By its nature, stemmatics favours simplicity. It seeks to derive a plurality of nodes from a single archetype, and prefers to award every node a single parent. Accordingly, a close analysis of the sort here conducted is bound to conclude that reality is more complex. Part I of this article series drew attention to the existence of parallel independent development across branches of the kinsmen tradition, a pattern that can doubtlessly be found in the transmission history of

---

[67] See Stephen Pelle, 'Continuity and Renewal in English Homiletic Eschatology, *ca.* 1150–1200' (unpublished doctoral dissertation, University of Toronto, 2012), pp. 167–68.
[68] Ed. by F. S. Schmitt, in *S. Anselmi Cantuarensis opera omnia*, 2nd edn, 6 vols (Stuttgart: Frommann, 1984), III, 76–79.
[69] Schmitt, pp. 78–79; Pelle, pp. 167–68.

any widely copied motif. The present article adds to this the high incidence of contamination, when homiletic compilers rely on multiple sources to synthesise different versions of the same motif.

Scragg has previously proposed that contamination took place when the kinsmen motif was transmitted from *HomU 9* to *HomU 27* with memory relay of a grammatical construct from *HomS 4*. I have adduced evidence in the present article that the compiler of *HomU 55* had access to manuscript copies of both Pseudo-Ephraem and Pseudo-Isidore, which he combined in his rendering of the kinsmen motif, while the *HomM 8* compiler seems to have read *HomU 27* as well as Pseudo-Isidore. I have also shown that the *HomS 44* compiler appears to have worked directly with Pseudo-Ephraem but additionally echoes the motif's phrasing as found in the Macarius group, while its copyist in *HomS 33* seems to have had access to a text like *HomU 27* as well. Finally, Wulfstan appears to have merged a shorter version of the motif with elements of a gospel passage, thereby independently restoring it to a fuller length. Thus among the twenty-two textual nodes here consulted, fourteen of which are Anglo-Saxon, at least six may synthesise multiple sources in the transmission of the same motif. This finding sheds light not only on methods of homiletic compilation, but also on the availability of Latin and vernacular homilies in Anglo-Saxon England and the homilists' familiarity with them.

Above all, the complexity of the textual network here uncovered serves as a warning about the pitfalls of textual stemmatics in general and local stemmatics in particular. As the Wulfstan material demonstrates, derivation principles are especially unreliable if applied to short passages; as the kinsmen material at large suggests, authors frequently used more sources than we can account for. Indeed, we will often misread the signs, and my stemma is not meant as a reliable map of this motif's dissemination. Even so, the speculative science of local stemmatics is able to provide some insight into the spread of motifs from author to author, and consequently has a modest role to play in the field of source studies.

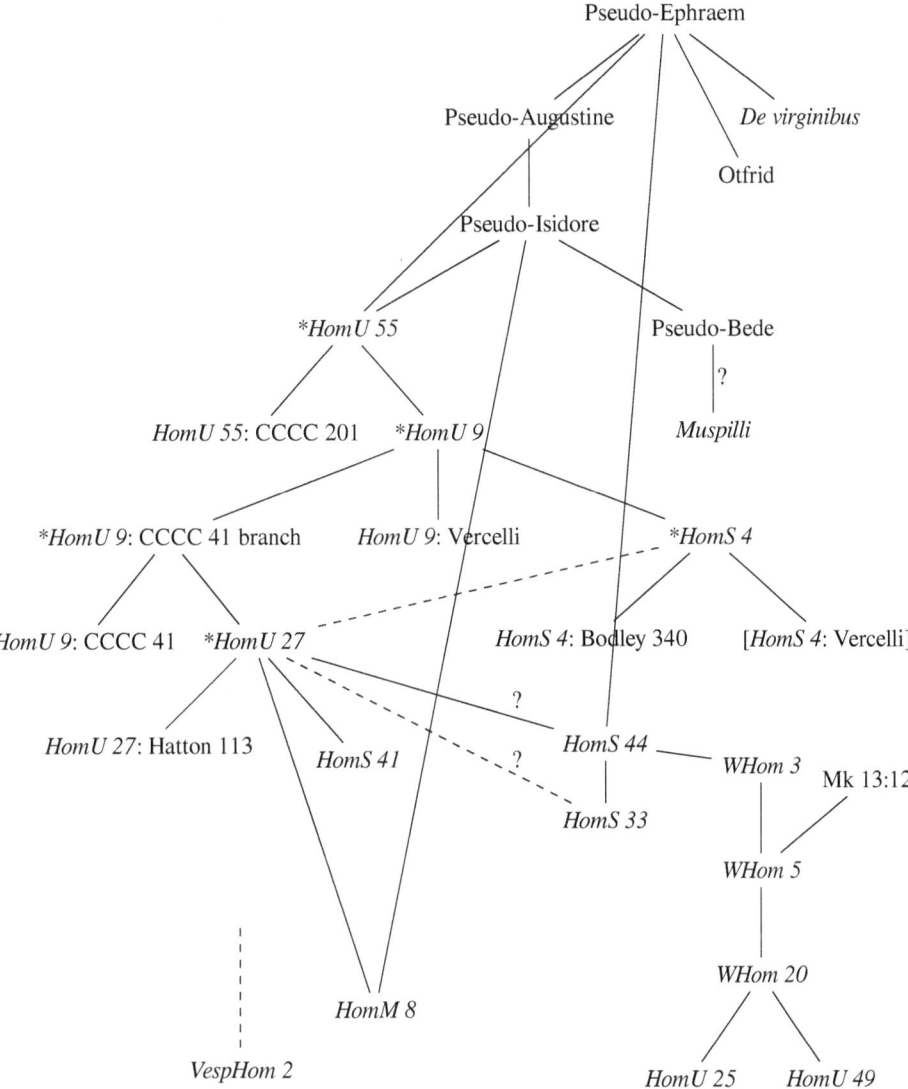

Figure 2: Full stemma. Asterisks indicate reconstructed witnesses; dashed lines indicate transmission by memory; square brackets indicate that the motif does not survive in the Vercelli copy of *HomS 4*. The immediate source of *VespHom 2* is uncertain, but it seems to derive from the *HomU 9* branch.

Appendix 1: configurations of the motif

Text	Setting	Verb	Agents:Beneficiaries
De paenitentia (Pseudo-Ephraem)	hell; (last judgement)	*liberare*	frater:fratrem; pater:filium
Sermo LXVI ad fratres in eremo (Pseudo-Augustine)	hell	*liberare*	pater:filium; filius:patre; amicus; frater
Sermo III (Pseudo-Isidore)	hell	*adiuvare*	pater:filium; filius:patrem; amicus:amicum; frater:fratri
Versus de contemptu mundi (Pseudo-Bede)	last judgement	*adiuvare*	pater:filium; filius:patrem
Evangelienbuch (Otfrid)	last judgement	*helfan*	manahoubit:hereren; kind; quene; themo filu richen manne
Muspilli	last days	*helfan*	mak:andremo
HomU 55	last judgement	*gefultumian*	fæder:suna; suna:fæder
HomU 9: Vercelli	last judgement	*helpan*	fæder:suna; sunu:fæder; nan mæg:oðrum
HomU 9: CCCC 41	last judgement	*gefultumian*	fæder:suna; sunu:fæder; dohtor:meder; nan mæg:oðrum
HomS 4: Bodley 340	hell	*gehelpan*	nan:oðres
HomU 27	last judgement	*gehelpan*	ænig man:oðrum; fæder:suna; sunu:fæder; modor:dehter; dohtor:meder; nan:oðrum
HomS 41	last judgement	*gehelpan*	nan mann:oþran; fæder:sunu; sunu:fæder; nan mann:oþrum
HomS 44, first occ.	last judgement	*helpan*	broðor:oðrum; fæder:suna; neahmagas; maðmgestreon; woruldæhta
HomS 44, second occ.	hell	*ongytan* etc.	fæder:sunu; sunu:fæder; dohtor:modor; modor:dehter
HomS 33, first occ.	last judgement	*gehelpan*	broþor:oþrum; fæder:suna; neahmagas; maðmgestreon; worulde æhta
HomS 33, second occ.	hell	*ongytan* etc.	fæder:sunu; sunu:fæder; dohter:modor; moder:dohter
HomM 8	hell	*gehelpan*	fæder:suna; suna: fæder; moder:dohter; nan oðer freond
WHom 5	last days	*beorgan*	broðor:oðrum; fæder:bearne; bearn:fæder; gesibb:gesibban
WHom 3	last days	*beorgan*	gesibba:gesibban
WHom 20.1	present time	*beorgan*	gesib:gesibban; fæder:suna; bearn:fæder; broðer:oðrum
HomU 25	present time	*beorgan*	gesib:sibban; fæder:bearne; bearn:fæder; broðor:oðrum
HomU 49	present time	*beorgan*	gesibba:gesibban; broðor:breðer; bearn:fæder/meder
VespHom 2	last judgement	*helpen*	non frend:oðre
De virginibus	last judgement	*gehelfen*	niemen:dem anderen

Table 1

Appendix 2: index of English homilies

(*DOE*) Short Title	Traditional Title	Editor; *Manuscripts*	Passages Discussed
HomM 8	Fadda VII	Fadda, pp. 139–57 *CUL Ii. 1. 33*	32–61
HomS 4 (Bodley 340)	Vercelli IX (Bodley 340)	Förster, 'Der Vercelli-Codex', pp. 100–16 *Bodley 340*	111.6
HomS 33		Förster, 'Der Vercelli-Codex', pp. 128–37 *Hatton 116*	131.3–134.13 134.19–135.4 135.14–18 135.29
HomS 41	Bazire–Cross VII	Bazire and Cross, pp. 90–100 *CUL Ii. 4. 6*	16–28
HomS 44	Bazire–Cross III	Bazire and Cross, pp. 40–55 *CCCC 162*	53–88 95–101 115–18 125–26
HomU 9	Vercelli IV	Scragg, *Vercelli*, pp. 90–107 *Vercelli; CCCC 41*	58–77
HomU 25	Napier 27	Napier, pp. 128–30 *CCCC 201; Cot. Tib. A. 3*	128.10–13
HomU 27	Napier XXX	Napier, pp. 143–52 *Hatton 113*	148.28–149.31
HomU 49	Napier LX	Napier, pp. 309–10 *York Minster*	310.7–10
HomU 55	Macarius Homily; *Ecclesiastical Institutes*; *Canons of Theodulf*	Sauer, pp. 411–16 *CCCC 201*	12–30 55–57 69–112
VespHom 2	Vespasian Homily 2	Morris, I, 230–41 *Cott. Vesp. A. xxii*	1.239
WHom 3	*Secundam Lucam*	Bethurum, pp. 123–27 *3 MSS (see Bethurum, p. 123)*	54–55
WHom 5	*Secundum Marcum*	Bethurum, pp. 134–41 *3 MSS (see Bethurum, p. 134)*	98–100
WHom 20.1	*Sermo Lupi ad Anglos*	Bethurum, pp. 255–60 *5 MSS (see Bethurum, pp. 22–24)*	56–61

Table 2. Short referencing for Old English homilies (but not *VespHom 2*) follows the practice in *Dictionary of Old English: A to G Online*, ed. by Angus Cameron and others (2007) <http://tapor.library.utoronto.ca/doe/> [accessed 1 February 2015].

Saint as Seer: Structure and Style in Ælfric's Life of St Cuthbert

Hiroshi Ogawa

Ælfric's life of St Cuthbert, which is the tenth item in the Second Series of *Catholic Homilies* (*Depositio Sancti Cuthberhti Episcopi*; the *Dictionary of Old English* short title *ÆCHom* II, 10),[1] has been a focus of Ælfrician scholarship chiefly owing to the position it holds in the development of the homilist's prose style. It is the first work in Ælfric's outstanding career as a vernacular prose writer in which he experiments in a sustained manner with the new style of rhythmical prose for which he was to become a renowned master in his subsequent writing. In J. C. Pope's words, this prose style 'emerges first in certain homilies of Ælfric's Second Series. [...] The Cuthbert homily, which occurs first in the set, may be among the earliest in date of composition and certainly exhibits an interesting mixture.'[2] Pope's full analysis of the prose in the Cuthbert homily, both in relation to the homilist's 'ordinary prose', which precedes it, and his rhythmical prose in its mature form, shows clearly how important the homily is as an experimental stage. This importance, however, should not draw attention away from other dimensions of the work that are equally important in considering Ælfric's prose style. In a seminal study of Ælfric's hagiographies in the *Catholic Homilies*, M. R. Godden has persuasively argued that the homilist's experimentation with rhythmical prose is part of the emergence of a new pattern that clearly points to his 'change of heart' about hagiography. While his earlier saints' lives such as those of John the Apostle and Peter and Paul use a narrative that is interspersed with passages where Ælfric the homilist has almost replaced Ælfric the narrator, later lives within the *Catholic Homilies* and those in the *Lives of Saints* for which they set the pattern 'concentrate on narrative rather than preaching and debate' and 'use the universalizing hagiographic diction and employ the balanced, succinct, rhythmical style'.[3] Godden convincingly shows that the Cuthbert homily is one of these later saints' lives. This

---

[1] *Ælfric's Catholic Homilies: The Second Series*, ed. by Malcolm Godden, Early English Text Society, s. s. 5 (London: Oxford University Press, 1979), pp. 81–91.

[2] *Homilies of Ælfric: A Supplementary Collection*, ed. by John C. Pope, Early English Text Society, o. s. 259–60, 2 vols (London: Oxford University Press, 1967–68), I, 113.

[3] M. R. Godden, 'Experiments in Genre: The Saints' Lives in Ælfric's *Catholic Homilies*', in *Holy Men and Holy Women: Old English Prose Saints' Lives and Their Contexts*, ed. by Paul E. Szarmach (Albany, NY: State University of New York Press, 1996), pp. 261–87 (p. 280). As for the earlier saints' lives, I have examined the one on Peter and Paul in 'Hagiography in Homily — Theme and Style in Ælfric's Two-Part Homily on SS Peter and Paul', *Review of English Studies*, 61 (2010), 167–87. On the homily on John the Apostle, see Godden, 'Experiments in Genre', pp. 266–69.

perspective suggests the importance of considering the Cuthbert homily in a different light by discussing its stylistic features in relation to the style of hagiographical narrative, rather than as a problem of prose style *per se*. In particular, it stimulates a reconsideration of the homily focusing on Ælfric's narrative technique in it: how, apart from experimenting with rhythmical prose, does he adapt the hagiographical material to the larger end of a preaching homily and its overall structure, when he has abandoned the homiletic discourse in the relevant writing? Following this line of approach, I shall examine the full details of the homily's narrative and discuss how the style enhances its structure in a way that attests to the working of a conscious stylist.

In considering the structure and style of Ælfric's Cuthbert homily, we must first understand clearly the preceding works he used as sources for creating a new life of the saint. Here, the situation is rather complicated. There are three Latin *Vitae* of the saint: the prose *Vita* by an anonymous monk of Lindisfarne, Venerable Bede's *Vita* in verse, and his own expansion of it in prose, all written not long after the saint's death,[4] with part of this last work later included in a few chapters of the *Historia ecclesiastica* (Bk IV, chs. 27–32). Ælfric seems to have had all of these available in one way or another for his use, and which of them he used as his source has been a matter of dispute. However, it is now generally agreed that Bede's metrical *Vita* is Ælfric's main source, which he supplements mostly with Bede's prose *Vita* and occasionally with the anonymous *Vita* and the *Historia*. Thus, in his introductory note to the homily Godden speaks of Ælfric's 'primary use of Bede's verse Life', adding 'that the parallels with the anonymous Life [...] are clearly there, and that there are also definite borrowings from Bede's prose Life for the material that is not reproduced in the *Historia*'[5] — a view which is partly based on the evidence adduced by Gordon Whatley.[6] The conclusion the two scholars share and the details Godden gives of the closest parallels between the *Vitae* and individual passages from Ælfric's Life serve as the point of departure for my analysis of this Old English homily.

Godden goes on in his introductory note to ask about Ælfric's homily and its sources: 'how much did the different structures and stylistic techniques of the three lives affect his own writing?'[7] Godden does not dwell on this problem but mentions Bede's verse Life as the main influence upon Ælfric's structuring:

---

[4] The short titles for the three are, respectively, *VCA*, *VCM*, and *VCP*, as commonly used. The editions of the *Vitae* used in this study are *Bedas metrische Vita Sancti Cuthberti*, ed. by Werner Jaager (Leipzig: Mayer & Müller, 1935), and *Two Lives of Saint Cuthbert*, ed. and trans. by Bertram Colgrave (Cambridge: Cambridge University Press, 1940). The translations of the passages from the two prose *Vitae* cited below are Colgrave's in this latter book.

[5] *Ælfric's Catholic Homilies: Introduction, Commentary and Glossary*, ed. by Malcolm Godden, Early English Text Society, s. s. 18 (Oxford: Oxford University Press, 2000), pp. 412–13.

[6] E. Gordon Whatley and others, 'Acta Sanctorum', in *Abbo of Fleury, Abbo of Saint-Germain-des-Prés, and Acta Sanctorum, Sources of Anglo-Saxon Literary Culture I*, ed. by F. M. Biggs and others (Kalamazoo, MI: Western Michigan University, 2001), pp. 22–486 (p. 159). On Ælfric's sources, see also Mechthild Gretsch, *Ælfric and the Cult of Saints in Late Anglo-Saxon England*, Cambridge Studies in Anglo-Saxon England, 34 (Cambridge: Cambridge University Press, 2005), pp. 101–7. Gretsch gives another dimension to the study of the Cuthbert homily by considering it and its sources in the context of the cult of the saint which developed in England in the few centuries before the eleventh century. She argues that the homily shows Ælfric 'specifically aiming to promote the cult' (p. 101). How this aspect would have affected the structure and style of his homily is a problem I cannot consider in this study.

[7] Godden, *Commentary*, p. 413.

> Bede's verse Life is written in 46 chapters which focus on individual miracles and omit most of the context of events [...] As Lapidge says, 'it is part of Bede's purpose to remove the episodes of Cuthbert's life from the temporal and local and to situate them in a timeless, placeless framework'. [...] Ælfric clearly follows the model of Bede's verse Life as much as possible. He focuses on the miracles and gives very little sense of the context and place.[8]

This apparent parallelism prompts further questions about Ælfric's homily and its method. If such is the purpose and framework of the work that Ælfric follows as his model, how does he recast these aims in his own work as he transforms its narrative (and that of the other *Vitae*) into a homily? How much does he alter the structure of his model for his own purpose? What are the narrative and stylistic techniques he deploys to achieve his purpose? My contention in the sections that follow is that Ælfric shows a clear sense of structure designed to emphasize Cuthbert's position as one of God's elect. He places the main emphasis on the role of the saint as a seer and, in doing so, represents the saint in the early life as foreshadowing the kindly bishop that he is predestined to be, while often rearranging the events and details of events found in the *Vitae* in a way which uncovers a certain pattern of development in the hagiography. These points will become clear as we analyse his homily in comparison with the narratives in the *Vitae*.[9]

II

As Godden notes in the quotation above, of the three preceding lives of Cuthbert, the one that served as Ælfric's main source uses little overall structure in telling the story of the saint. This feature of the verse Life has been repeatedly pointed out by previous scholars. For example, Werner Jaager asserts: 'das Gedicht zeigt in seinem Aufbau keine Steigerung' ('the poem shows no climax in its structure').[10] Michael Lapidge's reference to the poem's 'timeless, placeless framework' (as quoted by Godden; see above) indicates a similar opinion, as does his concluding remark that 'it is wrong to look to this poem for narrative history of any sort'.[11] This point has been discussed more recently in greater detail by Carole E. Newlands. Comparing the verse Life with the other *Vitae*, Newlands argues convincingly that while Bede's prose life 'is developmental in its structure', his verse Life essentially 'sees the saint's career in terms of accretion, not development'. In this, it is more like the anonymous Life, which 'illustrates this given fact [of Cuthbert's predestined sainthood] through its paratactic structuring of a series of wondrous events'. 'The poetic Cuthbert', she concludes, '[...] is essentially a static character who lives out his predestined holiness', in a treatment that 'views Cuthbert's sanctity as preordained and Cuthbert himself as mature in faith almost from the beginning'.[12] Newlands also notes that the anonymous Life 'opens by establishing the notion of predestination. Bede's metrical vita elaborates on this concept by explaining at the start of this [first] episode that Christ singled out Cuthbert and guided him in his early years to

[8] Godden,*Commentary*, p. 414.
[9] Obviously, the alliterative style and other poetic features are also an important part of Ælfric's stylistic techniques in this homily, but these cannot be considered in this study except in passing.
[10] Jaager, *Bedas metrische Vita*, p. 16.
[11] Michael Lapidge, 'Bede's Metrical *Vita S. Cuthberti*', in *St Cuthbert, His Cult and His Community to AD 1200*, ed. by G. Bonner, D. Rollason and C. Stancliffe (Woodbridge: Boydell, 1989), pp. 77–93 (p. 93).
[12] Carole E. Newlands, 'Bede and Images of Saint Cuthbert', *Traditio*, 52 (1997), 73–109 (pp. 82, 84 and 91).

ensure his reception in heaven'.[13] Drawing on the representation in the *Vitae*, Ælfric phrases this notion of special election as *his gecorenan* 'God's chosen one', as he refers to Cuthbert in the first episode and the final doxology; see below and the final section.

As in Bede, from the beginning of Ælfric's homily, Cuthbert is described as a saint with preordained holiness. To be noted in this connection is the passage Ælfric adds prior to the first episode as the opening of the homily:

> *ÆCHom* II, 10.1 Cuthberhtus se halga biscop scinende on manegum geearnungum and healicum geðincðum. on heofenan rice mid þam ælmihtigum scyppende on ecere blisse rixiende wuldrað.
>
> (Cuthbert the holy bishop, shining with many merits and high honours, reigning in the kingdom of heaven with the Almighty Creator in everlasting blessing, lives in glory.)

Here, Ælfric gives a striking initial characterization of his protagonist saint, depicting him as a living bishop in heaven (with the present tense *wuldrað*) rather than, say, an ignorant child (with a verb in the narrative past tense); he also portrays Cuthbert as reigning with God ('mid þam ælmihtigum scyppende [...] rixiende'), emphasizing his oneness with God. These features, both unparalleled in any of the hagiographical homilies in the *Catholic Homilies*,[14] uniquely set the general tone of the homily, foreshadowing the nature of the subsequent narrative.

The notion of Cuthbert's preordained sanctity is best seen, as Newlands suggests, in the first episode, in which the eight-year-old Cuthbert is reprimanded by a God-sent boy of three years for behaving like other boys and not in a way worthy of a future bishop (ll. 7–27). Here, the closest parallel is the passage in the verse Life, and Ælfric on the whole follows it closely but makes some notable changes.[15] For instance, he makes the boy tell Cuthbert, described as 'his gecorenan' (l. 10): 'geðeod þe to gode. ðe ðe to biscope his folce geceas. þam ðu scealt heofonan rices infær geopenian' ('attach yourself to God, who has chosen you as a bishop for his people, to whom you shall open the entrance of the kingdom of heaven'; ll. 18–19), where the poetic *infans* says more plainly: 'Quid te [...] / Quem deus [...] sacravit / Praeficiens populis, caeli quibus atria pandas?' ('why [...] you whom God has consecrated, setting you over the people for whom you would lay open the dwelling of heaven?'; c. 1, 63–65). With the distinctive use of particularizing phrases such as 'to biscope [...] geceas' and 'heofonan rices infær', Ælfric represents Cuthbert's special election by God and his preordained bishopric more pointedly and with more specific details, while at the same time he uses *scealt* to represent the bishopric as unambiguously prophetic. The verse Life is vaguer about Cuthbert's bishopric and uses the subjunctive present *pandas* to refer to this future career. This direction of change has in fact been initiated in the immediately preceding reference to Cuthbert's behaviour being unworthy of a bishop; Ælfric rephrases it as a general truth using the third person pronoun ('ne gedafenað biscope þæt he beo on dædum folces mannum gelic'; 'it is not befitting to a bishop that he should be like the common people in deeds'; ll. 16–17)) and not as being directly relevant to young Cuthbert, as in the two prose *Vitae*, which use the second

---

[13] Newlands, 'Bede and Images', p. 85.
[14] With the single exception of the Cuthbert homily, Ælfric always opens his relevant homilies by referring either to the feast of his protagonist saint or the Latin author whose work is his source.
[15] B. A. Blokhuis is right to call Ælfric's lines 14–16 'an almost exact copy of the words in [*VCM*]' ('Bede and Ælfric: The Sources of the Homily on St Cuthbert', in *Beda Venerabilis: Historian, Monk and Northumbrian*, ed. by L. A. J. R. Houwen and A. A. MacDonald (Groningen: Egbert Forsten, 1996), pp. 107–38 (p. 115)). But she

person pronoun (*VCA* 64.26–27; *VCP* 156.30–158.1);[16] both prose versions also address the young Cuthbert literally as 'bishop' (*VCA* 64.25 'episcope'; *VCP* 156.30 'antistes'). All this shows that Ælfric's representation of Cuthbert's preordained bishopric is more factual, both in the specific details it gives and its unambiguous reference to the future career.

To register his emphasis, Ælfric also rearranges the details of the story.[17] Thus, in the verse Life (as in the other *Vitae*) the God-sent boy's first words of admonition are disregarded and, when given soothing kisses by young Cuthbert and told to stop his wailings, he renews his admonition with the prophecy of a bishopric for Cuthbert. Ælfric instead places the prophesying at the beginning of the boy's admonition, as quoted above, launching straightaway into the heart of the episode without even mentioning at this point Cuthbert's actions which prompted it in Bede. The significance of this rearrangement becomes clearer as we go on to find the kisses focused on at the end of the story, where we read that Cuthbert's playmates tried to soothe the child in vain, until at last 'cuðberhtus hit mid arfæstum cossum gegladode' ('Cuthbert gladdened him with kindly kisses'; ll. 24–25).[18] This last description is a close rendering of Bede's in the verse Life ('hunc pia complexum Cuthbertus ad oscula mulcet'; 'Cuthbert embraces this boy and soothes him with kindly kisses'; c. 1, 60). However, lifted from its original context, the description is endowed with a new force in Ælfric's representation, depicting the climax of the episode: young Cuthbert now makes the boy happy by giving *arfæstum* kisses — not unlike a holy man, an analogy the word *arfæstum* seems to imply. The word probably means here, as it usually does in the *Catholic Homilies*,[19] 'virtuous, honourable' rather than 'kind' (as Thorpe translates it).[20] All this suggests that Ælfric represents Cuthbert as an understanding youth (unlike Cuthbert in the anonymous Life, who did not clearly understand (64.27–66.1)) who is envisaged as a kindly bishop that he is prophesied to be. Hence perhaps Ælfric concluding the episode with a note on the effect of the event, saying that the youth for his part 'syððan [...] on healicere stæððignysse symle ðurhwunode' ('afterwards [...] always remained in intense steadiness'; ll. 26–27, with *healicere*, literally meaning 'high', possibly also suggesting holiness). This final remark, absent in the verse Life, is derived from Bede's prose Life, where the youth 'stabilior [...] animoque adolescentior existere coepit' ('began [...] to be steadier and more mature in mind'; 158.6–7). What Newlands says with respect to the representation in this version applies to Ælfric's as well: 'Cuthbert the chastised becomes the comforter, and the roles of the prophetic

---

does not take cognizance of the alteration I discuss below.

[16] The verse Life is closer to Ælfric: 'Fas erit aut vulgi antistes similabitur actis?' ('Or will it be proper that the bishop should resemble the deeds of the common people?'; c. 1, 67). For analyses and interpretations of this episode in the *Vitae*, see Newlands, 'Bede and Images', pp. 84–86; Eric Knibbs, 'Exegetical Hagiography: Bede's Prose *Vita Sancti Cuthberti*', *Revue Bénédictine*, 114 (2004), 233–52 (pp. 240–41).

[17] For details, see Godden, *Commentary*, p. 416, note on lines 7–27.

[18] On the word *arfæstum*, see below.

[19] Ælfric uses the adjective fourteen times in the *Catholic Homilies*, mostly in reference to God and holy saints or with such nouns as *weorc*, *dæd* and *geleafa*. The *Dictionary of Old English* (s.v. *arfæst*) distinguishes two senses with some subdivision: '1. pious, dutiful; virtuous, honourable; 2. merciful, compassionate; kind, benevolent, gracious', citing under 1 three examples from the *Catholic Homilies*; on the other hand, the one example of the second sense from Ælfric refers to God. Blokhuis ('Bede and Ælfric', p. 115) translates the word as 'honourable'.

[20] *The Homilies of the Anglo-Saxon Church: The First Part, Containing the Sermones Catholici or Homilies of Ælfric*, ed. by Benjamin Thorpe, 2 vols (London: Ælfric Society, 1844–46; repr. New York: Johnson Reprint, 1971), II, 135.

child and the schoolboy are dramatically reversed.'[21] Ælfric intensifies the reversal with his rearrangement and vocabulary.

The kindly, virtuous bishop which the young Cuthbert is predestined to become may be seen at different points in the subsequent narrative, but most prominently in the well-known passage where he, while still a monk, prays at night on the shores (ll. 74–94). Part of the interest of the passage lies in its diction, including 'on ðam sealtan brymme' ('in the salt sea'; l. 75) and 'on fealwun ceosle' ('on the yellow sand'; l. 85).[22] But more important, in terms of the figure of a future bishop, is the use of distinct patterns of syntax whereby Ælfric gives a contrastive treatment to the kindliness that the holy youth shows to the two different parties surrounding him — the sea-animals, on one hand, coming from the depths, obediently drying and warming him with their fur and breath and asking for his blessing, and, on the other, a spy monk who is curious about his nocturnal walks and watches him. The first half describes Cuthbert and the seals using largely parallel clauses marked by two shared features, which are the adverb *syððan* and a participial construction:

> ÆCHom II, 10.78 Ða dyde cuþberhtus swa his gewuna wæs. sang his gebedu on sælicere yðe. standende oð þone swyran. and syððan his cneowa on ðam ceosle gebigde. astrehtum handbredum to heofenlicum rodore; Efne ða comon twegen seolas of sælicum grunde. and hi mid heora flyse his fet drygdon. and mid heora blæde his leoma beðedon. and siððan mid gebeacne his bletsunge bædon. licgende æt his foton on fealwun ceosle; Þa cuðberhtus ða sælican nytenu on sund asende. mid soðre bletsunge. and on merigenlicere tide mynster gesohte.
>
> (Then Cuthbert did as was his habit, sang his prayers in the sea-wave, standing up to the neck, and afterwards bent his knees on the sand, with palms outstretched to the heavenly firmament. Behold, then came two seals from the sea-ground, and they dried his feet with their fur and warmed his limbs with their breath, and afterwards begged his blessing by a sign, lying at his feet on the yellow sand. Then Cuthbert sent the sea-animals to the sea with a true blessing, and on the morning tide he sought the monastery.)

Two additional details, both shared by the saint and the seals — the word order ða VS ('Ða dyde cuþberhtus [...] Efne ða comon twegen seolas [...]') and the word *bletsung* ('hi [...] his bletsunge bædon [...] cuðberhtus [...] asende. mid soðre bletsunge') — intensify the parallelism and the affinity between the man and the animals which the parallelism enhances. The parallelism is then broken in the next sentence by the word order VS without an initial

---

[21] Newlands, 'Bede and Images', p. 86.

[22] For a discussion of these phrases, see Godden, 'Experiments in Genre', p. 279. Godden defines the former phrase as 'poetic' in 'both phrasing and vocabulary' and the adjective in the latter phrase as 'a colorful dramatic language'. The presence of *sea*-terms of similar phrasing ('sælicere yðe', 'sælicum grunde', and 'sælican nytenu' (ll. 79–85)) and the selective use of *fealwe* (for it does not occur with the noun *ceosl* when the latter first appears in this passage (l. 80)) seem to confirm this view. The phrase *sealt brym* also occurs in lines 164 and 189. It may also be relevant to note that the adjective *fealwe* corresponds to *fealu* in Bede's poem, which Lapidge ('Bede's Metrical Vita', p. 91, n. 46) translates as 'golden'. For the view that the adjectives in the two phrases mentioned above have 'a generalising force', see Peter Clemoes, 'Ælfric', in *Continuations and Beginnings: Studies in Old English Literature*, ed. by E. G. Stanley (London: Nelson, 1966), pp. 176–209 (p. 206). On poetic words in Ælfric, see further Thomas A. Bredehoft, 'Ælfric and Late Old English Verse', *Anglo-Saxon England*, 33 (2004), 77–107 (pp. 97–105), and the same author's *Authors, Audiences, and Old English Verse* (Toronto: University of Toronto Press, 2009), pp. 154–59. Bredehoft does not discuss the passage from the Cuthbert homily under consideration. However, on the evidence of poetic words and other features such as alliteration and rhythmical scheme and also metrical pointing on the manuscript, he argues that Ælfric wrote the Cuthbert homily and other rhythmical works not as 'rhythmical prose' but as verse. See further n. 32.

adverb, which announces the transition to the second half of the story: 'wearð þa se munuc micclum afyrht' ('then the monk became much frightened'; l. 87).²³ There are no more parallel clauses but disparate types of description for the two parties now put in focus — a rapid succession of parataxis for the monk who becomes ill for his sin of curiosity and begs the saint to have mercy ('wearð þa se munuc [...] hine geeadmette [...] biddende [...]'; 'the monk then became [...], prostrated himself [...], praying [...]'; ll. 87–90) and direct speech for the saint who agrees to do so ('ic ðinum gedwylde dearnunge miltsige'; 'I will secretly pardon your error'; ll. 90–91), albeit conditionally. The two descriptions are linked by a word they share — the verb *miltsian* (as opposed to the preceding *bletsung* for the seals), which emphasizes at once the monk's difference from the seals and the holy youth's kindliness which transcends that difference. The condition Cuthbert imposes on the monk — that he should tell nothing of what has happened until he (Cuthbert) dies — foreshadows the words he is later to give to an abbess when prophesying his own election as bishop (ll. 237–38; see p. 31). Cuthbert's reference to his own death is couched in generalized terms with homiletic echoes ('oð þæt min sawul heonon siðige. of andwerdum life gelaðod to heofonan'; 'until my soul journeys hence, invited from the present life to heaven'; ll. 92–93), expanding the verse Life's factual 'quousque / Decedam mundo' ('until I depart from the earth'; c. 8, 243–44). When Ælfric concludes the passage, he does so by representing young Cuthbert as a saint who is powerful enough to heal a man by prayer and remit his sin ('Cuðberhtus ða mid gebede his sceaweres seocnysse gehælde. and his fyrwites ganges gylt forgeaf'; 'Cuthbert then healed his observer's illness by prayer and forgave the guilt of his walk of curiosity'; ll. 93–94). That Ælfric here again slightly expands the verse Life ('tum prece languorem pellit culpamque relaxat'; 'then he drives away the illness by prayer and remits the sin'; c. 8, 247) and uses the homiletic *gehælde* for Bede's plain *pellit* suggests his insistence on the figural significance of the event.

III

The representation of Cuthbert as a preordained bishop and its implication of a powerful saint is a feature that sustains the homily from its opening to the final doxology (on the doxology, see the final section). However, within this larger pattern, Ælfric's approach to the individual events he narrates varies. I would argue that Ælfric deploys varying narrative patterns as his protagonist develops from a learning youth to a seer and a bishop. Through this narrative technique and the thematic use of linguistic details we shall discuss later, Ælfric registers his sense of the structure of the saint's *vita*. His Life is not static but has a structure of its own which requires detailed analysis. Alex I. Jones says that Ælfric's text has 'a very different structure from Bede's' and 'falls very clearly into three parts'.²⁴ But he says this in terms of what the protagonist is and does — he is first 'the recipient of grace', then 'contends with the devil', and finally 'is spiritual leader, seer, and thaumaturge'.²⁵ What is more important is to examine the narrative and stylistic techniques Ælfric deploys to give thematic expression to this development.

We may begin with one of the earliest episodes in the life of young Cuthbert. Immediately following the God-sent boy's prophecy, this episode (ll. 28–47) recalls how an angel of God

---

[23] On this use of the VS word order to mark a transition or turning-point in narratives, see Bruce Mitchell, *Old English Syntax*, 2 vols (Oxford: Clarendon Press, 1985), II, 976 (§3933).

[24] Alex I. Jones, 'Ælfric's Life of Saint Cuthbert', *Parergon*, n. s., 10 (1992), 35–43 (p. 40).

[25] Jones, 'Ælfric's Life', p. 40.

healed Cuthbert's injured leg. Ælfric first calls the heavenly visitor 'sum arwurðe ridda' ('a worthy horse-rider'; l. 32) but soon identifies him as an angel ('ðam engle', l. 35), repeating this narrative explanatory phrase again ('þæs engles', l. 44) and reinforcing it with a reference to 'his halwendum handum' ('his healing hands'; l. 40). This authorial intervention at once emphasizes Cuthbert's ignorance at that time and the knowledge he will soon acquire. In fact, he does learn the truth at the end of the event, where Ælfric explains that Cuthbert 'ongeat þæt god þurh his engel hine geneosode' ('realized that God had visited him through his angel'; ll. 45–46). As Godden has pointed out, this firm statement 'gives the agency to God more clearly than in the *Vitae*.'[26] By placing such emphasis on the direct agency of God, Ælfric registers his point that the young Cuthbert foreshadows what he is predestined to become — the holy man who has a special status with God.

The same pattern is also sustained in another early episode, which is the first episode after Cuthbert becomes a monk (ll. 59–73). As the guest-master of the monastery, he one day welcomes a visitor, whom Ælfric 'identifies [...] as an angel at the outset'.[27] But young Cuthbert does not become aware of the truth until later when, on coming back from outside to the room, he finds the visitor gone:

> *ÆCHom* II, 10.66 he ne gemette nænne cuman ða ða he inn com. ac lagon ðry heofenlice hlafas on lilian beorhtnysse scinende. and on hrosan bræðe stymende. and on swæcce swettran þonne beona hunig; Þa sceawode se halga cuðberhtus on ðam snawe gehwær. hwyder se cuma siðigende ferde. ac ða ða he nane fotswaðe on þam snawe ne geseah. ða ongeat he þæt se cuma wæs engel and na mann. se ðe ðone heofenlican fodan him brohte. and ðæs eorðlican ne rohte.

> (He did not find any visitor when he came in, but there lay three heavenly loaves, shining with the lily's brightness and giving off the rose's fragrance and sweeter in taste than bees' honey. Then the holy Cuthbert looked everywhere in the snow to see where the visitor had gone travelling, but when he saw no foot-traces in the snow, then he realized that the visitor was not a man but an angel, who had brought him the heavenly food and did not care for the earthly food.)

Cuthbert is here shown to be guided to the truth by the loaves left in the room and the snow on the ground outside. The white colour the two nouns both imply is obviously symbolic of the heavenly visitor, as it is in the 'snawhwitum horse' ('snow-white horse'; l. 32) on which the visitor arrives in the previous episode, and to that degree it ties in with the preceding authorial identification. The symbolism is reinforced by a comparison of the loaves to a lily and two other things with similar associations.[28] For all this and the epithet 'heavenly' for the loaves, Ælfric had the model in Bede's verse and prose Lives (*VCM* c. 7, 208–9, *VCP* 178.6–7; *VCM* and *VCP* c. 7, chapter heading). However, Ælfric gives a final touch of his own to the narrative flow by rearranging the details. In Bede's two versions, Cuthbert first looks out to find no footprints in the snow and only then (and two sentences later in the prose Life) discovers the loaves in front of him; there is apparently little narrative development between the two discoveries. Ælfric not only reverses this order but makes the one discovery immediately consequent on the other, producing a sharper account of the climax. The account

---

[26] Godden, *Commentary*, p. 417, note on lines 44–47.
[27] Godden, *Commentary*, p. 418, note on lines 59–73.
[28] Ælfric also uses rhyme in this passage ('scinende [...] stymende' and 'him brohte [...] ne rohte'); see Pope, *Homilies of Ælfric*, I, 115 and Godden, *Commentary*, p. 419, note on lines 59–73. For a third example, a sequence of five rhyming words in lines 232–34, see p. 31.

ends, as in the previous episode, with the statement that Cuthbert now realized the truth ('ða ongeat he').

The narrative pattern used to tell the stories of young Cuthbert soon begins to give way to a new mode. This new pattern first emerges in the third episode of Cuthbert's life as a monk, in the account of how Cuthbert was fed miraculously by an eagle while travelling and preaching with a companion (ll. 97–112). In an earlier similar story of a miraculous gift of food (ll. 51–58), Cuthbert does not know about the gift until it suddenly appears before him. In contrast, in the eagle episode as Ælfric recounts it Cuthbert foresees the gift from God before it arrives. To render the point clearly, Ælfric 'places the eagle a little earlier in the story than any of the *Vitae*'.[29] Whereas in all the *Vitae* Cuthbert had started talking about the meal of the day with his companion before the eagle came into his sight, Ælfric describes Cuthbert as seeing the eagle first and then starting the conversation about the meal. It appears as if, in Ælfric's narrative, the sight of the eagle prompted Cuthbert to recall the precedent of Elijah's raven (which in fact the saint quotes as he explains his trust in God to his companion) and to think about the meal and foresee the solution for the problem that he is going to be favoured with. All the *Vitae*, too, describe Cuthbert as trusting in God's favour, but only rather vaguely and before he sees the bird (*VCA* 86.3–4; *VCM* c. 10, 298–301; *VCP* 196.5–7). To that extent, Ælfric has woven subtle hints of Cuthbert's foreknowledge into the narrative. But he does not say anything explicitly about it (as Bede does, saying 'praescius ipse futuri' ('himself prescient of the future'; *VCM* c. 10, 293) at the outset), thereby rendering the foreknowledge all the more effective when it is finally revealed. Whereas in the two earlier events discussed above, Cuthbert is innocent while we are given the truth, he now foresees God's favour before we read about it in the eagle episode: Cuthbert has now become a seer. This development is of course evident in all of the *Vitae*. But Ælfric's use of the new pattern (and the rearrangement of narrative material upon which it hinges) at this point emphasizes his sense of the protagonist's development.

The emergence of this new narrative pattern is reinforced by the next miracle that Ælfric recounts, which describes how Cuthbert, foreseeing an illusion of fire conjured by the devil, warns the people to whom he is preaching (ll. 113–26). As before, Ælfric makes a change in the narrative details. All the *Vitae* describe Cuthbert as evidently foreseeing the devil's illusion and warning the crowd against it through direct speech. Ælfric does not explicitly mention Cuthbert's foreknowledge at this point. On the contrary, he transforms Cuthbert's original direct speech into indirect speech and renders his warning in such general terms that the devil's temptation is put vaguely as *leasung* 'lying, falsehood' and buried in the embedded clause of purpose, hinting at no impending danger: 'cuðberhtus [...] bodade. þæt hi wære wæron wið deofles syrwum. ðy læs ðe he mid leasunge heora geleafan awyrde. and fram ðære bodunge. heora mod abrude' ('Cuthbert [...] preached that they should be wary of the devil's wiles, lest he should damage their faith with lying and draw their minds from the preaching'; ll. 113–16).[30] That Ælfric's Cuthbert was here actually warning against a foreseen illusion of fire is disclosed only at the end, when Ælfric uses the word *foresæde* 'predicted' in making the people, now ashamed of having disregarded the warning, refer to it and pray for Cuthbert's pardon in an indirect speech: 'biddende æt ðam lareowe. liðe miltsunge. þæt hi his lare ær to

---

[29] Godden, *Commentary*, p. 420, note on lines 97–112.
[30] The anonymous Life, for example, says more specifically: 'inludentis fantas iam predicens, [...] ait [...] si aliqua temptatio exorta foris repente extiterit, uos tamen stabiles estote' ('so foretelling the illusion of the deceiver, he said [...]: "[...] if any temptation should suddenly arise outside, be steadfast" '; 88.2–4).

lyt gymdon. ða ða he ða fræcednysse him foresæde' ('praying the teacher for kind mercy for having heeded his teaching too little before, when he predicted the danger for them'; ll. 125–26). The verb in this last clause reveals that Cuthbert had foreseen and foretold the danger of the illusion; none of the *Vitae* has anything approaching this *ða ða* clause as a narrative technique of disclosing Cuthbert's foreknowledge. It should be added that the people's indirect speech in part ('hi [...] gymdon') echoes the preceding authorial narrative ('hi ðære lare to lyt gymdon', l. 118), suggesting the manipulative use of speech on Ælfric's part, whereby the people are made to speak the same language and hold the same view of Christian truth as the narrator-homilist himself.

IV

Cuthbert the seer, who has emerged in two events during his monkhood, becomes a dominant theme in the subsequent part of Ælfric's life of the saint. This theme is accompanied by another development in his characterization which is also first seen clearly in this subsequent part: Cuthbert now speaks and acts with authority. It is in Cuthbert after he has moved to the island of Farne to live as a hermit that we find those two features combined to uncover a new figure of the saint. This new development demands a detailed examination, with a view to seeing how it is revealed through a series of miracles and events that take place on Farne.

The Farne section opens with what is one of the most renowned passages in the homily, describing the island amidst the sea to which Cuthbert is now determined to retire. It is noted largely for its alliterative style.[31] The heavy alliteration, reinforced by subjectless asyndetic parataxis for Cuthbert's actions and special diction for 'sea',[32] gives poetic heightening and tension to the passage, enhancing the representation of the island as a place of austere life and the determined asceticism of the man who will inhabit it. It is in this context that Cuthbert arrives as a man of power with whom the devils on the island do not dare to contend. In fact, the devils do not come into Ælfric's narrative of the scene. This absence is in part a feature of Ælfric's source text at this point, Bede's prose Life, where no conflict between Cuthbert and his foes takes place. But the prose Life gives at least some details of the 'wicked foe' with his demons and their oppressions, as in 'demorantium ibi phantasias demonum' ('the phantoms of demons who dwelt there'; 214.25–26) and 'omnia tela nequissimi ignea' ('all the fiery darts of the wicked one'; 214.28). Ælfric omits or shortens these, leaving almost nothing to mention about the devils except that they gave up the island entirely ('þæt igland. eallunge rymdon', l. 168) to the newcomer. Ælfric's Cuthbert is the 'æðela cempa' ('noble champion'; l. 168) without fighting against the 'ðeowracan. sweartra deofla' ('threats of the dark devils'; l. 167).

---

[31] For a discussion, see James Hurt, *Ælfric* (New York: Twayne, 1972), pp. 128–31.
[32] (Subjectless asyndetic parataxis) 'begann ða on mode [...]; wolde ða [...]; ferde ða to farne [...]' ('began then in his mind [...]; wished then [...]; went then to Farne [...]'; ll. 159–63); (diction for 'sea') 'on flowendre yðe [...] mid sealtum brymme' ('in the flowing wave [...] with the salt sea'; ll. 163–64). It may be relevant to note that this passage is given dense pointing on the manuscript, as in Godden's edition. On the basis of this, Hurt (*Ælfric*, pp. 128–29) arranges the passage in metrical lines to emphasize the alliterative and rhythmical scheme of 'rhythmical prose' in which it is written. Bredehoft (see n. 22) would see the pointing as evidence of verse writing here, as he does the pointing in the opening passages of the Cuthbert homily and another Second Series homily ('Ælfric and Late Old English Verse', pp. 77–78 and 97–98). Whether to be accepted as evidence of rhythmical prose or verse, the pointing in the opening of the Farne section and the poetic effects it implies endorse my view about the elevated use of language in the passage.

Inhabiting the place alone after the devils' retreat, Cuthbert now performs a succession of miracles through which his power is revealed. Remarkably, in his account of the first two miracles Ælfric uses the verb *het* 'commanded' in succession when describing the saint:

> *ÆCHom* II, 10.172 ac se halga wer. ða sona het. þa heardnesse. swiðe holian. onmiddan ðære flore. his fægeran botles. and ðær wæter æddre ða wynsum asprang. werod on swæcce. þam were to brice. se ðe hwilon wæter. to winlicum swæcce. wundorlice awende. ða ða hit wolde god; Se halga ða het. him bringan sæd. wolde on ðam westene. wæstmes tilian. gif hit swa geuðe. se ælmihtiga god. þæt he mid his foton. hine fedan moste; He seow ða hwæte. on beswuncenum lande. ac hit to wæstme. aspringan ne moste. ne furðon mid gærse. growende næs; Þa het he him bringan. bere to sæde. and ofer ælcne timan. ða eorðan aseow; Hit weox ða mid wynne. and wel geripode.

> (But the holy man then immediately commanded the hardness to be hollowed thoroughly in the middle of the floor of his fair dwelling, and there a pleasant water-source sprang up then, sweet in taste, for the use of the man, who once wonderfully turned water to wine-like taste when God willed it. The saint then ordered seed to be brought to him, wishing to labour to raise a crop in the waste, if Almighty God should grant it so, that he might feed himself with his feet. He then sowed wheat on tilled land, but it was not allowed to spring up to fruit, nor was it even growing with shoots. Then he commanded barley to be brought to him to sow and sowed the earth beyond any appropriate time. It then waxed joyfully and well ripened.)

In the anonymous Life and Bede's prose Life, in the first miracle Cuthbert has his monks dig into the rocky ground to find water (*VCA* 98.12–13; *VCP* 218.7), while in the verse Life he has no monks to assist him but succeeds in obtaining water by his prayers ('sanctus amoenam / Excutit insolita precibus dulcedine limpham'; 'by his prayers the saint sends forth water pleasant for its uncommon sweetness'; c. 16, 406–7). Ælfric's Cuthbert uses none of these expedients but just commands, like God in his Creation, and then 'ðær wæter æddre [...] asprang'. The miraculous nature of the event is intensified by the abstract mode in which the command is made through the verb *het*. For one thing, the verb has no direct object denoting a person who is commanded, as a necessary result of the absence of any available monks in this narrative. More significant is Ælfric's use of the noun *heardnesse* 'hardness' as the direct object of the verb *holian* 'to hollow out', instead of a factual noun for the concrete object, such as *terram* in the anonymous Life ('fodite in medio pauimento domus meae hanc saxosam terram'; 'dig this rocky ground in the middle of the floor of my dwelling'; 98.7–8); Bede's prose Life has no expressed object of *fodiamus* 'let us dig'. Ælfric's preference for an abstract noun here seems deliberate in light of the two parallel expressions he uses in the neighbouring sentences: 'wæteres wynsumnysse' ('water's sweetness'; ll. 171–72) and 'winlicum swæcce' ('wine-like taste'; see above).[33] Ælfric's choice of language enhances his representation of Cuthbert's miraculous command and the power of the saint. The same mode of expression continues into the next miraculous episode in which he grows crops out of season. Where in Bede's prose Life Cuthbert asks his brethren first for tools and wheat and then for barley

---

[33] Ruth Waterhouse pays attention to the first two of these abstract nouns, saying with respect to the first that Ælfric 'chooses the noun "þa heardnesse" to stress the abstract quality of the conditions' ('"Wæter æddre asprang": How Cuthbert's Miracle Pours Cold Water on Source Study', *Parergon*, n. s., 5 (1987), 1–27 (p. 13)). But exactly what she means by this is not explained. Ælfric's preference for this kind of abstract expression may be compared with the Latin 'aequoreum [...] frigus' ('watery cold'), as Bede puts it in the metrical *Vita* (c. 8, 230), describing the seals drying Cuthbert's body. Lapidge ('Bede's Metrical *Vita*', p. 92) calls this phrase 'suggestively abstract',

(220.15–22),³⁴ Ælfric's Cuthbert, as before, simply commands with a similar effect (in the last two lines above). The verb *het*, again as before, lacks any agent noun, granting the command a level of abstraction that has a similar elevating effect. By describing Cuthbert and his miracles in this way, Ælfric represents him as a man of absolute power, a type of Christ. It should be added that in the first miracle he reinforces this representation by echoing the biblical account of Christ's miracle at the wedding at Cana, most obviously when he refers (in the third line above) to the saint's own example of a similar miracle, implying that there is no wonder about the water miracle coming from such a saint.³⁵ The biblical echo is not original to Ælfric but comes from the verse Life ('qui quondam [...] / In meracum latices valuit convertere nectar'; 'who at some time [...] had the power to turn water into pure nectar'; c. 16, 411–12), which he translates almost verbatim.³⁶ But the successive use of the verb *het* and its abstract mode of expression are Ælfric's own addition, and his representation is all the more clear and effective.

Cuthbert as a man of authority continues to be a dominant theme in the next two miracles, both of which are wrought against ravens which persistently annoy him. Ælfric's characterization of the hermit saint is seen particularly clearly in the second of these miracles, when he recounts how Cuthbert banishes the birds for damaging his abode but forgives them when they come back repentant. The miracle is told in both Bede's verse and prose Lives. As Newlands has argued, the birds in the verse Life 'are banished for ever, "per aevum" (436). Such harsh words are not found in Bede's prose vita. Instead, true to Bede's prose characterization of Cuthbert as a kind, moderate man, the saint admonishes the ravens in gentler words'.³⁷ In this respect, Ælfric is closer to Bede in the verse Life. But Ælfric goes even further. His hermit banishes the birds 'mid ealle [...] mid anum worde' ('entirely with one word'; ll. 193–94), where the verse Cuthbert is given two lines of direct speech to admonish the birds. The birds in turn are described as 'swearte hremmas' ('dark ravens'; l. 191), like those in the first miracle called 'wælhreowe fugelas' ('cruel birds'; l. 188). The attitude of the hermit (and the homilist Ælfric) towards the birds is expressed clearly by these affective terms;³⁸ the adjective *wælhreow* is Ælfric's own addition.

Ælfric's insistence on the austere hermit and his authority is no less obvious when the pair of birds come back with a token of repentance. Here Ælfric characteristically humanizes the birds:

> *ÆCHom* II, 10.194 Ac an ðæra fugela. eft fleogende com. ymbe ðry dagas. þearle dreorig. fleah to his foton. friðes biddende. þæt he on ðam lande. lybban moste. symle unscæððig. and his gefera samod; Hwæt ða se halga. him þæs geuðe. and hi lustbære. þæt land gesohten. and brohton ðam lareowe. lac to medes. swines rysl his scon to gedreoge. and hi ðær siððan. unscæððige wunedon.

---

seeing in it 'Bede's striving for abstract, generalized expression'.

³⁴ No monks appear in the verse Life, while the anonymous Life lacks the entire episode.

³⁵ Cuthbert's conversion of water into wine is given an independent account in a later chapter in the two prose *Vitae* (*VCA* lib. 4, c. 18; *VCP* c. 35).

³⁶ This echo in Bede is discussed in John C. Eby, 'Bringing the Vita to Life: Bede's Symbolic Structure of the Life of St. Cuthbert', *American Benedictine Review*, 48 (1997), 316–38 (p. 329). Waterhouse notes Ælfric's use of it (' "Wæter æddre asprang" ', p. 17).

³⁷ Newlands, 'Bede and Images', pp. 96–97.

³⁸ The phrase 'swearte hremmas' may be compared with 'sweartum gastum' ('dark spirits'; l. 165) and 'sweartra deofla' (l. 167; see p. 28), both referring to the devils on the island of Farne. On the other hand, Ælfric uses the phrase 'dark raven' for Elijah's raven ('ðone sweartan hremm', l. 105). But the symbolism Ælfric attaches to the word *sweart* seems obvious in context in the Farne passage being discussed. In contrast, Ælfric calls Cuthbert's apparently humble hermitage 'fair' ('his fægeran botles', l. 173).

(But one of those birds came flying back after three days very sad, flew to his feet, asking for peace so that he might live in that land unharmful ever after, and his mate with him. Lo! then the holy man granted that to them, and they gladly sought that land and brought the teacher a gift as reward, swine's fat for the softening of his shoes, and they afterwards dwelt there unharmful.)

The raven who first came back alone begged pardon, lying at the saint's feet, not unlike a human penitent and quite unlike the raven in Bede's prose Life which uses 'quibus ualebat indiciis' ('such signs as it could'; 224.6) to pray for pardon. When the hermit accordingly gives remission, he does so with a verb of forgiving (*geuðe*) as in Bede's prose Life, and the term *lustbære* for the ravens may come from the verse Life ('ambo veniunt alacres'; 'both came back happy'; c. 18, 441). But the use of the two words together in contrast is original to Ælfric. Their combined use emphasizes the contrast between the two sides, the forgiving and the forgiven, enhancing the characterization of the saint as a hermit with absolute authority. It should be added that Ælfric's narrative obviously registers a contrast between the birds in the two miracles — those who came back repentant three days later and those who did not dare to do so. That may well be the reason why Ælfric emphatically says 'oðre twegen swearte hremmas' ('two other dark ravens'; ll. 190–91) in the second miracle, where the verse Life ('rescindunt corvi [...] pactum'; 'the ravens rescind [...] the agreement'; c. 18, 431) seems to imply that the birds in the two miracles are the same ones.[39]

These miracles are finally followed by one in which Cuthbert the seer emerges clearly, far more clearly than in the two events in his early life. Ælfric now for the first time in this homily calls the saint *se witega* 'the prophet' as he recounts the story of Ælfflæd the abbess's visit to the saint on Farne and the ensuing dialogue between the two (ll. 212–38). During the dialogue Cuthbert, prompted by the abbess's questions, makes his first public prophecies, regarding the demise of King Ecgfrith and the name of his successor, and further his own election as a bishop. It is at this last point that the saint is called *se witega*:[40]

> *ÆCHom* II, 10.231 Ða cwæð se witega þæt he wurðe nære. swa miccles hades. ne ðæs heahsetles. ac swa þeah nan man godes mihte ne forflihð. on nanum heolstrum. heofenan. oþþe eorðan. oþþe sæ ðriddan; Ic gelyfe swa ðeah. gif se ælmihtiga me hætt þæs hades beon. þæt ic eft mote ðis igland gesecan. æfter twegra geara ymbrene. and ðyses eðeles brucan; Ic bidde þe ælflæd. þæt ðu uncre spræce. on minum life. nanum ne ameldige.
>
> (The prophet then said that he was not worthy of so great an office, nor of the exalted seat, but, nevertheless, no man flees from God's power in any hiding-places of heaven or of earth or, thirdly, of sea. 'I believe, nevertheless, that if the Almighty commands me to be of that office, I shall be allowed to seek this island again after the course of two years and enjoy this homeland. I beg you, Ælfflæd, that you would not reveal our discourse to anyone during my life.')

As Ælfric starts the passage, the prophet's words are couched in indirect speech, heightened by the poetic 'heolstrum' and a succession of rhymes: 'hades [...] heahsetles [...] heofenan [...]

---

[39] See Godden, *Commentary*, p. 423, note on lines 184–90.

[40] The word *witega* is used subsequently two more times: 'ðæs witegan word' (l. 290) and 'swa swa se witega cwæð' (l. 300), both in reference to a miracle the saint worked. The Latin equivalents *vates* and *propheta* are often used prior to the Farne passage in the verse Life. According to Newlands ('Bede and Images', pp. 103–4), in the verse Life the commonest word 'used to refer to Cuthbert is *vates* [...], used 32 times in this poem of 979 lines', while 'the word *vates* is never used of Cuthbert' in Bede's prose Life, which uniquely describes the saint as *pater*; and the anonymous Life 'refers to the saint commonly as "homo Dei" [...] and less commonly as "servus Dei/Domini" '.

eorðan [...] ðriddan'.⁴¹ Here many of the ideas are derived from the *Vitae*. Halfway through the saint's words, however, Ælfric suddenly switches to direct speech,⁴² thereby giving the prophecy of his election and his subsequent retirement in two years the dramatic force and immediacy appropriate to what may be seen as a central point in the structure of the homily. The prophecy anticipates the rest of the homily both in content and structure. It provides much of the material that remains to be narrated in the homily and the structural framework for that narrative, which places the seer-saint at its centre. The word *witega*, introducing the prophecy in the first instance and then framing all that follows it, upholds the significance of this subsequent development of the homily. The details of this structuring will be discussed in the next section.

V

As the previous two sections have shown, Ælfric's narrative has its own structure. It is a structure that embodies the homilist's sense of Cuthbert's development as he changes, in the parts examined so far, from a youth who only learns the truth after the event, to a foreseeing monk and then a *witega*, who is also a man of power, as seen in the Farne section. How Ælfric continues to give a similar structured expression to his narrative in the subsequent part of the homily remains to be examined in this section. But before going into the analysis, we may as well have a look at an earlier part of the homily to see how Ælfric has already attempted to restructure the narratives of the *Vitae*. The method Ælfric employs there is rather local and not directly related to the larger framework we are going to discuss. However, it requires examination to help us understand the full nature of the narrative technique of the Cuthbert homily.

The earlier part that calls for attention is lines 97–157, which recount the stories of the miraculous feeding by the eagle and three other miracles in succession. Ælfric tells these four events in the same sequence as the *Vitae* but links them more closely. Thus, the second event, in which Cuthbert extinguishes an illusory fire the devil creates before a crowd of people (see above, p. 27), is presented as occurring after the saint eating the meal provided by the eagle ('ða æfter gereorde'; 'then after the meal'; l. 113) and hence on the same day and during the same preaching journey. The *Vitae*, on the other hand, are all vague about the sequence of the two events, with no clearer link between them than, for example, 'eodem tempore' ('at the same time') used to introduce the second event in Bede's prose Life (198.3). This event in turn is linked thematically, in Ælfric's narrative, to a similar story about the saint standing in front of a fire, which immediately follows, using the phrase *swa ðeah* 'however', implying 'another fire, though not a phantom but a real fire this time' — a verbal link that Æfric adds in place of the looser sequence in the *Vitae*.

Æfric then makes a larger adaptation to the sequence of the four events. Where all of the *Vitae* move directly to the last of the events, Ælfric instead inserts a 'brief intervening

---

⁴¹ See Roberta Frank, 'Poetic Words in Late Old English Prose', in *From Anglo-Saxon to Early Middle English: Studies Presented to E. G. Stanley*, ed. by M. Godden, D. Gray and T. Hoad (Oxford: Clarendon Press, 1994), 87–107 (pp. 104–5). Of the five rhyming words, the last (*ðriddan*) is Ælfric's own addition to the verse Life ('caeli terraeve marisve latebris'; 'in the hiding-places of heaven or earth or sea'; c. 21, 529).

⁴² I discuss in detail the transition from indirect to direct speech in this passage in 'Ælfric's Shifting Mode of Speech: Postscript on *Wite Ge* in the Peter and Paul Homily', *Studies in English Literature* (Tokyo), English Number, 54 (2013), 1–10.

comment on Cuthbert's preaching [which] is perhaps based on an earlier chapter found only in VCP c. 9' and which 'is oddly placed in Ælfric's version, in the middle of a sequence of miracle stories'.[43] Godden's remark that 'possibly it marks the end of a sequence of events associated with Cuthbert's preaching expeditions'[44] seems to give a convincing explanation for the rearrangement, bringing to light an aspect of Ælfric's method of restructuring the narratives. In terms of the story itself, one may note that the last of the four events is a story about a woman whose husband, when asking for the saint's help, would have liked to conceal her madness, though the saint had already seen the circumstances of her condition. Ælfric accordingly places the focus on the saint's foresight by using much the same wording in the authorial narrative ('Cuðberhtus [...] cwæð þæt se deofol [...] forlætan sceolde. and mid micelre fyrhte aweg fleon'; 'Cuthbert [...] said that the devil [...] should [...] leave her and flee away in great fright'; ll. 149–52) and the wife's report after being healed ('cydde hu se deofol. hi dearnunge forlet. and swiðe forhtigende. fleames cepte'; 'reported how the devil secretly left her and, greatly fearing, took flight'; ll. 155–56). He makes a similar manipulative use of language when he refers, in corresponding terms, to how the saint predicts about the wife and how the healed wife behaves (ll. 152–54), and inserts the phrase 'be ðæs lareowes wordum' ('in accordance with the teacher's words') to emphasize the correspondence. Such an emphasis on the saint's foresight may be an early expression of the theme which is subsequently seen more clearly to be central to the structuring of the *vita* as a whole.

To return to this larger structure, its thematic centre is, as I suggested above, Cuthbert as a seer and man of authority, a theme which continues to sustain much of the narrative subsequent to the Farne section. The passage that immediately follows it (ll. 239–58) is an account of how the three public prophecies he made on Farne came true. Ælfric first gives a full account of the saint's promotion to bishopric of Lindisfarne, recounting how the King and other high representatives of the church and the state unanimously elected and persuaded him to accept the office and how the saint at last agreed to do so very reluctantly. Ælfric says that all this had long been predicted by the God-sent boy and Bishop Boisil, though he never mentions the bishop elsewhere in his narrative. However, his main aim in this passage is to relate these events to the saint's prophecies made on Farne in the immediately preceding passage. Ælfric brings this relation emphatically into focus by framing the passage verbally, saying 'æfter ðisum wordum' ('after these words') referring to the saint's prophecies at the opening and 'þa wæs gefylled. seo foresæde spræc. swa se halga wer. sæde þam mædene' ('then the prophetic speech was fulfilled, as the holy man had said to the maiden') at the end, with the *swa* clause referring back again to the saint's prophesying. These phrases are absent in the *Vitae*; Ælfric's narrative frame clearly reflects the intention to emphasize the events as a fulfillment of a prophecy rather than to give a chronological account. To reinforce this frame, Ælfric makes a slight but important change in the details. Unlike Bede, who places it a year or so after in his *Vitae* (*VCM* c. 21, 545; *VCP* 238.21), Ælfric represents King Ecgfrith's death and his brother's succession as taking place in the same year as the election ('on ðam ylcan geare', l. 252), making the saint's prophecy and its fulfillment more immediately and dramatically related. His opening phrase, 'æfter ðisum wordum', itself points to this intention, since it apparently locates the events it introduces more closely together in time than Bede's 'nec multo post' ('not long afterwards'; *VCP* 238.4) and its equivalents in the other *Vitae* (*VCA*

---

[43] Godden, *Commentary*, p. 421, note on lines 131–36.
[44] Godden, *Commentary*, p. 421, note on lines 131–36.

110.2; *VCM* c. 21, 536). All these adaptations stress the overall narrative structure into which Ælfric recasts the three events. It is also important to note that the frame, with the closing *swa* clause affirming the fulfillment, represents a new pattern, succeeding the earlier two, in Ælfric's narrative of miracles; this is soon to become the standard pattern for the subsequent narrative, as we shall see.

Adaptations along the same lines are made in much of the subsequent narrative of the miracles the saint works when he was a bishop. In the story of a half-dead boy whom he heals, Ælfric omits much of the circumstantial detail given by Bede but instead ends the story with a firm statement that his prophecy was fulfilled ('ðæs witegan word. wurdon gefyllede'; 'the prophet's words were fulfilled'; ll. 290–91), bringing into focus the saint and his power of foresight. Again, in the story of the second dialogue with Ælfflæd, when questioned about his curious behaviour at the meal, the saint is described as answering that he has just seen the death of a certain man in her monastery and prophesies that the man's name will be made known to her the next morning, instead of being made known to him by her, as in all of the *Vitae* (*VCA* 126.14–15; *VCM* c. 31, 669–71; *VCP* 262.29–30). One feels inclined to ask if Ælfric might possibly be implying that the saint knows who the dead was when he tells the abbess about him, so great is his power as a seer. At any rate, Ælfric does not forget to extol the saint's power by saying at the end of the story that the truth then became widely known just as he had prophesied ('hit wearð ða gewidmærsod. swa swa se witega cwæð', ll. 300–1).

The last of the passages in which Cuthbert the seer is central to the narrative is found towards the end of the homily in an account of the deaths of the saint and his disciple Hereberht (ll. 308–31). Here Ælfric makes the most drastic rearrangement, omitting most of the events between the two deaths that occur in widely separated chapters in the *Vitae*. In the fullest account given by Bede in the prose Life, for example, Chapter 28 describes the saint meeting Hereberht and telling him about his own death which he had foreseen, followed by the latter's plea to be allowed to die on the same day and his subsequent departure granted after a long illness. The chapter is followed by further miracles and stories of the saint's last days after he returns to Farne, before he dies in Chapter 39. Ælfric omits this intervening material, moving some of it to an earlier point in the narrative, in order to represent the deaths of the two literally as a continued story, almost as one death — an intention which is expressed symbolically and beautifully by the phrase 'swiðe onette' (l. 324), literally meaning 'greatly hastened', referring to the saint hurrying back to Farne to await what is now described as his own impending death. These rearrangements show a clear sense of structure, leading to 'a moving conclusion' to the story.[45]

Ælfric's rearrangement of the story of Cuthbert's death in the *Vitae* is so obvious that it has attracted the attention of much previous study. Jones, for example, argues that Ælfric's final third section, where the saint is primarily a seer, 'loses the variety of miracles at the time of and subsequent to Cuthbert's death: the concern is with the death itself'.[46] Similarly, Hurt discusses Ælfric's omissions of the material in the *Vitae* from a structural point of view, saying that they 'are chiefly in the last sections of the life, where Bede's narrative is structurally weakest. [...] Ælfric's treatment of Cuthbert's death is structurally quite independent of Bede's prose life'.[47] Both are right as far as their comparison of Ælfric and Bede goes. But neither of

---

[45] Godden, *Commentary*, p. 429, note on lines 308–22.
[46] Jones, 'Ælfric's Life', p. 40.
[47] J. R. Hurt, 'Ælfric and the English Saints' (unpublished PhD. dissertation, Indiana University, 1965), pp. 67–68. See also Gretsch, *Ælfric and the Cult*, p. 106.

them notes that Ælfric's 'independent' structure in this part of the narrative hinges on Cuthbert the seer whose foresight it is designed to highlight. The saint first foresees his own death. This may be nothing singular in hagiographical narratives. What is unique to Ælfric's narrative is that the saint foresees that through the grace of God he and his disciple are to be granted their wish. When Hereberht makes his plea anxiously, the saint kindly responds to it and reassures him with his foresight: 'se biscop. his cneowa gebigde. to ðissere bene. mid bliðum mode. and syððan ðone sacerd. sona gefrefrode. cwæð þæt him geuðe. se ælmihtiga wealdend. þæt hi ætsomne. siðian moston' ('the bishop bent his knees to this prayer with cheerful mind, and then immediately comforted the priest, saying that the Almighty Ruler had granted them that they might depart together'; ll. 317–20). Significantly, the saint does not pray to God here. Ælfric represents Cuthbert as confident in God's mercy without praying for it, unlike the saint in the *Vitae*, who prays before he knows that their request has been granted (*VCA* 124.19; *VCM* c. 30, 650; *VCP* 250.14). The material in the *Vitae* is severely pruned in Ælfric's narrative as detailed above in order to focus on this foreseeing scene, particularly the saint as its centre. Ælfric reinforces this image of the seer-saint by ending the story with a statement, in what is now his usual narrative pattern, confirming the relevance of the saint's foresight: the saint 'to drihtne gewat. and hereberhtus samod [...] swa swa hi [...] ær geleornodon. þurh godes gast' ('departed to the Lord, and Hereberht with him [...], just as they had learnt before [...] through the spirit of God'; ll. 329–31).

Representing Cuthbert's foresight in this way, Ælfric also emphasizes the saint as a man specially elected by God, who has a special relationship to God; his promise to Hereberht may even be seen 'like Christ's to the repentant thief', as Jones argues.[48] The emphasis on this aspect of the story makes the passage a fitting conclusion to the *vita* of the saint who is described as coeternal with God in both the opening and closing lines (see below). That might also explain why Ælfric apparently felt little need to elaborate on the post-mortem miracles; he summarizes the profuse material for this in the *Vitae* briefly in a few lines (ll. 331–38) before going on to the doxology.

VI

Ælfric's homily on St Cuthbert has been studied primarily for the author's incipient rhythmical prose, and its other aspects have not been granted the full examination they deserve. This essay has focused on the structure of this hagiographical homily and the narrative techniques that sustain it. As I have shown in the previous sections, Ælfric's life of Cuthbert has a structure that, though differently conceived than in the preceding *Vitae*, is clearly demonstrable and deserves appreciation in its own right. In this regard, Ælfric's *vita* differs from the anonymous Life and Bede's verse Life, which, as the previous studies have shown, are 'static' and use little structuring. It is more like the 'developmental' prose Life by Bede.[49] But Ælfric structures the development in his own way, seeing it primarily as the protagonist's progress to a seer-saint, from a lay youth who does not know the truth until after the event, to a foreseeing monk and then a seer, a 'witega', who is 'wis ðurh witegunge. wisdomes gastes' ('wise through prophecy of the spirit of wisdom'; l. 307) and makes his first public prophecies while a solitary on Farne and continues to dominate the subsequent narrative. The development itself and most of the

---

[48] Jones, 'Ælfric's Life', pp. 40–41.
[49] See the second section, p. 21.

details Ælfric uses to illustrate it are in the preceding *Vitae*. Ælfric, however, gives a new form to the development, deploying a narrative method and linguistic usage to register his sense of structure, and reveals the development more emphatically than the preceding versions do. Central to this new form are the three successive patterns Ælfric uses in recounting miracles and Cuthbert's changing perceptions of them. The last of the three, emphasizing Cuthbert the *witega* by starting the account with the saint's own words of prophecy and closing it with authorial words of affirmation that it came to pass as he had prophesied, becomes the standard pattern for the later part of the narrative, as in the saint's first public prophecies made on Farne, and the story of the saint's death, where Ælfric drastically prunes and rearranges the individual events told in the *Vitae* and creates a memorable ending of his *vita*.

Cuthbert's development as Ælfric recounts it with changing narrative patterns is accompanied by other features which reflect it. Most prominent of these is the emphasis Ælfric places on the saint as a man of power, speaking and acting with authority — a figure which first takes shape in the first episodes of the Farne section in conjunction with the emergence of the saint as *witega* later in the same section. Remarkably, Ælfric intensifies the representation with a biblical echo and the thematic use of language, notably using an expression of commanding rather than asking, as used in the *Vitae*, in order to describe the saint as a type of Christ. The representation takes a slightly varied form in the story of the deaths of the saint and his disciple, where the saint is represented as a man with a special relationship to God, who is allowed to know, without praying to God, that their wish has been granted. All these features reinforce the successive narrative patterns Ælfric deploys and his structuring of the *vita* they are used to uphold.

Significantly, all this development is ultimately a development that embodies the preordained sanctity the protagonist is blessed with in the *vita*. Ælfric treats this aspect in the earliest part of the narrative, particularly in the first episode, following the *Vitae* in the main. What is Ælfric's own is the opening lines of the homily he adds prior to the narrative, where he describes the saint as living in the present tense and emphasizes his oneness with God (see the second section). This opening has a closing counterpart in the final doxology, which matches it both in intent and language: 'sy wuldor and lof. þam welegan drihtne. se ðe his gecorenan. swa cystelice wurðað. æfter deadlicum life. mid him lybbende .a. on ecnysse. ealra worulda. amen:—' ('glory and praise be to the prosperous Lord, who so generously honours his chosen one after mortal life, living with him forever for all eternity. Amen'; ll. 339–41). Like the opening, the doxology describes the two living together, though it is God here who reigns in the present tense and honours the saint, 'his gecorenan', living with him for all eternity. The opening affirms oneness by focusing on the saint, as appropriate to the introduction to a hagiography; the doxology focuses on God, as appropriate to the ending of a homily. Taken together, they emphasize the saint's special status with God. Within this framework of the homily, the saint develops, within the *vita*, from his earliest youth to his last day in this world. The saint is in progress in one sense and yet is one with God from the outset in another sense. This double structure Ælfric gives his homily is obviously a result of the adaptation of the hagiographical material to a preaching purpose. Seen, however, in the larger context of what Godden has elucidated as Ælfric's 'experiments in genre', it may also be part of the answer the homilist has reached in this piece of the *Catholic Homilies* in his experiments with the form of

---

[50] For a convincing explanation of this later development, see Godden, 'Experiments in Genre', pp. 277–82.

hagiography, before finally moving on to a more distinct form of separation of the homiletic discourse from the narrative in the *Lives of Saints*.[50]

There is another sense in which the Cuthbert homily can be considered in a wider context. If, as I have shown above, Ælfric's telling has produced a 'developmental' saint's life in this homily, how does it fit with what he does with other saints in the *Catholic Homilies* and the *Lives of Saints*? The 'developmental' life of Cuthbert appears to be far removed from, for instance, the treatment in another Second Series homily on St Martin (*ÆCHom* II, 34), though the protagonist here too develops, from a heathen soldier to a devout man of prayer and from a monk to a bishop who foresees his own death.[51] How would this apparent variation in narrative style (and other ones that may possibly be brought to light) be related to Ælfric's changing attitude to hagiographical writing and/or the individual Latin sources he draws upon and the way he rewrites them? And how can it be related to trends in Anglo-Saxon hagiography more generally? These questions remain to be pursued in understanding the history of the genre in the period. That eventual understanding may reinforce the results of my present study, emphasizing the position of the Cuthbert homily both as an important subject of study in its own right and as a point in Ælfric's changing attitude to hagiography and the development of his narrative styles.

---

[51] I have discussed Ælfric's Martin homily in comparison with his later telling of the saint in the *Lives of Saints*, in 'Sententia in Narrative Form: Ælfric's Narrative Method in the Hagiographical Homily on St Martin', *Leeds Studies in English*, n. s., 42 (2011), 75–92.

The Virgin's Kiss: Gender, Leprosy, and Romance in the Life of Saint Frideswide

Gary S. Fuller

Sweet Helen, make me immortal with a kiss.[1]

Medieval hagiographic texts often produce a peculiar delight when their holy subject confronts an unusual situation in unexpectedly human fashion, creating a breach in the saint's halo of sanctity but also a stronger shared identity with the fallible audience. One such moment occurs in the long version of a thirteenth-century Middle English verse legend of the life of St Frideswide, the Anglo-Saxon princess and abbess (*c.* 650–727). This poem, found in the collection of saints' lives known as the *South English Legendary* (*SEL*), concludes with Frideswide's return to Oxford after an extended absence. According to the text, as the saint entered the city, surrounded by joyous townspeople,

> A mesel com among that folc, swythe grisliche myd alle,
> That hadde yare sik ibe and ne mighte no bote valle.
> Loude he gradde and ofte inough, 'Levedi, bidde ic thee,
> Vor the love of Jhesu Crist, have mercy of me
> And cus me with thi suete mouth, yif it is thi wille!'
> This maide was sore ofschame and eode evere vorth stille.
> This mesel gradde evere on and cride 'milce' and 'ore,'
> So that this maide him custe and was ofscamed sore.
> A suete cos it was to him, vor therwith anon
> He bicom hol and sound, and is lymes echon,
> And vair man and clene inou was, and of thulke cosse there
> Me thencht the maide nadde no sunne, of ordre thei heo were! (ll. 143–54)

> (A leper came among that people, very hideous indeed,
> That had been sick for a long time and unable to acquire a remedy.
> He called out loudly and repeatedly, 'Lady, I bid thee,
> For the love of Jesus Christ, have mercy on me
> And kiss me with thy sweet mouth, if it is thy will!'
> This virgin was sorely ashamed and continued quietly walking.
> This leper called out incessantly and cried for mercy and help,

---

[1] Christopher Marlowe, *Doctor Faustus*, in *English Renaissance Drama: A Norton Anthology* (New York: W. W. Norton, 2002), pp. 245–85 (p. 280) (v.1.92).

So this virgin kissed him and was sorely ashamed.
It was a sweet kiss to him, for immediately thereby
He became whole and sound, and all his limbs,
And was a beautiful and clean man, and as for that kiss
It seems to me that the virgin committed no sin, even though she was in a religious order!)[2]

Three elements of this event in the *SEL* legend particularly draw the attention of the reader: the sensuous nature of the leper's request for a kiss; the reluctance of the virgin saint to offer it; and her shame both before and after the healing act. Kissing of lepers had become a hagiographical convention by the time of the *SEL*'s composition; however, these three elements in Frideswide's story were not part of that convention and, indeed, cannot be found in any accounts of similar miracles.[3] Moreover, this episode in Frideswide's life is the only known instance in which a male leper requests a kiss from a female saint, and the *SEL*-poet has enhanced the event's exceptionality by making changes to the Latin source which fundamentally transform the interaction between saint and supplicant. Yet, in spite of this remarkable incident, the longer *SEL* life of Frideswide has received little critical attention.[4] The purpose of this essay is to explore the tension between saintly compassion and romantic love introduced as the *SEL*-poet negotiates intersections of conventional portrayals of leprosy, gender, and religious authority; this tension, I propose, can provide new insight into the medieval conflation of hagiography and romance and suggest new ways of thinking about the construction of romantic identity in thirteenth-century England.

Latin Sources for the *SEL* Lives of Frideswide

Latin hagiographic texts were used as source material for the creation of the *South English Legendary*, a collection of liturgically-ordered saints' lives in Middle English verse. The *SEL* was first composed in the last half of the thirteenth century; the best estimate of the date of the initial collection is *c.* 1270–85.[5] The fact that the collection exists with some variation in over sixty surviving manuscripts, dating from *c.* 1300 to *c.* 1500, is evidence of its popularity.

---

[2] 'The Legend of Frideswide of Oxford, an Anglo-Saxon Royal Abbess', in *Middle English Legends of Women Saints*, ed. by Sherry L. Reames (Kalamazoo: Medieval Institute Publications, 2003), pp. 23–50 (p. 42). The Modern English translation is my own, as are all subsequent Modern English translations of Middle English verse in this essay. The longer *SEL* life of Frideswide is found in only four manuscripts: Oxford, Bodleian Library MS Ashmole 43 (*c.* 1300–30); Cambridge, Magdalene College MS Pepys 2344 (*c.* 1325–50); London, British Library MS Cotton Junius D IX (early fifteenth century); and Oxford, Bodleian Library MS Bodley 779 (*c.* 1400–50); see Manfred Görlach, *The Textual Tradition of the South English Legendary*, Leeds Texts and Monographs, n. s. 6 (Leeds: School of English, University of Leeds, 1974), p. 196.

[3] See Carole Rawcliffe, *Leprosy in Medieval England* (Woodbridge: Boydell, 2006), pp. 144–46, and Catherine Peyroux, 'The Leper's Kiss', in *Monks & Nuns, Saints & Outcasts*, ed. by Sharon Farmer and Barbara H. Rowenstein (Ithaca: Cornell University Press, 2000), pp. 172–73 and 180–85, for detailed discussions and examples of the hagiographical convention of the kissing of lepers.

[4] See 'The Legend of Frideswide', p. 47, and Anne B. Thompson, *Everyday Saints and the Art of Narrative in the South English Legendary* (Aldershot: Ashgate, 2003), pp. 148–49. Also see Oliver Pickering, 'Black Humour in the *South English Legendary*', in *Rethinking the South English Legendaries*, ed. by Heather Blurton and Jocelyn Wogan-Browne (Manchester: Manchester University Press, 2011), pp. 427–42 (p. 433).

[5] Görlach, pp. 37–38; see also Thomas R. Liszka, 'Talk in the Camps: On the Dating of the *South English Legendary*, *Havelok the Dane*, and *King Horn* in Oxford, Bodleian Library, MS Laud Misc. 108', in *The Texts and Contexts of Oxford, Bodleian Library, MS Laud Misc. 108: The Shaping of English Vernacular Narrative*, ed. by Kimberly K. Bell and Julie Nelson Couch (Boston: Brill, 2011), pp. 31–50, in which Liszka summarizes pre- and post-Görlach scholarship on the dating of the *SEL*.

The Virgin's Kiss: Gender, Leprosy, and Romance in the Life of Saint Frideswide

Composed largely in septenary rhyming couplets and characterized by simple, direct language, its intended purpose appears to have been the religious instruction of largely uneducated laity, accomplished via oral recitation of the legends; more recently, scholars have proposed that the collection may have been meant for 'private reading or reading aloud to small groups in the homes of the rural gentry of western England'.[6] Although the poets who composed the legends are not known, it is generally agreed that they belonged to a religious order, since the original source material of the legends was mostly in Latin. The poems in the collection often expand upon the original narratives, making comments or explanations to the reader in such a way that the saints' lives become more memorable and accessible to the intended audience. Relative to other collections of hagiographic texts, Klaus Jankofsky notes that the legends of the *SEL* can generally be said to possess the following characteristics:

> a simplification of theological-dogmatic and hagiographical problems; an explanatory, interpretive, and didactic expansion of subject matter; a process of concretization through the creation of enlivening dialogues and scenes where the sources have plain third-person narrative, that is, dramatization; and a process of acculturation, the adaptation of essentially Latin sources to an English audience, thereby creating a distinctive flavor and mood, *Englishing* […] Its singularity consists in the new tone and mood of compassion and warm human empathy for the lives and deaths of its protagonists.[7]

Recent scholarship has also focused on the *SEL*'s emphasis on narrative and concludes that its storytelling function seems to overshadow even its supposed didactic purposes.[8] As an important part of their poetic project, the writers of the *SEL* blended the conventions of hagiography with conventions from other genres already popular in English, such as romance. Both the longer *SEL* version of Frideswide's life already cited and a shorter verse version of her life found in other *SEL* manuscripts are examples of this sort of creative literary translation, which is one of the distinguishing characteristics of the entire *Legendary* and which provides an important contextual lens through which to view the expanded account of the leper's healing.[9]

The shorter life of Frideswide, although not the focus of this essay, differs in its presentation of the virgin's kiss and must be mentioned here. It is one of the rarest texts in the Legendary, existing in only two surviving manuscripts, plus a fragmentary copy in a third.

Latin Lives A and B were used by one or more poets to create the shorter and longer *SEL* verse legends of Frideswide's life, respectively. The shorter version is one of the rarest texts in the *Legendary*, existing in only two surviving manuscripts, plus a fragmentary copy in a third.[10] Its version of the leper's healing consists of a compact pair of couplets that portrays

---

[6] Thompson, p. 193.

[7] Klaus P. Jankofsky, 'National Characteristics in the Portrayal of English Saints in the *South English Legendary*', in *Images of Sainthood in Medieval Europe*, ed. by Renate Blumenfeld-Kosinski and Timea Szell (Ithaca: Cornell University Press, 1991), pp. 81–93 (pp. 82–83).

[8] O. S. Pickering, 'The *South English Legendary*: Teaching or Preaching?', *Poetica: An International Journal of Linguistic-Literary Studies*, 45 (1996), 1–14 (pp. 3, 10–11). Pickering notes that while the *SEL* legends are 'in almost all cases straightforward narratives' (p. 3), the creative changes made by an 'outspoken' late reviser moves them moderately closer to the sermonizing end of the teaching-preaching continuum (pp. 10–11).

[9] 'The Legend of Frideswide', pp. 27–36.

[10] Görlach, p. 196. The two manuscripts containing complete copies of the shorter life of Frideswide are Cambridge, Trinity College MS 605 (*c.* 1400) and London, British Library MS Stowe 949 (late 14th century); the fragmentary copy is found in Aberystwyth, National Library of Wales MS 5043 (*c.* 1400?).

the event in a very straightforward way, meeting the expectations of hagiographic readers by preserving the conventional roles of saint and supplicant:

> As heo yede a day in the toune, a mysel heo mette.
> To hure the mysel felle adoune, and on knes hure grette,
> And bysoght that lady that heo hym cusse scholde.
> Heo custe hym, and he was hole, ryght as God hit wolde. (ll. 111–14)
>
> [As she walked one day in the town, a leper met her.
> The leper fell down before her, and on his knees greeted her,
> And begged that lady that she would kiss him.
> She kissed him, and he was whole, just as God wished it.][11]

No confusion of feeling or ambiguity of motivation is present, and the relative communal positions of the protagonists are made clear by the added visual detail of the leper falling to his knees before the abbess (a detail found in no other version of the legend). The natural assumption by the reader is that Frideswide has kissed the leper on the forehead or face in a chaste and benevolent manner. The simpler description of the kiss and lack of interiority in both protagonists as portrayed in the shorter *SEL* life are in marked contrast to the account found in the longer *SEL* life, reinforcing the exceptionality of the latter.

Apart from her *vitae*, historical records reveal very little about Frideswide. She was, as far as can be determined, a royal Mercian lady who founded and headed a monastery in Oxford in the late seventh century that was already richly endowed before the end of Anglo-Saxon times. She later was adopted as Oxford's patron saint, and the rebuilt Priory of St Frideswide became the foundation of the current Christ Church in Oxford.[12] Historical certainty ends with these meager biographical data, and further details of her life are only to be found in hagiographic texts. Three surviving Latin texts of the life of Frideswide are considered possible sources for the *SEL* versions: a short summary of her life by William of Malmesbury in *Gesta Pontificum Anglorum*, *ca.* 1125; a longer text with several miracle stories, written *c.* 1100–30 in 'bald, rather clumsy Latin' and designated by John Blair as 'Life A'; and a 'longer and more elegant re-working of Life A', designated as 'Life B' and written *c.* 1140–70, almost certainly by Robert of Cricklade, Prior of St Frideswide's.[13]

Using the designators M, A, and B for each of the respective sources, a composite of the events in the Latin *vitae* may here be presented. Frideswide was born to a king of Oxford [MAB] named Didan, of the Anglo-Saxons, and his wife Safrida [AB].[14] The young princess showed remarkable spiritual and mental prowess when at age five she memorized all 150 psalms over the course of a few months [AB]. After the death of her mother [AB], Frideswide, having reached a marriageable age, instead renounced the world and became a nun, living in

---

[11] 'The Legend of Frideswide', p. 31.
[12] *Saint Frideswide, Patron of Oxford: The Earliest Texts*, ed. and trans. by John Blair (Oxford: Perpetua, 1988), p. 9.
[13] Blair, *Saint Frideswide*, pp. 9–11; here Blair refutes the premise put forward by F. M. Stenton in 'St. Frideswide and her Times', *Oxoniensia*, 1 (1936), 103–12 that the details of Frideswide's legend were mere inventions added to Malmesbury's simple story. Stenton's verdict was that the extra miracles were a late addition in the late twelfth or thirteenth century and could not have come from an earlier tradition. But Blair shows conclusively that Stenton must not have been aware of Life A, which was produced at the same time or earlier than Malmesbury's narrative and seems to have been independent of it, using at least one older source that is now lost. Görlach also believed that the longer and shorter *SEL* versions of Frideswide's life were based on independent sources, although at the time his book was written (1974) Life A had not yet come to light; see Görlach, p. 197.
[14] It should be noted that the longer *SEL* version of Frideswide's life presents her father only as a nobleman, 'Sire Didan', whereas the shorter *SEL* version and all Latin sources discussed in this essay identify him as a king.

the strictest asceticism [MAB]; her father, before his own death, built a church in Oxford and gave it to her [AB]. After becoming abbess, she rejected the devil, who, appearing as Christ, had invited her to worship him [AB]. The wicked king Algar tried to take her by force to be his wife, but was miraculously stricken by blindness as he pursued her [MAB]. She fled to a wood near Bampton, where she lived three years while evading the king and healed a blind girl [AB]. Frideswide then moved much closer to Oxford, being led to a secluded spot in Binsey, where she lived with her companion sisters and miraculously located a well to sustain them [B]. While there, she healed a young man who had been cursed for chopping wood on a Sunday and cast a demon out of a fisherman [AB]. When she felt that her death was near she returned to Oxford, healing the young leper with her kiss as she entered the city [AB]. Being informed by an angel that she would die on Sunday, 19 October 727, she asked for a grave to be dug on the day before so that no one would be obligated to work on Sunday [AB]. When the hour of her death arrived, she looked heavenward and saw the holy virgins Catherine and Cecilia, who had come to guard her on her way back to the Lord; after her passing, a light blazed through Oxford and a sweet scent filled the town [AB]. As further proof of her holy status, a paralyzed rich man was healed after dragging himself to her grave, and a crippled nobleman named Athelwold threw away his crutches and leapt into the church after interrupting her funeral [AB].[15]

Admittedly, much of Frideswide's legend seems familiar to experienced readers of hagiography; the figure of the lustful king miraculously struck down while pursuing a holy virgin, for example, is quite common in lives of virgin martyrs and often dismissed by scholars as a homiletic invention, although Blair notes that the abduction of noblewomen was not uncommon in early medieval times, and that 'King Algar' may have had a historical precedent in King Æthelbald of Mercia.[16] A comparison of the Latin sources of the Frideswide story reveals the way in which details from the earlier texts (Malmesbury's summary and Life A) are modified, enhanced, or corrected in the later Life B. For instance, in Malmesbury's brief text the blinded king's sight is restored after he sends messengers to seek the saint's forgiveness, but Algar receives no such merciful treatment in Life B.[17] Also, an error regarding the geographical location of Binsey, introduced unknowingly by the writer of Life A, is corrected by Prior Robert in Life B, who obviously was well familiar with Oxford and the surrounding countryside.[18]

A comparison of individual events narrated by the Latin sources of the Frideswide legend reveals that some of the greatest differences are found in the incident of the leper's healing. Malmesbury's account does not mention it at all. Life A is the earliest text to record the miracle, presenting it in a very straightforward fashion:

> Cum autem ingrederetur beata Fritheswitha in supradictam urbem, occurrit ei quidam iuvenis plenus lepra, dixitque ei, 'Adiuro te, O Frithesuuitha virgo, ut des mihi osculum in nomine Iesu Cristi.' Illa, ut semper erat repleta Sancto Spiritu, faciens signum crucis dedit ei osculum in nomine Domini, et statim mundatus est a lepra.[19]
>
> (Blessed Frideswide had just entered the town when a young man full of leprosy ran up to her and said, 'I beseech you, virgin Frideswide, to give me a kiss in the name of Jesus

---

[15] John Blair, 'Saint Frideswide Reconsidered', *Oxoniensia*, 52 (1987), 71–127 (pp. 74–79).
[16] Blair, *Saint Frideswide*, p. 15.
[17] Blair, *Saint Frideswide*, p. 27.
[18] Blair, *Saint Frideswide*, pp. 12–13.
[19] Blair, 'Saint Frideswide Reconsidered', p. 100.

Christ.' Filled as she always was with the Holy Spirit, she made the sign of the cross and gave him a kiss in the Lord's name, and at once he was cleaned of his leprosy.)[20]

Life B, on the other hand, seems to be the product of a conscious and determined effort on the part of Prior Robert to give Frideswide a richer and more interesting history, and this version of the leper's healing is significantly expanded:

> Repedanti ergo sacrosancte virgini, tota ilico in obviam ruit civitas et ecce inter *cler*i populique utriusque sexus congratulantium turbas, adest *iuvenis lepra* immanissima adeo tabe et pustulis toto deformatus corpore. [...] Sic enim ulcera, sic tumors, sic iniquus color cuncta obduxerant, ut monstrum potius putaretur quam homo. Iste profecto non modo miserabilis verum extra modum horribilis, cum appropinquaret ad sanctam, quanta potuit voce horribiliter quidem rauca emisit sonitum satis confusum, verba tamen exprimentem, dicens, '*Adiuro te, virgo Frideswida*, per Deum omnipotentem, *ut des mihi osculum in nomine Iesu Cristi* Filii eius Unigeniti.' [...] O dura sane postulatio! Petis, iuvenis leprose, virginem natura uti regiam sed, quia Cristi ancillam, non moribus delicatam, tibi dare osculum, in quem mares animo prorsus duriores figere abhorrent obtutum? Plane postulatio tua, ni fides eam magnifica proferri compulsisset, forte putaretur insanientium improbitate prolata. Quidni? Homines, ut dixi, te intueri pre horrore nequeunt, pro sanie profluente tangere, pro fetore intolerabili tibi appropinquare, et osculum petis a regia virgine? Esto. Nisi leprosus fueris, attamen masculus, num tibi porrigere poterit osculum, que virilem ab inuente etate non novit attactum? Sed inquis, 'Morbi mei intolerabilis estus, et non quem tu commemoras sexus, hoc me petere compellit. Credo enim quod ad tactum oris eius mundissimi, fugiet morbida immunditia corporis mei.' O res miranda et seculis inaudita preteritis! Caritatis igne succensa virgo, contra opinionem omnium ilico accessit et *signo crucis* prius impresso, leproso contulit *osculum*. Facile etenim proculdubio sit quod a caritate vera procedit. Abhorrent intuentes, et cum admiratione non modica rei exitum expectant. Stupendum plane miraculum! Non enim minus quam Naaman Siro septena et mistica iuxta sermonem Helisei in Iordane ablutio, quantum ad corporis sanitatem spectat, huie una pia cum humili devotione puelle sacratissime deosculatio contulit. Ore etenim virginis os leprosi tangitur, et continuo toto corpore *mandatur*. Cutis aspera ad squamarum modum solvitur et velud exuvie colubrine deponitur, ac statim fit caro ipsius sicut caro pueri parvuli.[21]

> (When the most holy virgin returned, the entire town immediately rushed to meet her in the way, and, behold, among the crowds of rejoicing clergy and people, both men and women, there is a young man so deformed by monstrous leprosy with pus and blisters on his entire body [...] Thus ulcers, tumors, and uneven complexion so covered everything, that it was easier to believe him a monster than a man. That one certainly was not only pitiable in manner but very frightful; when he approached the holy one, how horribly with a raucous voice he was able to emit a quite disordered sound, yet still expressing words, saying, 'I adjure thee, virgin Frideswide, by Almighty God, that thou give me a kiss in the name of Jesus Christ, His Only Begotten Son.' [...] Oh truly hard request! Do you, leprous youth, at whom men of entirely hard character shudder to fasten their gaze, ask this virgin to give you a kiss, who is not only of royal birth but also Christ's handmaid, and not of wanton character? Clearly your request would be considered an insane wickedness, unless great faith prompted it to be brought forth. Why not? Men, as I said, cannot look at you because of the dread of touching the flowing gore, of approaching your insufferable stink, and you ask a kiss from the royal virgin? So it is. If you were not a leper, but

---

[20] Blair, *Saint Frideswide*, p. 37.
[21] Blair, 'Saint Frideswide Reconsidered', p. 113. Italicized words are direct quotations from Life A.

simply male, you would never be able to offer a kiss to her, who does not know the touch of one who has arrived at a manly age. But you say, 'Remember, the insufferable heat of my disease, and not any such thing as my sex, compels me to ask this. For I believe that at the touch of her pure mouth the diseased foulness of my body will flee away.' A wonderful thing, and unheard of in the past! Kindled with the flame of charity and against the opinion of everyone present, the virgin immediately approached, first making the sign of the cross, and bestowed a kiss upon the leper. Truly it is without a doubt that she proceeded by true charity. Those observing shrink back and anticipate the outcome of the event with no moderate admiration. A truly amazing miracle! For indeed, what the seven and secret washings in Jordan according to Elisha's sacred word did for the health of the body of Naaman the Syrian, so did one holy kiss bestowed by the consecrated maiden with humble devotion. Since the mouth of the leper is touched by the mouth of the virgin, he is immediately cleansed in his whole body. His skin, rough like scales, is loosened and shed just like a molted snake skin, and immediately his flesh is like the flesh of a very small child.)[22]

Notable changes in this version include the emphasis on the leper's horrible appearance, the narrator's questioning of the leper for his audacity in requesting a kiss from Frideswide, and the explanation of the leper's possible motives for making the request.

Medieval Conceptions of Leprosy

As the writer of the longer *SEL* life of Frideswide adapted his Latin sources for a lay English audience, he was drawing upon a medieval worldview in which leprosy was understood symbolically. The symbolism was dual in nature, with one meaning rooted in the Bible and the other in early Christian hagiographic texts. Mosaic law treated leprosy not only as a danger to public health, but also as a representation of sin and spiritual disease; thus, a leper who had been pronounced clean of the plague was required to have both sin and trespass offerings performed in his behalf.[23] Additionally, there are biblical stories of individuals who are miraculously afflicted with leprosy as divine retribution for personal wickedness or rebellion.[24] These scriptural accounts, coupled with the natural revulsion felt by people of all classes when confronted by a leper in the advanced stages of the disease, led, in Carole Rawcliffe's words, to 'the assumption that spiritual deformity would somehow leave its trace upon the body as well as the soul insidiously [finding] its way into religious and secular literature alike'.[25] In their sermons, medieval clergy used not only Bible stories but also popular tales and moral anecdotes that connected leprosy to wickedness, often interpreting the stories on multiple levels; such preachers, for example, might refer to the lepers in the tales as allegorical figures representing specific sins, such as the 'leper of bakbityng'.[26] Many in the Middle Ages, then, assumed that leprosy was a natural result of sin and spiritual decay and that a leper's wickedness was unmistakably inscribed on his own body as a warning for all to see.[27]

---

[22] Blair, 'Saint Frideswide Reconsidered', p. 78. The Modern English translation is mostly my own, with valuable assistance from Miranda Wilcox, for which I am grateful.
[23] See Leviticus 13–14.
[24] See Numbers 12:10, 2 Kings 5:27, and 2 Chronicles 26:19-21 as examples.
[25] Rawcliffe, p. 48.
[26] Rawcliffe, pp. 48–49.
[27] Peyroux, p. 174.

These negative connotations of leprosy inherited from the Bible sharply contrast with favorable representations of leprosy in hagiographic texts beginning in the fourth century, in which the ravages of the disease are symbolic of the suffering and sorrow of Christ himself. By the late medieval period, iconography of Christ included 'images of His beaten and abused body, which shared many of the features conventionally deployed in the depiction of lepers'.[28] Hagiographers and medieval theologians were also influenced by St Jerome's somewhat liberal translation of Isaiah 53:4 in the fourth-century Vulgate Bible: 'vere languores nostros ipse tulit, et dolores nostros ipse portavit: et nos putavimus eum quasi leprosum, et percussum a Deo et humiliatum' ('surely he hath borne our infirmities and carried our sorrows: and we have thought him as it were a leper, and as one struck by God and afflicted').[29] Jerome's interpretation of Isaiah's Messianic prophecy led to the long-lasting concept of *Christus quasi leprosus*: that Christ had assumed the most wretched and abject physical condition possible, through his bruises, wounds, and putrefying sores, and therefore had close affinity with the leper.[30]

Christus quasi leprosus was reinforced through incidents recorded in saints' lives, in which a saint is asked for alms or other assistance by a leper, after which the leper either mysteriously disappears or transforms into Christ and ascends to heaven.[31] Thus, service to lepers, including embracing, kissing, and washing their sores, became a way for a saint to access the divinity of Christ and show love to him, actions which are motifs in the legends of several saints. The Thuringian princess Radegund, who, like Frideswide, had founded a monastery after spurning a royal marriage, embraced the women in a group of lepers seeking charity, 'and kissed even their faces, loving them with her whole soul'.[32] Matilda, the wife of King Henry I of England, was found one night washing and kissing the feet of lepers; when asked what the king would think if he knew that her lips had touched the feet of lepers, she replied, 'who does not know that the feet of the Eternal King are to be preferred to the lips of a king who must die?'[33] Some saints were even portrayed as being eager to contract the disease themselves in order to experience Christ's suffering and rejection more intimately.[34] Thus, hagiographers constructed their narratives of saints kissing lepers to demonstrate that these kisses were a means by which saints might attain a more profound spiritual fulfillment. Yet Frideswide's healing kiss in the longer *SEL* version of her life departs from these conventions, and functions in a radically different way from the expected hagiographic treatment of kissing lepers.

The virgin's kiss and the construction of romantic identity

In the longer *SEL* version of Frideswide's legend, the poet crafts the scene of the leper's healing using conventions not only of hagiography but of romance as well, thus creating tension between sanctity and secular love in the scene. This tension is essentially rooted in the reader's expectations of competing genres: in hagiography, a suffering leper requests healing from a maternal and compassionate abbess, and, in romance, a courtly lover begs his beloved to heal

---

[28] Rawcliffe, pp. 60–61.
[29] All Latin Bible quotations are taken from *Biblia sacra iuxta vulgatam versionem*, ed. by B. Fischer and others (Stuttgart: Deutsche Bibelgesellschaft, 1994). All English Bible quotations are taken from *The Holy Bible: Douay-Rheims Version*, ed. by James Gibbons (Rockford, IL: TAN Books, 1989).
[30] Rawcliffe, pp. 60–63.
[31] Peyroux, pp. 173, 184–85; also see Rawcliffe, p. 63. One such incident occurred in the life of Francis of Assisi.
[32] Peyroux, p. 181.
[33] Peyroux, p. 183.
[34] Rawcliffe, p. 59.

his lovesickness with her favor. When the saint kisses the leper, the didactic purposes of the hagiographic text are instantly subverted by the secular, sexual complexities of romance. The kiss thus activates two modes in the narrative simultaneously: saintly compassion and romantic love, and Frideswide's body becomes the nexus where generic tensions are instantiated.

In light of the prevailing hagiographic tradition and symbolism of leprosy, the longer *SEL* account of Frideswide's kiss is strikingly unconventional. When the leper makes his initial request for a kiss, the abbess tries to ignore him and continues to walk along quietly, rather than seek union with Christ through service to his earthly counterpart in suffering. Instead of viewing the request as an opportunity to follow in the footsteps of Jesus, Frideswide surprisingly feels shame and seeks to avoid the leper altogether; this, of course, proves to be impossible because their encounter takes place in front of all the townspeople of Oxford. In fact, the presence of a great crowd of witnesses is the only additional detail that the Frideswide story shares with another medieval account of a saint healing a leper. The fourth-century life of Martin of Tours records how the bishop healed a leper by kissing him in the crowded city gates of Paris, but the leper does not ask for healing, and Martin is portrayed as kissing the leper's face and not his mouth.[35] Indeed, it is the method of contact between the saint and the leper in Frideswide's story that stands out as its most unusual feature. In the New Testament, Jesus heals lepers with a simple touch of his outstretched hand.[36] Of known accounts of the kissing of lepers in medieval hagiography, the Frideswide legend is the only one in which a kiss is demanded by the leper and not offered unsolicited by the saint; it is also the only story in which the leper is male and the saint is female.[37]

The gender difference between the saint and the leper is highlighted when the male leper makes specific reference to the female saint's 'suete mouth' (147); his familiarity introduces an element of eroticism and seems to provoke her shame. It is highly improbable that the leper would have made the same request in the same way had the saint entering the city been male. The overall effect of the longer *SEL* version of the healing is to highlight the gender of Frideswide and bring her femininity to the forefront; it seems to the reader that the leper requests a kiss from her, not only because she is holy, but because she is a holy *woman*. The intimate nature of the requested kiss between a woman and a man will bridge not only the gulf between holy and unholy, between health and disease, but also between female and male. Other hagiographic accounts of kissing lepers, as we have seen, involved the saint kissing feet or faces of the diseased persons; only in the Frideswide legend does the healing kiss involve mouth-to-mouth contact. Even Robert's Life B makes it clear that the saint didn't simply kiss the leper's face: 'Ore etenim virginis os leprosi tangitur, et continuo toto corpore mandatur' (since the mouth of the leper is touched by the mouth of the virgin, he is immediately cleansed in his whole body). Only the act of kissing the saint *as* a woman, the *SEL* poet seems to imply, can bring about a complete union, complete wholeness, and complete reconciliation between how things are and how they ought to be, overcoming the fragmentation of the leper's diseased body. The efficacy of this union is shown by the magnified scale of the healing in the longer *SEL* account, in which the leper goes from 'swythe grisliche myd alle' (143) to 'hol and sound' (152), a 'vair man and clene' (153).

---

[35] Peyroux, p. 180.
[36] See Mark 1:41 and Matthew 8:3 for examples of Jesus' healing lepers.
[37] See Rawcliffe, pp. 144–46, and Peyroux, pp. 172–73, 180–85, for a detailed list of accounts of the kissing of lepers.

In fact, the expanded Frideswide story is a compelling example of how the religious worldview in the later Middle Ages is characterized by a yearning to bridge gaps and reintegrate fragmented parts into a meaningful whole. Caroline Walker Bynum has shown how Western European religious thinkers of the twelfth and thirteenth centuries were often concerned with how various body parts, such as pared fingernails, would be reassembled in the resurrection, and notes that 'it was a period in which the overcoming of partition and putrefaction — either through reunion of parts into a whole or through assertion of part *as part* to *be* the whole — was the image of paradise'.[38] Leprosy itself could then be seen as a powerful symbol of fragmentation, in which the sufferer, in a half-living state, is experiencing a preview of death's disintegration. The fragmentation is vividly manifest not only in the physical breakdown of the leper's body, whose horrible appearance is emphasized in Latin Life B, but also in the breakdown of community through his exclusion from the town's social environment.

In the longer *SEL* poem, Frideswide's gendered and holy body becomes the means to satisfy the medieval desire for reintegration. Her status as a *virgo intacta* represents wholeness according to the patristic writers, who described the female virgin body as 'a jewel, a treasure, a sacred vessel, a temple of God which was to be cherished and honored'.[39] The saint's untarnished purity and her gendered wholeness confront the decay of the leper's body and restore it to completeness in so powerful and miraculous a fashion that the healing also expresses figuratively for the townspeople of Oxford the glory of the final resurrection. Although the patristic writers vigorously debated which body parts would be preserved in the resurrection, they did not consider gender itself to be a fragmentation that would be removed or recombined in resurrected bodies; risen human beings would retain their sex, because, 'for reasons [theologians] could not fully explain, God's creation was more perfect in two sexes than in one'.[40] So Frideswide's gender, unlike the temporary, temporal nature of the leper's diseased disintegration, is an enduring part of her identity and personhood and, as portrayed by the poet, becomes a vital component of her miraculous healing power.

Although Frideswide's gender informs and helps define her sanctity in the longer *SEL* poem, it also is inextricably connected to the shame she feels throughout the incident of the leper's healing. Whether the leper's request for a kiss was intended as a sexual advance is not as important as the fact that Frideswide, at least partially, interpreted it as one. The shame and hesitation she shows would indicate that she considered the leper's request as a possible breach of her vow of chastity, or at least inappropriate physical contact between an abbess and a lay man. There are certainly other possible explanations for her feelings, such as the natural revulsion one would feel when faced with the prospect of mouth-to-mouth contact with a leper; one can also imagine her hesitating, for modesty's sake, to perform a charitable act in front of the entire town that she would be quite willing to do in the private confines of her abbey. A telling piece of evidence that her shame was connected to her vow of chastity, however, is the fact that she was 'sorely ashamed' *after* the kiss. Other reasons for embarrassment or shame would have disappeared once the kiss was complete and, indeed, would have been replaced by joy and gratitude when the man's leprosy vanished. However, after introducing ambiguity

---

[38] Caroline Walker Bynum, *Fragmentation and Redemption: Essays on Gender and the Human Body in Medieval Religion* (New York: Zone Books, 1992), p. 13.

[39] Jane Tibbetts Schulenberg, *Forgetful of Their Sex: Female Sanctity and Society, ca. 500–1100* (Chicago: University of Chicago Press, 1998), pp. 127–28.

[40] Bynum, p. 230.

concerning the motivation and emotions of the participants, the poet intervenes in the narrative and offers his opinion that Frideswide was not guilty of sin 'even though she was in a religious order'. An important result of concluding the story in this way is that it emphasizes not only the femininity of the abbess but also her humanity. Rather than a sanctified caricature of unchanging benevolence, removed from earthly care and weakness, she becomes accessible through her display of uncertainty, shame, and embarrassment, and her emotional response draws the reader into an unexpected and compelling moral dilemma. The leper has constrained Frideswide, by her vows of devotion and piety, to help him; she is obligated, as a servant of Christ, to show mercy and render aid to all who ask for it. Her shame at being asked to submit to unwanted physical contact with a man is trumped by the leper's very public insistence on mercy. The kiss then becomes, for her, a stern test of devotion and surrender of free will that is unlikely to have been required of a male cleric in the same situation.

Why, then, did the poet make these changes in the longer *SEL* life of Frideswide? One possibility is that the poet was crafting the narrative for a lay female audience. Considerable scholarship in recent years has established that vernacular saints' lives were read by large numbers of women, and many were written explicitly for female readers, especially those whose subjects were virgin martyrs.[41] Lay women readers were urged by moralists and hagiographers to read the legends as exemplary biography; however, since closely imitating the sufferings and miraculous deeds of the virgin saints was not possible, they were encouraged to find and emulate virtues in the stories consistent with contemporary social expectations and feminine devotional practice.[42] These interpretive readings were often figurative in nature, and readers were sometimes quite flexible in their mapping of heroic behavior onto practical daily routines. Thus, in addition to viewing Frideswide's act as an exemplar of compassion to suffering souls, the healing could also be read more generally as a victory of Christ's compassion (as symbolized by the saint) over sin and wickedness (as symbolized by the leper). Alternately, viewing the leper as Christ (through the lens of *Christus quasi leprosus*) and Frideswide as the betrothed of the Bridegroom, 'refined gentlewomen' might see how compassionate sacrifice might bring healing benefits to their own marriages.[43]

The notion that some *SEL* legends were written largely for female readers illuminates possible reasons for the poet's changes, and the history of Frideswide's cult prior to the composition of the *SEL* also suggests a female audience. Pre-Norman historical details of the saint's monastery are practically nonexistent; the reason, as recorded in a royal charter restoring the title-deed to St Frideswide's in 1004, is that Danes fleeing Æthelred's extermination order in 1002 took refuge in the monastery and set fire to it.[44] Even before the fire, the monastery had apparently been converted into a minster of non-monastic male clerics. By the early twelfth century the restored monastery was refounded as a priory of disciplined Augustinian monks, and it was probably in connection with this change that Life A was written

---

[41] See Jocelyn Wogan-Browne, *Saints' Lives and Women's Literary Culture c. 1150–1300: Virginity and its Authorizations* (Oxford: Oxford University Press, 2001); Karen A. Winstead, *Virgin Martyrs: Legends of Sainthood in Late Medieval England* (Ithaca: Cornell University Press, 1997); and Catherine Sanok, *Her Life Historical: Exemplarity and Female Saints' Lives in Late Medieval England* (Philadelphia: University of Pennsylvania Press, 2007).

[42] Sanok, pp. 2–9; also, see Andrea Hopkins, 'Female Saints and Romance Heroines: Feminine Fiction and Faith among the Literate Elite', in *Christianity and Romance in Medieval England*, ed. Rosalind Field, Phillipa Hardman, and Michelle Sweeney (Cambridge: Brewer, 2010), pp. 121–38 (pp. 126–27).

[43] Winstead's phrase, p. 113.

[44] Blair, *Saint Frideswide*, pp. 18–19.

in an attempt to recover and memorialize the origins of both the community and the saint. However, because St Frideswide's had been held for some time by Abingdon Abbey prior to the installation of the Augustinians, the new residents feared that the Abingdon monks had stolen Frideswide's remains. A fourteenth-century manuscript chronicles how the fears of the Augustinians were put to rest after a secret nighttime excursion to the church; not only did the excursion uncover the saint's remains, but it was attended by a miraculous extinguishing and rekindling of their torches as the bones were uncovered. Impressed by this heavenly sign and by the fact that the number of visitors and miracles at the gravesite had increased markedly, Prior Philip of St Frideswide's had the saint's bones transferred to a raised shrine with great publicity in 1180. The Archbishop of Canterbury himself came to Oxford to perform the ceremony.[45] The translation of the relics and dozens of miracles reported soon thereafter seem to be the culmination of an effort begun much earlier by Prior Robert, who expanded the earlier Life A and corrected its faulty geographical references when he produced Life B c. 1140–70.

When the *SEL* was first compiled c. 1270–85, nearly a century had elapsed since most of the healing miracles had been recorded at the shrine of Frideswide; the great majority had occurred in the last two decades of the twelfth century. Henry Mayr-Harting, in a detailed study of miracles recorded at the saint's shrine, notes that in cases of healing, sixty-seven involved females and only thirty-two involved males.[46] This female-male ratio is highly unusual when compared to the shrines of other saints. Moreover, a great number of the maladies healed were related to the psychological effects of the onset of puberty in girls and sexual fear or rejection in adult women. Mayr-Harting concludes:

> one sees […] in the Miracles of St. Frideswide the perennial dislocations and illnesses caused by sexual problems, compounded for women by their being regarded in that society as inferior to men and having far fewer alternative outlets for their energies and emotions.[47]

It is thus quite probable that the longer *SEL* life of Frideswide was composed at a time when she had acquired a considerable reputation for being especially merciful to women and quick to grant their supplications for relief, and therefore reasonable to assume that suffering girls and women had a long-established rapport with the saint and had adopted her as a patroness. If this was indeed the case, the poet may have wanted to strengthen Frideswide's cult by portraying her as being obligated to kiss a leprous man against the delicate dictates of her own conscience, thereby creating empathy in a female lay audience. Such a sympathetic treatment of women beset by unwanted male advances would be consistent with a section of another, lengthy *SEL* poem, *Southern Passion*, which lauds the fidelity of women and argues against categorizing them as fickle and lecherous, since lechery invariably originates with men.[48]

Another possible reason for the poet's alterations is that they may constitute a reaction against the existing religious institutional landscape, in which conceptions of female monas-

---

[45] Blair, *Saint Frideswide*, 19–20.
[46] Henry Mayr-Harting, 'Functions of a Twelfth-Century Shrine: The Miracles of St Frideswide', in *Studies in Medieval History Presented to R. H. C. Davis*, ed. by Henry Mayr-Harting and R. I. Moore (London: Hambledon, 1985), pp. 193–206 (pp. 197–98).
[47] Mayr-Harting, p. 198.
[48] O. S. Pickering, 'The "Defense of Women" from the *Southern Passion*: A New Edition', in *The South English Legendary: A Critical Assessment*, ed. by Klaus P. Jankofsky (Tübingen: Francke, 1992), pp. 154–76 (p. 156). It is not known whether the poet who composed *Southern Passion* is the same who wrote the longer *SEL* life of Frideswide.

ticism had changed so much during the five centuries since Frideswide's death that abbesses of her stature were now completely unknown. The Benedictine reform movement that had begun in the tenth century, over three centuries before the composition of the *SEL*, resulted in substantial restrictions of female ecclesiastical power and influence.[49] The original community of St Frideswide appears to have changed as a result of the reform: it was probably founded as a double monastery led by a female abbess but, as has been noted, was later refounded as a male-only monastery, eliminating the position of abbess altogether.[50] As the monastic reform movement continued into the eleventh century, it became less common for abbesses to attend synods and for nuns to receive the same rigorous training in Latin and the scriptures as monks.[51] As a result, dynamic abbesses such as Frideswide, who organized missionary work, advised monarchs, and ruled with complete ecclesiastical authority over both male and female monastics, had completely disappeared from religious establishments by the time of the *SEL*'s composition.

Indeed, the roots of an ideology that limited female ecclesiastical power can be traced to writings of early Christian Fathers, who depicted the ideal spiritual being as male and reasoned that in order to achieve relevance in Christian dialogue a woman must surpass her own nature and become male, at least symbolically.[52] Helene Scheck offers the tenth-century lives of two saints, Euginia and Euphrosyne, as examples: the female saints dress and masquerade as male monastics in order to live a more righteous and holy life, and when their true gender is inevitably discovered, the monks are amazed that women could be so righteous.[53] Consequently, female monastics were often denied access to the scriptural study and commentary available to male monastics and were increasingly confined to physical expressions of piety, such as fasting or other forms of physical penance and self-denial.[54]

Further evidence that ecclesiastical institutions limited feminine influence is found in the conventions of hagiography itself, which tended to portray female saints as passive or reactive rather than active. Male hagiographers, already viewing their female subjects as 'other' *because* they were female and therefore mysterious, were reluctant to portray the saints' worldly, everyday assertiveness, choosing instead to focus on 'the women's proximity to the supernatural realm, a holy intimacy the men admired but felt incapable of imitating'.[55] It is important to recognize that the Latin sources used by the *SEL*-poet to create his Middle English life of Frideswide were not written soon after her death in 727, but dated from the twelfth century and had thus already passed through the male authorial filter of experienced

---

[49] Helene Scheck, *Reform and Resistance: Formations of Female Subjectivity in Early Medieval Ecclesiastical Culture* (Albany: State University of New York Press, 2008), pp. 83–85. A detailed treatment of the Church's attempt to limit female leadership and influence can be found in Jane Tibbetts Schulenberg, 'Female Sanctity: Public and Private Roles, ca. 500–1100', in *Women and Power in the Middle Ages*, ed. by Mary Erler and Maryanne Kowaleski (Athens: University of Georgia Press, 1988), pp. 102–25 (pp. 115–21).

[50] Blair, *Saint Frideswide*, p. 18.

[51] Scheck, pp. 83–84.

[52] See Margaret R. Miles, *Carnal Knowing: Female Nakedness and Religious Meaning in the Christian West* (Boston: Beacon Press, 1989), pp. 55–56; also see Schulenburg, *Forgetful of Their Sex*, pp. 128–29. Schulenburg references St Jerome, who said that when a woman 'wishes to serve Christ more than the world, she will cease to be a woman and will be called man', and St Ambrose, who said that 'she who believes progresses to perfect manhood, to the measure of the adulthood of Christ' (p. 453).

[53] Scheck, pp. 85–90.

[54] Schulenburg, *Forgetful of Their Sex*, pp. 377–79, 395.

[55] Catherine M. Mooney, 'Voice, Gender, and the Portrayal of Sanctity', in *Gendered Voices: Medieval Saints and Their Interpreters*, ed. by Catherine M. Mooney (Philadelphia: University of Pennsylvania Press, 1999), pp. 1–15 (pp. 10–11).

hagiographers who sought to portray female saints not as exceptional leaders and ecclesiastical rulers, but as resisters of male lust and sufferers of fleshly trials. Also, the basic narrative framework of the leper's healing had already been established in the sources, and even the *SEL*-poet's expanded version retains elements of female passivity. For instance, it was the male leper who dictated the terms of his interaction with Frideswide by choosing the manner of the healing, and, uncomfortable though she was with it, she is presented as unable to find another option.

In fact, the original Latin Lives A and B contain a far greater number of depictions of Frideswide's passivity than the longer *SEL* version of her life. Life B in particular contains several instances in which the virgin receives instructions from a heavenly messenger on where to go or how to proceed, thus presenting her own agency as limited. The *SEL* version, in contrast, contains fewer instances of direct divine intervention, and the corresponding events show the abbess possessing a greater power of action. Anne Thompson notes that while 'Robert's description [Life B] of Frideswide conspires to remove her from the human sphere',[56] in the *SEL* versions '[Frideswide's] travels are constructed as positive events, which she undertakes through her own volition, rather than being imposed on her by God and the narratorr'.[57] By returning the saint to an active role in her own story, the *SEL*-poet has reclaimed some small part of the lost female dynamism of medieval narrative and permitted a glimpse of the power and influence of Anglo-Saxon abbesses.

Yet, even as medieval conceptions of leprosy, gender, and religious authority collide and provide an underlying tension in the longer *SEL* life of Frideswide, the poetic art that is likely to have made it appealing to a medieval audience is largely achieved through the infusion of the hagiographic narrative with the language and conventions of romance. That the poet had access to romance texts is not only plausible but likely, since many abbeys had libraries that contained them, not only among the Augustinian canons regular and the Benedictines, but among other orders as well, such as the Gilbertines and Cistercians.[58] Writers of Middle English hagiography often absorbed the stylistic conventions of romance while rejecting much of its subject matter, which is vividly demonstrated in several *SEL* manuscripts. No fewer than fifteen contain a poem called 'Banna Sanctorum' that was written to serve as a prologue to the collection in later manuscripts and which seeks to prove the superiority of saints' lives over romance stories:

> Men wilneþ muche to hure telle of bataille of kynge
> And of kniȝtes þat hardy were þat muchedel is lesynge
> Wo so wilneþ muche to hure tales of suche þinge
> Hardi batailles he may hure here þat nis no lesinge
> Of apostles & martirs þat hardy kniȝtes were
> Þat studeuast were in bataille & ne fleide noȝt for fere
> Þat soffrede þat luþer men al quik hare lymes totere (ll. 59–65)
>
> (Men greatly desire to hear of the battles of kings
> And of knights who were brave, much of which is lying.
> Whoever would like to hear tales of such things
> May hear of hardy battles here which are not lies;

---

[56] Thompson, p. 145.
[57] Thompson, p. 151.
[58] Melissa Furrow, *Expectations of Romance: The Reception of a Genre in Medieval England* (Woodbridge: Brewer, 2009), p. 223.

Of apostles and martyrs who were bold knights,
Who were steadfast in battle and fled not for fear
And suffered evil men to tear their living limbs to pieces.)[59]

The poet here employs a conscious rhetorical strategy, asking the reader to exchange the stories of popular romance (which he characterizes as 'lying') for the legends of the *SEL* saints (which are 'not lies'); rather than reject the style and motifs of romance, however, he embraces them, and in a manner reminiscent of the earlier Old English poetic tradition casts the holy martyrs as knights and heroic warriors. At a stroke, the poet has claimed the best qualities of a popular literary genre and fitted them with what he considers to be proper subject matter.

One particular *SEL* manuscript blurs the line between hagiography and romance even further, as it includes in the compilation actual romances that involve saint-like protagonists, such as *King Horn* and *Havelok the Dane*. A recent collection of essays on Oxford, Bodleian Library, MS Laud Misc. 108 shows how 'genres are critical constructions after the fact of writing', and are very much in the eye of the manuscript compiler.[60] Kimberly Bell and Julie Nelson Couch, in their assessment of this manuscript, argue that, rather than viewing it as being clearly divided into a *vita* section and a romance section, it should be read as a whole book, noting that the consecutive numbering of all the texts in the manuscript and its mostly uniform decoration indicate a desire on the part of the compilers to frame the romances as part of 'a continuum of saints' lives and religious matter'.[61] Andrew Lynch continues this argument by noting that in the juxtaposition of *vita* and romance, new combinations of images and ideas could form in the mind of the reader, reinforcing but also varying and enhancing themes of heroic virtue.[62] The direction of the connections is framed by the compiler of the collection and the choices of what texts to include, and in which order. Legends of martyrs and confessors in the *SEL* are linked to the exile-prince romances *Horn* and *Havelok* by 'the special prominence they give to the nature and disposition of heroic bodies'; divine power is registered corporeally in both types of protagonists 'through signs of divine origin, providential preservation, and ultimate heavenly endorsement'.[63] The inclusion of these romances in a notable *SEL* manuscript such as Laud Misc. 108 seems to highlight two genres that in the thirteenth century were being drawn ever closer together, as authors and compilers, responding to a changing readerly aesthetic, sought to redefine the artistic boundaries of hagiographic narrative.[64]

In general, the verse lives of saints found in the *SEL* are splendid examples of the romanticization of vernacular hagiographic texts, and the *SEL* versions of Frideswide's legend

---

[59] *The South English Legendary, Vol. 1*, ed. by Charlotte d'Evelyn and Anna J. Mill (Woodbridge: Boydell and Brewer, 2004), p. 3. The 'Banna Sanctorum' is found in two of the four *SEL* manuscripts containing the longer life of Frideswide: Cambridge, Magdalene College MS Pepys 2344 and London, British Library MS Cotton Junius D IX.

[60] Andrew Lynch, 'Genre, Bodies, and Power in Oxford, Bodleian Library, MS Laud Misc. 108: *King Horn*, *Havelok*, and the *South English Legendary*', *Texts and Contexts*, pp. 177–96 (p. 179). Although the manuscript focused on in these essays does not contain either the shorter or longer life of Frideswide, the collection addresses connections between genre and manuscript compilation that are pertinent to the discussion at hand.

[61] Kimberly K. Bell and Julie Nelson Couch, 'Introduction: Reading Oxford, Bodleian Library, MS Laud Misc. 108 as a Whole Book', *Texts and Contexts*, pp. 1–18 (pp. 7–9); also see Murray J. Evans, ' "Very Like A Whale": Physical Features and the "Whole Book" in Oxford, Bodleian Library, MS Laud Misc. 108', *Texts and Contexts*, pp. 51–69.

[62] Lynch, pp. 177–78, 182.

[63] Lynch, p. 187.

[64] See Jocelyn Wogan-Browne, ' "Bet ... to ... rede on holy seyntes lyves ...": Romances and Hagiography Again',

are no exception. In comparing the account of the leper's healing in the longer *SEL* life of Frideswide to its principal source, Robert's Latin Life B, certain elements found in the former have the effect of making it feel like a romance. While Life B draws attention to the disfiguring ulcers, tumors, and horrible smell of the leper, creating in the reader's mind the image of a rotting, inhuman monster, the *SEL* version chooses instead to emphasize his humanity and courage. Though his hideous appearance is mentioned in passing, sympathy is created on his behalf with the newly added details of his having been sick for a long time and having tried unsuccessfully to find a remedy for his condition. This sympathetic treatment of the *SEL* version also extends to how the leper's request is voiced. While the leper in Life B makes his demand once in a 'raucous' voice, the leper in the *SEL* version cries loudly and insistently for 'mercy' and 'help'. Also, the narrator of Life B questions the leper for his audacity in asking the saint to kiss him in his condition and takes great pains, through an imagined conversation, to make clear to the reader that the leper is compelled to request a kiss by the 'heats' of his disease and not because of sexual desire; if he were 'simply male', his request would shockingly sinful. In contrast, the *SEL* version is resoundingly silent on the leper's possible motivations for requesting the kiss, and the poet only presents his judgment that Frideswide was not guilty of sin, as if her virtue were somehow in doubt. The resulting ambiguity is another means of creating tension between sacred love and sexual desire, a tension common in medieval romances.

Even more striking than the narrative changes, however, is the poet's recasting of the language itself in the longer *SEL* version to make it more like a romance than its source. In Life B, the hagiographer uses *adjurare* to frame the leper's request, a verb with legal connotations involving a binding under oath.[65] The leper also addresses Frideswide in Life B using the word *virgo*, a term that could simply mean 'a maiden', but was often used in ecclesiastical discourse to signify the elevated spiritual status of virginity.[66] The leper's strict charge to Frideswide while publicly recognizing her chaste sanctity thus bestows a sense of formal religious ceremony upon the leper's healing in Life B. In the *SEL* version, on the other hand, the leper makes his request in the language of medieval romance, with himself cast as a wooer in the courtly love tradition: 'Levedi, bidde ic thee, | [...] have mercy of me | And cus me with thi suete mouth, yif it is thi wille!' The term of address, 'Lady', is quite common in medieval romance. And the Middle English verb used, 'bid', is more versatile than *adjurare*: it can mean 'to address a prayer or entreaty to (God, a saint); supplicate, pray; also, worship', but it can also simply mean 'to request or beg (sth. of sb.).'[67] In addition, a lover in a courtly romance will often ask his lady to have mercy on him because of the suffering that his love for the lady is causing him. The idea of mercy is often expressed in romances using the Middle English word 'reuth(e)', which means 'pity, compassion, sympathy; also, mercy'.[68]

---

in *Readings in Medieval English Romance*, ed. by Carol M. Meale (Cambridge: Brewer, 1994), pp. 83–97, for a useful discussion of the similar functions and relations to cultural context exhibited by hagiographic and romantic texts.

[65] 'To swear to, to confirm by an oath'; see Charlton T. Lewis and Charles Short, *A Latin Dictionary Founded on Andrews' Edition of Freund's Latin Dictionary* (Oxford: Clarendon Press, 1879), s.v. 'adjuro', <http://www.perseus.tufts.edu/hopper/text?doc=Perseus:text:1999.04.0059>, accessed May 2, 2012. The Middle English definition of 'adjure' is 'To bind (sb.) by oath (to do sth.); also, to entreat (in the name of, or for the sake of, sth. holy)'; see *Middle English Dictionary* (Ann Arbor: University of Michigan Press, 1952–2001), s.v. 'adjuren', <http://quod.lib.umich.edu/m/med/>, accessed May 2, 2012.

[66] *A Latin Dictionary*, s.v. 'virgo'.

[67] *Middle English Dictionary*, s.v. 'bidden'.

[68] *Middle English Dictionary*, s.v. 'reuth(e)'.

The Virgin's Kiss: Gender, Leprosy, and Romance in the Life of Saint Frideswide

This language of romance and courtly love, with its repeated address of 'Lady' and its plea for mercy or pity, by the thirteenth century permeated religious texts that praised the Virgin Mary, as can be seen by the following lyric:

> Mi swete levedi, her mi bene [prayer]
> And reu of me yif thi wille is.
> [...]
> Swete levedi, of me thu reowe
> And have merci of thin knicht.
> [...]
> Levedi milde, softe and swote,
> Ic crie thee merci, ic am thi mon.[69]

A century later, Chaucer uses the same language in a secular context to undermine courtly love traditions, when Absolon tries unsuccessfully to woo Alisoun in *The Miller's Tale*: 'Now, deere lady, if thy wille be, | I praye yow that ye wole rewe on me' (3361–62).[70] Yet it was not the convention to make use of this language when addressing female saints in hagiographic texts. The *SEL*-poet's infusion of the formal language of courtly love into a hagiographic narrative demonstrates a popular departure from the conventions of Latin saints' lives and results in a recasting of the roles of the protagonists, with the leper as courtly lover and Frideswide as his love interest.[71] When used in this way in a hagiographic text, the language of romance becomes transformational, able to confront and alter readers' expectations of social transactions between the holy and the afflicted.

The word 'suete', in particular, conveys multiple meanings to medieval readers, and its two appearances in the *SEL* healing (each functioning differently from the other) are responsible for much of the ambiguity in the poem. In one sense, the reference to Frideswide's 'suete mouth' is an example of the romantic language common to secular love lyrics of the thirteenth and fourteenth centuries; one of these, entitled 'When þe Nyhtegale Singes,' seems to closely parallel the language in the saint's legend: 'Wiþ þy loue, my suete leof, mi blis þou mihtes eche; | A suete cos of þy mouþ mihte be my leche' ('with thy love, my sweet dear, thou mightest increase my bliss; | A sweet kiss of thy mouth might be my healer').[72] But 'suete' can also mean 'of God, Christ, Mary, a saint, etc.: blessed, holy; gracious', or 'spiritually refreshing'; the resolution of the sacred-or-secular ambiguity depended largely on the life experience and devotional practices of the reader. When the kiss is described as being 'suete' to the leper, other definitions of the word are activated, such as 'precious, valuable', and 'of

---

[69] *Middle English Marian Lyrics*, ed. by Karen Saupe (Kalamazoo: Medieval Institute Publications, 1998), p. 52.

[70] The connection between the Marian lyric and Absolon's wooing couplet is convincingly laid out by Peter G. Biedler in ' "Now, Deere Lady": Absolon's Marian Couplet in the "Miller's Tale" ', *Chaucer Review*, 39 (2004), 219–22.

[71] As the use of the language of romance casts the protagonists in new roles, the saint's first refusal to grant the leper's request brings to mind the lady's initial rebuff of the lover in some courtly love literature. Another compelling use of romantic language occurs earlier in the longer *SEL* Frideswide legend, when the devil addresses the saint as 'my lemman' (35), a Middle English romantic term of endearment. It is worth noting that the sexual tension introduced in the longer SEL life of Frideswide seems to have made a later writer uncomfortable: in a Middle English prose recasting of the legend made in or after 1438 and added to the *Gilte Legende*, the writer renders the kiss, 'and than this holy virgyn fulle mekely kyssyd hym' (see *Supplementary Lives in Some Manuscripts of the 'Gilte Legende'*, ed. by Richard Hamer and Vida Russell (Oxford: Oxford University Press, 2000), p. 155). The use of the word 'mekely' (meaning, variously, 'humbly', 'respectfully', 'courteously', 'quietly', or 'graciously') sanitizes the intrusion of romance into the hagiographic account.

[72] *The Harley Lyrics*, ed. by G. L. Brook (Manchester: Manchester University Press, 1948), p. 63.

the harmony or accord of parts'.[73] Mary Carruthers has shown that a medieval understanding of 'sweetness', while sometimes understood as a medicinal property that restores the balance of the body's humors ('þe swete accorde'), also includes a component of bitterness that fights against wholesomeness, yet is inseparable from it. She notes that 'sweetness characteristically occasions and exploits irony, oxymoron, paradox [...] [its] very essence is ambiguous'; this notion is encapsulated in medieval awareness by the apostle John, who in vision eats a scroll that is sweet in his mouth but bitter in his belly, and by the tree in Eden, whose sweetest fruit also introduced the bitterness of death.[74] In the *SEL* version of Frideswide's story, tension is produced at a climactic moment because the kiss is sweet only to *one* of the protagonists; the poet thus skillfully uses the compound and contrary nature of the medieval concept of sweetness to great effect by introducing the appearance of shame as the bitter fruit of sweet healing.

With the addition of the language and narrative elements of romance to the Latin sources of Frideswide's legend, the cleansing of the leper, in which he is restored from a state of repulsive degeneration to a state of primal purity, performs an important generic function in the longer *SEL* poem. Having reversed the conventional hagiographic roles of the participants, so that the leper is now the protagonist and the virgin saint his love interest, the poet uses the kiss to reveal the leper's true identity, a central theme of medieval romance. Simon Gaunt argues that, in contrast to the epic, in which the hero's identity is constructed primarily in relation to other men, 'romance constructs masculinity in relation to femininity, developing a strong sense of alterity.'[75] This alterity is vividly displayed in the contrasting reactions of the leper and Frideswide to the kiss, and in the reader's realization that the leper's recovery of identity is counterbalanced by the diminution or loss of the saint's self-identity. The use of shame as a device leading to self-knowledge is also prominent in the romance *Sir Gawain and the Green Knight*, when the revelation of Gawain's hidden cowardice and dishonesty results not only in his deep shame but in a greater self-awareness and dedication to the chivalric code. However, the *SEL* poem departs from *Sir Gawain* in that the shame does not participate in the construction of romantic masculine identity, as it does for Gawain, but in the deconstruction of sacred feminine identity, as Frideswide's chastity is portrayed as potentially suspect. The conflict and ambiguity arising from these intersections of gender and genre suggest that the *SEL* saints' lives might contain more insight into the construction of romantic identity than has been considered previously.

It must be remembered that the *South English Legendary*, while its author or authors remain unknown, was intended to provide religious instruction to the unlettered, whether lay or religious. The longer *SEL* account of St Frideswide's healing of the leper brings together three facets of medieval awareness that would have been familiar to that audience: leprosy, with its symbolism of wickedness and holiness; chastity, as embodied most commonly in the female virgin saint; and Christian service to afflicted and suffering souls. The tension between these potentially conflicting elements and the recasting of the legend using the

---

[73] *Middle English Dictionary*, s.v. 'swet(e)'.
[74] Mary Carruthers, 'Sweetness', *Speculum*, 81 (2006), 999–1013 (p. 1010).
[75] Simon Gaunt, *Gender and Genre in Medieval French Literature* (Cambridge: Cambridge University Press, 1995), pp. 73–75. Robert W. Hanning neatly summarizes the matter of identity in romance in the following statement: 'the great adventure of chivalric romance is the adventure of becoming what (and who) you think you can be, of transforming the *awareness* of an inner self into an *actuality* which impresses upon the external world the fact of personal, self-chosen identity, and therefore of an inner-determined identity' (quoted by Furrow, p. 57).

language and narrative elements of romance make the *SEL* poetic rendering of the story accord better with thirteenth-century English readerly tastes than its earlier and more conventional Latin versions. The surprising moment when Frideswide kisses the leper is simultaneously transgressive and transcendent, revealing God's power in the joining of holiness with disease, in the struggle between shame and faith, and in the union of woman and man. The shame and reluctance felt by the abbess regarding the requested kiss in this account also forge an important link between saint and laity, especially suffering girls and women. The poet's compelling humanistic depiction of the leper's healing in the longer *SEL* legend of St Frideswide, with its profound explorations of gender and sanctity, makes it a truly unique and fascinating event in medieval hagiography.

The Terror of the Threshold: Liminality and the Fairies of *Sir Orfeo*

Piotr Spyra

Although fairies are not very difficult to find in the extant body of medieval English romances, there is something about the Middle English lay of *Sir Orfeo* that makes it a particularly good starting point for exploring the romance fairy tradition. *Sir Orfeo* boasts not only characters whose fairy identity, contrary to that of the Green Knight in *Sir Gawain and the Green Knight* or the dancing ladies of Chaucer's 'The Wife of Bath's Tale', is never to be doubted, but also a full-fledged vision of the fairy otherworld, 'more concretely evoked [...] than in any other romance'.[1] While the descriptions of Sir Bertilak or the Loathly Lady only hint at their true nature, or their realms of origin, *Sir Orfeo* has it all: an explicit case of fairy abduction, a woodland encounter with the fairy cavalcade, not merely one but two different portals leading to the land of Faerie,[2] and the fairy king himself (perhaps atypically so, in light of the more usual, though by no means exclusive, references to fairy queens, as in Chaucer's parody of the genre in the tale of Sir Thopas).

One common approach to the study of fairies in both literature and folklore is to invoke the notion of liminality. Derived from Latin *limen* ('threshold'), the term *liminality* has often been applied in both fairy scholarship in general and the criticism of *Sir Orfeo* in particular; in fact, the majority of the sources cited in this article make use of the concept to a greater or lesser degree. It denotes a space, time or state that can be best characterized as being 'betwixt and between'.[3] Originating in anthropology, it has found its way into both cultural and literary studies, and can serve as a useful tool for capturing the sense of ambiguity that, according to the post-New Critical paradigm, defines the nature of literature.[4] As a useful piece of critical vocabulary, it does come with a caveat, however. Just as the notions of irony or paradox in

---

[1] Corinne Saunders, *Rape and Ravishment in the Literature of Medieval England* (Woodbridge: Brewer, 2001), p. 228.
[2] The term as used here, capitalized and in the Spenserian spelling, refers to the land, or kingdom of fairies. With regard to the creatures inhabiting this realm, the standard dictionary spelling shall be used.
[3] Lizanne Henderson and Edward J. Cowan, *Scottish Fairy Belief: A History* (East Linton: Tuckwell, 2001), p. 17. The phrase is a reference to a seminal article by Victor Turner — see below.
[4] As a term in literary criticism, liminality may be seen as a modern variant of the notions of ambiguity, tension, or paradox, all of which have become a staple mark of post-New Critical literary hermeneutics. William Empson's seminal *Seven Types of Ambiguity* (London: Chatto and Windus, 1930) may itself be read as an unwitting exploration of the interpretive fringes of liminality and an attempt at classifying its role and function in literary texts.

the early days of modern literary criticism, it can be applied sweepingly to a whole array of texts and interpretive problems. In an overview of the applications of liminality in literary studies, Manuel Aguirre provides a lengthy list of problems addressed by the concept; these include ideas as diverse as literary investigations of the theological notion of the Numinous, structuralist analyses of the fantastic in literature, the very nature of postmodernism, concepts of heteroglossia and paratexts, and various others issues that cut across theoretical paradigms and historical periods.[5]

In this article my aim is to show that liminality can serve as a particularly potent tool for understanding the reader's hermeneutic encounter with the text of the lay of Orfeo — indeed, that the text not only consistently incorporates the idea of the liminal in its various formulations but that it also forces its readers to engage with the idea. The concept of liminality has often guided *Orfeo* scholarship in terms of its thematic preoccupation. Much has already been made, for instance, of the grafting of the tree from under which the fairies snatch Queen Heurodis[6] or of the uncertain nature of her madness.[7] This article investigates and re-examines these and a number of other issues to posit liminality as a principle that underlies and permeates the entire fabric of the tale. Not only does it argue that taking recourse to the notion of liminality is a useful and productive practice in dealing with the text of *Sir Orfeo*, which has already been suggested by earlier criticism, but it also suggests that invoking liminality is virtually indispensible if one wishes to understand how all the elements of this particular story fit together. The choice of the theoretical apparatus will therefore be shown to be invited by the text itself. This approach will not only help to appreciate the complexity of the ways in which *Sir Orfeo* exposes the reader to the liminal, but also posit the tale as a unified whole, where even those details which apparently have little to do with the presence of fairies in the story do, under closer scrutiny, appear to spring directly from it.

Although the term *liminality* originally derives from the work of the French anthropologist Arnold van Gennep, it was the British scholar Victor Turner who formulated the idea in a way that lent itself easily to applications beyond the study of proper rites of passage.[8] Describing the position of neophytes within the dynamics of such rites, he notes that they 'are neither living nor dead from one aspect and both living and dead from another'.[9] This is a key issue, and a striking feature of liminality itself at work, for a commonsensical approach would require that one favours either one reading or the other, rather than the conclusion that the neophytes are *both* and *neither* living and/or dead. Still, Turner suggests that to understand the ritualism in question one has to entertain both readings at the same time, and this insight into the mechanics of liminality, together with the logical tension it brings, will be shown to permeate the lay of Orfeo far beyond the context of rites of passage themselves.

Before dealing with how the fairy element intertwines with the idea of liminality in the lay, it is useful to look at the general interconnections between fairies and the liminal, as attested by folklore studies. Thus fairies are to be found in locations that belong neither wholly

---

[5] Manuel Aguirre, 'The Lure of the Limen', *Trellis Papers*, 1 (2006), 3–16.
[6] Curtis E. H. Jirsa, 'In the Shadow of the Ympe-tre: Arboreal Folklore in *Sir Orfeo*', *English Studies*, 89 (2008), 141–51.
[7] Ellen M. Caldwell, 'The Heroism of Heurodis: Self-Mutilation and Restoration in *Sir Orfeo*', *Papers on Language and Literature*, 43 (2007), 291–310.
[8] See Arnold van Gennep, *The Rites of Passage*, trans. by Monika B. Vizedom and Gabrielle L. Caffee (Chicago: University of Chicago Press, 2011) [first published in 1909] for the original formulation.
[9] Victor Turner, 'Betwixt and Between: The Liminal Period in *Rites de Passage*', in *The Forest of Symbols: Aspects of Ndembu Ritual* (Ithaca: Cornell University Press, 1967), pp. 93–111 (p. 97).

to the familiar world nor to the unfamiliar — borderland areas, whose relationship to their surroundings is in some way problematic. This conclusion can be corroborated by observations pertaining to different historical periods. For instance, the status of fairy mounds in Ireland, which in many cases escaped destruction over the centuries owing to the unwillingness of the local population to interfere with them, provides a good example: the ambivalent status of these places guaranteed their survival to a large degree and may be compared with the immunity conferred on modern day diplomatic missions in foreign countries by virtue of their recognized special status.[10] The ambivalence here arises primarily from the combination of alien and familiar characteristics which such places exhibit. Very often they lie immediately beyond the familiar world of the home, school or church, and yet, there is an aura about them of something 'very special'.[11] Margaret Bennett managed to capture this duality in writing of the mysterious 'fairy knowe'[12] behind the church in Balquhidder, the Scottish village where the Reverend Robert Kirk (1644–92), author of *The Secret Commonwealth of Elves, Fauns and Fairies*, lived before allegedly being taken away by the same mysterious race whose secret society he investigated.[13] It was, as the Balquhidder children that she interviewed knew very well, a place where Kirk had seen the fairies, and the knoll was even suspected by some of the pupils of the local school of harbouring 'a secret hollow in the bottom' or a graveyard. Still, it was for them as well 'a favourite place to visit during the leisurely lunch break'.[14]

Although definitely marked as different from their surroundings,[15] such haunts of fairies hardly ever lie beyond the easy reach of the local population. In these traditions, the land of fairies is never the far-off country of literary fairytales that requires a seven-league-boots journey across distant mountains; quite the opposite, it is right there, right next to the most familiar, or even mundane spaces of everyday life, and may perhaps best be visualized as a sort of a parallel universe, to which places such as fairy mounds or local hilltops provide immediate access.[16] Folk beliefs have in this respect changed very little over the centuries; Kirk himself wrote in the late seventeenth century about the subterranean fairy realm that was, in geographical terms, clearly identified as local, or, in his words, 'Scotish-Irish', with a 'Fayriehill' to be found beside practically 'everie Churchyard'.[17] With his many references to people

[10] Patricia Lysaght, 'Fairylore from the Midlands of Ireland', in *The Good People: New Fairylore Essays*, ed. by Peter Narváez, Garland Reference Library of the Humanities, 1376 (New York: Garland, 1991), pp. 22–46 (pp. 31, 45). By referring to mounds that have survived until the present day, the author seems to be suggesting that the taboo surrounding the violation of fairy ground has continuously been at work and still persists.

[11] Margaret Bennett, 'Balquhidder Revisited: Fairylore in the Scottish Highlands 1690–1990', in *The Good People: New Fairylore Essays*, ed. by Peter Narváez, Garland Reference Library of the Humanities, 1376 (New York: Garland, 1991), pp. 94–115 (p. 106).

[12] Local term for hillock.

[13] For an account of the alleged fairy abduction, see Walter Yeeling Evans-Wentz, *The Fairy-Faith in Celtic Countries* (London: Oxford University Press, 1911), pp. 89–90. Evans-Wentz reports the story to have long been in oral circulation in the area as part of the local tradition (p. 89).

[14] Bennett, pp. 106–8 (quoting p. 108).

[15] One often finds that places with particularly lush vegetation are believed to be fairy circles. Cairns or hillocks are also likely candidates for fairy haunts. In all cases the particular place stands out in one way or another. See Bennett, p. 108. Cf. Robin Gwyndaf, 'Fairylore: Memorates and Legends from Welsh Oral Tradition', in *The Good People: New Fairylore Essays*, ed. Peter Narváez, Garland Reference Library of the Humanities, 1376 (New York: Garland, 1991), pp. 155–95 (p. 180).

[16] Katharine Briggs, *The Fairies in Tradition and Literature* (London: Routledge and Keegan Paul, 2002), pp. 23–24. All the stories about people abruptly disappearing in fairy circles only to reappear suddenly after months or even years also strongly suggest that the fairy realm is to be understood as being directly adjacent to ours. Cf. Briggs, pp. 124–25.

[17] Robert Kirk, 'The Secret Commonwealth of Elves, Fauns and Fairies', in *The Occult Laboratory: Magic, Science*

endowed with second sight suddenly catching a glimpse of the otherworld by encountering fairies face to face,[18] Kirk leaves his readers in no doubt whatsoever that the underground world he describes may be 'secret' and hidden, but actually lies closer than one may suspect, being both distinctly alien and uncannily familiar.

In literature, liminal spaces are often marked as such in more than one way at a time. The popular ballad of 'Tam Lin' furnishes a good example with its mention of a well in the woods and a crossroads.[19] That Tam Lin appears to Janet by the well is probably connected with the belief in fairies often making their presence felt next to a body of water, usually running water, as in *Lanval* by Marie de France. Folklorists have recorded numerous stories about encountering fairies by a brook,[20] and the border-like, liminal quality of running water seems self-explanatory: interestingly, crossing a stream is actually often believed to have apotropaic properties and guarantees safety in the event of being chased by a supernatural force,[21] which suspends rivers and streams half-way between danger and safety, both inviting a menace and dispelling it — a good instance of the liminal. What makes 'Tam Lin' a particularly good example of how liminal spaces can function in literature is that its various versions testify to the importance of the notion of in-betweenness in the ballad. Where Child's A version has Janet meet the fairy cavalcade at Miles Cross,[22] the F text mentions Chester Bridge.[23] It appears that what matters is the liminal character of the place, more than its particular realization in a given telling of the story.[24] This may also shed some light on the curious detail of mills being a preferred haunt of both fairies[25] and brownies,[26] for not unlike bridges, which invite wayfarers to enter a space existing 'betwixt and between' the two river banks they connect, mills are the locus of transformation, as within their walls grain *becomes* flour. The numerous bridge and river-ford guardians we find in medieval romance[27] may thus originate

---

and Second Sight in Late Seventeenth-Century Scotland, ed. by Michael Hunter (Woodbridge: Boydell, 2001), pp. 77–106 (pp. 78, 80, 85).

[18] Kirk, p. 84.

[19] 'Tam Lin', in *The English and Scottish Popular Ballads*, ed. by Francis James Child, 5 vols (Boston and New York: Houghton, Mifflin and Company, [1882–98]), I, pp. 335–58. The well is to be found in Child 39A, 39B and 39I, the crossroads in Child 39A, 39B, 39D, 39I, 39J and 39K.

[20] Evans-Wentz, pp. 124–25, 182. See also Barbara Rieti, ' "The Blast" in Newfoundland Fairy Tradition', in *The Good People: New Fairylore Essays*, ed. by Peter Narváez, Garland Reference Library of the Humanities, 1376 (New York: Garland, 1991), pp. 284–97 (p. 284).

[21] Evans-Wentz, p. 38. See also Peter Narváez, 'Newfoundland Berry Pickers "In the Fairies": Maintaining Spatial, Temporal and Moral Boundaries Through Legendry', in *The Good People: New Fairylore Essays*, ed. by Peter Narváez, Garland Reference Library of the Humanities, 1376 (New York: Garland, 1991), pp. 336–68 (p. 348).

[22] 'Tam Lin', p. 342.

[23] 'Tam Lin', p. 349.

[24] In most variants of the ballad the place is known as Miles Cross (sometimes in a corrupted form, such as 'Miles-Corse' in Child 39G or 'Blackstock' in Child 39E). Version F is the only one to provide an alternative to the crossroads.

[25] Briggs, p. 119. Briggs mentions Rothley Mill in Northumberland as an example.

[26] Briggs, p. 35. While Briggs refers to the English tradition, there is also the continental belief in the Killmoulis, a species of brownies to be found uniquely in mills. The belief was attested in Belgium, Germany and Holland. See Theresa Bane, *Encyclopedia of Fairies in World Folklore and Literature* (Jefferson: McFarland, 2013), p. 200.

[27] These abound already in Chretien's works, and *Le Chevalier de la Charrette* includes a memorable episode of the absent-minded Lancelot being set upon by one without even noticing. There are also plenty of these in Malory's *Morte*, but perhaps the best indication of how widespread the romance convention of having most fords guarded by belligerent figures was comes in *Sir Gawain and the Green Knight* (ll. 715–16). There, in a passage that plays with the convention on a meta-level and pushes it logically to the extreme, the narrator remarks that it was indeed a wonder ('ferly') if there was a ford or river crossing during Gawain's journey that had no guardian awaiting armed struggle.

from the same notion as the industrious mill brownies of British folklore — an understanding of both kinds of places as inherently liminal.

Instances of temporal liminality also tend to overlap in the ballads. Janet attempts to rescue Tam Lin not just on any night, but on Halloween,[28] and naturally at midnight.[29] This too has its source directly in folklore:

> the times for seeing fairies or getting into Fairyland are May Day and Hallowmas […]. The time of the full moon and the days before and after it are important to the fairies. Certain times of day belong to them — twilight, midnight and full moon are times when fairies are to be seen.[30]

One has the impression that what cuts through the thin veil separating the two worlds is precisely the liminality of the spatial and temporal alignments of a given setting, which overlap and thus enable mortals to interact with fairies and their realm.

The people who find themselves involved with fairies and the fairies themselves can too, however, be viewed as distinctly liminal. Diane Purkiss observes that 'fairies […] are like people who have become trapped at a certain indeterminate phase of life'[31] and provides numerous examples, such as that of fairy-like Greek nymphs forever poised on the cusp of womanhood.[32] One may also invoke the notion of 'fairy dependence', a defining mark of all fairy creatures according to Katharine Briggs.[33] Briggs devotes a lot of space to the issue, arguing that fairies ought not to be seen as living independently of ordinary people; instead, they are constantly observed to be in need of something that only human beings can provide — be it food, lovers, midwives or children — which is precisely what furnishes narrative material in stories of human-fairy interactions. Ontologically speaking, fairies are thus neither of this nor, in fact, of a different world, hovering for ever on the liminal fringes of reality. Helen Cooper, who analyzed the constructions of the fairy race in medieval romances, agreed with Briggs; in her view, fairies are 'an anomaly in the divine order of creation, and romances are rarely interested in defining their precise metaphysical or theological status except in terms of what it is not'.[34] Ontologically liminal, fairies also clearly belong to the spaces of 'betwixt and between' on the moral continuum, being neither angelic nor demonic, neither good nor evil. The famous description of not two but three roads in the ballad of Thomas the Rhymer, the first two leading, predictably, to heaven and hell, and the third one winding in a snake-like manner towards the land of Faerie, is perhaps the clearest manifestation of this popular belief. One should remember that if fairies have often been referred to as 'the good people', this is not because they are inherently good but rather out of fear of invoking their generic name and thus provoking them into action.[35]

---

[28] This detail is to be found in all main versions collected by Child (39A–K).
[29] Some variants do not mention the exact time, but if they do then it is invariably midnight, or the time between midnight and one, 'the dead hour o the night', as version 39I has it. Interestingly, in version 39H the fairy queen says that if only she had known about Janet's plan to rescue Tam Lin at noon, she would have prevented the attempt. Thus both midnight and midday are involved.
[30] Briggs, p. 125.
[31] Diane Purkiss, *At the Bottom of the Garden: A Dark History of Fairies, Hobgoblins, and Other Troublesome Things* (New York: NYU Press, 2000), p. 48.
[32] Purkiss, pp. 38–45.
[33] Briggs, pp. 113–22.
[34] Helen Cooper, *The English Romance in Time: Transforming Motifs from Geoffrey of Monmouth to the Death of Shakespeare* (Oxford: Oxford University Press, 2004), p. 179.
[35] This rationale behind the use of the name has long been known, with Kirk voicing it in the very first sentence of

The Terror of the Threshold: Liminality and the Fairies of Sir Orfeo

Liminality may also be said to characterize the status of human beings at the moment when they encounter fairies. Whether a given's person transitional state provokes contacts with fairies or is a result of their intervention in the stories in question is often difficult to gauge, yet this could, in fact, be a misguided question. What matters is that the liminal is not only to be seen as an external force that invades the human world but an essential element of the human experience as well, sometimes evident even prior to the fairy encounter. This is well illustrated by Marie's *Lanval*, where the knight who chances upon the fairy lady is simultaneously a member of the inner court and an outcast from an alien land forgotten by Arthur in his act of distributing largesse, still living in an inn and unable to become fully integrated into the court, neither its full-fledged member nor an outcast. In Marie's *Yonec*, in turn, the female protagonist may not immediately seem to be liminal in any sense of the word at the point when she is visited by her fairy lover, yet with her husband's decision to imprison her immediately upon marrying her, she is deprived of a life as such and seems forever frozen in time at the moment of her transition to womanhood, no longer a maid, yet not fully a wife either. The liminal status of human beings thus often appears to be a prerequisite for any involvement with fairies. Apart from finding oneself at the right place or time, it is a given's person transitional state that provokes contacts with fairies, often against the individual's will. Anthropological theories of liminality help understand the mechanics of fairy beliefs, and most tales of encounters involve a 'connection with critical junctures in the life cycle, among them the "liminal", in-between, transitional periods that occur during an individual's movement from one status to another' as understood by Arnold van Gennep.[36] Van Gennep's theory of liminality is founded on a double negative: one going through the liminal stage is neither what he or she used to be, nor the new entity he or she is yet to become. Victor Turner elaborated on this idea, stressing that 'the structural invisibility of liminal personae has a twofold character. They are at once no longer classified and not yet classified'.[37] This is why initiands in ceremonies of rites of passage are, as Mary Douglas pointed out, endowed with great power, tapping into the energies inherent in the formlessness of the state they are in.[38] According to Douglas, people in the liminal phase also tend to behave in anti-social ways, and 'for the duration of the rite they have no place in society. Sometimes they actually go to live far outside it'.[39]

Skjelbred mentions the 'churching' of women as a good example of such a rite of passage. She writes about a Norwegian custom following the period of isolation connected with labour, which included

> leading the woman who had given birth into church [...] The belief was that during her confinement the woman was not a worthy member of the church, although she was both christened and confirmed.[40]

---

the initial chapter of his 'Secret Commonwealth': 'These siths or fairies, they call [...] the good people: (it would seem, to prevent the dint of their ill attempts: for the Irish use to bless all they fear harme of)' (Kirk, p. 79).

[36] Ann Helene Bolstad Skjelbred, 'Rites of Passage as Meeting Place: Christianity and Fairylore in Connection with the Unclean Woman and the Unchristened Child', in *The Good People: New Fairylore Essays*, ed. by Peter Narváez, Garland Reference Library of the Humanities, 1376 (New York: Garland, 1991), pp. 215–23 (p. 215).

[37] Turner, p. 96.

[38] Mary Douglas, *Purity and Danger: An Analysis of Concepts of Pollution and Taboo* (London: Routledge, 2001), pp. 95–98.

[39] Douglas, p. 97.

[40] Skjelbred, p. 217.

There was something dangerous about such women, something 'heathen', as they were sometimes referred to, that required a special ritualistic remedy.[41] And indeed, according to Diane Purkiss, the notions of birth and infanthood are the conceptual nexus from which the world's beliefs in fairies and analogous creatures spring; Purkiss points to ancient Mesopotamian beliefs about stillborn demons 'trapped between states of being' as symptoms of the same anxiety that produced the idea of a changeling.[42] It should not come as a surprise that of all children it was those who were still awaiting baptism that were particularly prone, according to folklore, to being substituted by a fairy.[43] The same was observed with regard to children who were not yet given a name;[44] in both cases it was the liminal status of the infants, no longer in the womb of the mother but not part of the society as yet, that apparently invited the danger of fairy intervention.

Whether one deals with folklore or literature, liminality emerges as the single and most characteristic defining mark of fairies. While this could in truth be said of a number of other supernatural beings, what makes references to fairies unique in this respect is the sheer number of the overlapping senses of liminality which all work together to structure literary tales of fairy encounters, of which *Sir Orfeo* is a particularly apt example. What directs the reader's attention to the issue of in-betweenness in the tale is naturally the coexistence of the mortal world and Faerie, as well as Orfeo's and Heurodis's special, though unwitting, relations with the otherworld, which effectively render the royal couple liminal personae that belong neither fully to the human nor to the fairy plane. There is also the grafted tree, and this is where an analysis of how the text of the poem exposes its readers to the liminal must naturally begin. The first thing that happens in the tale is that, sleeping under the tree, Queen Heurodis suddenly awakes, only to startle her ladies-in-waiting with an ominous fit of madness:

> Ac, as sone as sche gan awake,
> Sche crid, & lothli bere gan make:
> Sche froted hir honden & hir fet,
> & crached hir visage — it bled wete;
> Hir riche robe hye al to-rett,
> & was reueyd out of hir witt. (ll. 77–82)[45]

The poem keeps the readers ignorant as to the actual course of events until the queen is taken to a chamber, where her husband solicits her to account for the terror she succumbed to. Only then is it revealed that in her sleep she became an inadvertent object of interest of the king of Faerie. Appearing in a fairy cavalcade,[46] he has forced her to accompany him on a quick tour of his domain and apprised her of his plans to abduct her. The meeting, she reports, concluded

---

[41] Skjelbred, p. 217.
[42] Purkiss, p. 15.
[43] Skjelbred, p. 219.
[44] Joyce Underwood Munro, 'The Invisible Made Visible: The Fairy Changeling as a Folk Articulation of Failure to Thrive in Infants and Children', in *The Good People: New Fairylore Essays*, ed. by Peter Narváez, Garland Reference Library of the Humanities, 1376 (New York: Garland, 1991), pp. 251–83 (pp. 275–76).
[45] *Sir Orfeo*, ed. by A. J. Bliss, 2nd edn (Oxford: Clarendon Press, 1966). The text is that of the Auchinleck manuscript. Since the article delves into the essential hermeneutic ambiguity of the text, only one version of *Sir Orfeo* is referred to in order to avoid focusing on interpretive problems arising solely out of the multiplicity of versions.
[46] See William Butler Yeats, *Fairy and Folk Tales of the Irish Peasantry* (London: Scott, [1888]). The term is glossed by Yeats as a translation of the Irish *Marcra shee* (p. 23). Since the favourite sport of fairies is hunting, such processions on horseback are also known under the name of the Wild Hunt (Briggs, p. 59).

The Terror of the Threshold: Liminality and the Fairies of Sir Orfeo

with the queen being commanded on pain of death to return to the tree on the following day, forever to depart from her lands.

Despite mustering a thousand knights in full battle gear and deploying them around the tree, Heurodis's husband fails to prevent the abduction. What follows is Orfeo's decision to abandon the life of a monarch, the story of his life in the wilderness and his eventual encounter with the fairy hunt, which he sees years later in the forest that he took for his hermitage. It is by following the fairy king's train that he arrives in the otherworld, passing through a huge rock that acts as a portal. Having made his way to the castle of the king, he beholds the lost Heurodis 'slepe vnder an ympe-tre' (l. 407). The text does not specify that it is the same tree, but does provide subtle hints that this is the case. The other people Orfeo sees in the castle, all of them frozen in time, were brought to the otherworld just before the moment of their death, or, if one reads the identification of Faerie with the classical Orphean Hades as far-going enough,[47] precisely at that moment:

> Sum stode wiþ-outen hade,
> & sum non armes nade,
> & sum þurth the bodi hadde wounde,
> & sum lay wode, y-bounde,
> & sum armed on hors sete,
> & sum astrangled as þai ete;
> & sum were in water adreynt,
> & sum wiþ fire al for-schreynt.
> Wiues ther lay on child-bedde,
> Sum ded & sum awedde. (ll. 391–400)

The picture Orfeo sees thus represents the actual scene from which they were all abducted, and just like the knights transported to the other side on horseback, Heurodis seems to have been taken together with the tree, with the general image of the queen and the other victims of the fairies acting like a grim tableau, faithfully reflecting the circumstances of their deathly capture. This would suggest that the tree Orfeo finds her under is the one she went to sleep under in the first place, and there she remains motionless, neither fully alive nor dead.

The text, however, in no way mentions that the tree in Orfeo's palace grounds disappeared. This apparent contradiction is further strengthened by an implied suggestion that the two trees are actually one, for in both cases the adjective 'ympe'[48] is used. Superficially, the detail seems hardly relevant, but its repetition in the story in its key moments foregrounds it and intimates that it has greater bearing on the tale than may be immediately obvious. And if there is just one tree, one has to conclude that it is growing in two places at the same time. Of course, this is quite a literal way of putting it, and one needs to inquire into what this might actually mean. The real issue here is whether or not Heurodis and the other figures Orfeo sees are dead, and this has proved to be a contentious issue in *Orfeo* scholarship. Peter Lucas argues strongly against reading these figures as dead, noting that the text itself tells us that Heurodis is to 'liue' with the fairy king 'euer-mo' (l. 168).[49] Such literal readings fail, however, to reconcile all the elements of the text, for one might just as easily note that some of the figures were

---

[47] Katharine Briggs points to the coalescence of beliefs in trooping faeries and the cavalcade of the dead; the association of Faerie with the land of the dead is not merely a result of the *Orfeo* poet's juxtaposition of Elfland with the notion of Hades from Greek sources, but features in Celtic lore itself (Briggs, pp. 58–65).

[48] ME *ympe*, OE *impa*, from *impian* (v.), 'to graft' (Jirsa, p. 142).

[49] Peter J. Lucas, 'An Interpretation of *Sir Orfeo*', *Leeds Studies in English*, n. s. 6 (1979), 1–9 (p. 3).

beheaded, and thus quite dead.[50] A look at the presentation of the fairy realm can help the reader understand the text's overall strategy.

It is tempting to read the fairy intruders as fiends, which is what John Block Friedman attempted in his investigation of a possible allegorical interpretation of the story. Friedman even goes so far as to state 'that the *Orfeo* poet has a conception of [Heurodis] which *required* her to be attacked by Satan'.[51] On the other hand, it has also been pointed out that the description of the fairy realm, and especially the castle of the fairy king, owes a lot to the imagery of heaven.[52] With its blinding luminosity and precious gems ('riche stones', l. 371), the fairy castle in *Sir Orfeo* is not so different from the city of New Jerusalem in *Pearl*, at least when seen from a distance. It is no wonder then that Orfeo himself thought at first to have found himself at the 'proude court of Paradis' (l. 376). Rather, this is neither heaven nor hell, but the text appears to play with both ideas, never dismissing them fully and prompting the readers to consider not only the possibility that this is neither this nor that, but also that, in some sense, the place is both.[53] This basic feature of liminality, as outlined by Turner, is also at work in the presentation of the still tableau of figures in the castle — they are neither alive nor dead, yet both alive and dead at the same time. This, in turn, serves to accentuate the virtual omnipotence of the fairy intruders, and, if one reads them as forces of fortune, to position the human protagonists, and by extension the human condition as such, *vis a vis* the unfathomable decrees of fate.

James Knapp suggests that *Sir Orfeo* owes a lot to the Boethian tradition,[54] pointing out that both Boethius and King Orfeo 'are seen at some point as suffering a reversal of Fortune' and that Orfeo, 'like Boethius, has been ravished of his happiness by an unexpected stroke of Fortune [...] which is baffling to him in its apparent senselessness'.[55] The poem indeed underscores the futility of human endeavours, as it is through submission to the decrees of fate rather than engaging in full-scale search efforts that the king reclaims his wife; he spots the fairy cavalcade by mere accident and the earlier attempts to stop the abduction with the help of his army reveal how utterly powerless he is. *Sir Orfeo* presents a world where calamities pose a terrifyingly real threat to human security and continually taint the sense of peace and order,

---

[50] Bruce Mitchell sees the text's lack of clarity as to whether these figures are alive or dead as evidence for the passage (present in roughly the same form in the Auchinleck and Ashmole MSS and missing from the Harley MS.) being a 'wildly incongruous' interpolation that ruins the harmony of the original narrative. His argument is that it is difficult to accept the paradox of the figures being both alive and dead, just as it is difficult to reconcile the 'sinister chill' of Faerie with images that suggest it is a rather pleasant place. See Bruce Mitchell, 'The Faery World of *Sir Orfeo*', *Neophilologus*, 48 (1964), 155–59. The present article aims to present a reading of the Auchinleck text of *Sir Orfeo* that allows one to avoid such definitive statements and to appreciate the contradictory character of the narrative and the moral ambiguity of the fairies in their own right.

[51] John Block Friedman, 'Eurydice, Heurodis, and the Noon-Day Demon', *Speculum*, 41 (1966), 22–29 (p. 26). Emphasis original.

[52] Ad Putter, 'The Influence of Visions of the Otherworld on Some Medieval Romances', in *Envisaging Heaven in the Middle Ages*, ed. by Carolyn Muessig and Ad Putter, Routledge Studies in Medieval Religion and Culture, 6 (London: Routledge, 2007), pp. 237–51 (pp. 240–41).

[53] A similar tension is at work in *Sir Gawain and the Green Knight*, with some critics reading the Green Knight as a devilish agent and other as a God-figure. For the former view, see Brian Stone, 'The Common Enemy of Man', in *Sir Gawain and the Green Knight*, trans. by Brian Stone, corr. repr. (London: Penguin, 1974), pp. 116–28; see also Claude Luttrell, 'The Folk-Tale Element in *Sir Gawain and the Green Knight*', *Studies in Philology*, 77 (1980), 105–27; for the latter, see Gerald Morgan, *Sir Gawain and the Green Knight and the Idea of Righteousness* (Dublin: Irish Academic Press, 1991). The Knight's fairy status seems to invite and provide for such an ambiguity of interpretations.

[54] It might be of significance that *The Consolation of Philosophy* itself contains an account of the story of Orpheus.

[55] James F. Knapp, 'The Meaning of *Sir Orfeo*', *Modern Language Quarterly*, 29 (1968), 263–73 (p. 266).

a world which in this respect mirrors the nature of human life, contingent upon unfathomable decrees of fate, embodied here in the king of Faerie and his whim to possess Heurodis.

Liminality helps to hyperbolize the power of fairies even more than the idea of fairy magic being unstoppable. Investigating the figures frozen in time in the fairy castle, Anne Marie D'Arcy points to the tradition of imperial displays of spoils of war and argues that 'in the manner of Xerxes, Alexander, Marcellus, Ptolemy Soter or Constantine, [the fairy king's] seizures are displayed as testament to the superior power of the Faerie realm and to his own imperium'.[56] This display of power amounts, however, to more than just a 'translation' of statues to a site of conquest, for in a sense Heurodis has not really moved — there she remains, under the same tree, still asleep in a kind of a dazed stupor — and yet, in another sense, she is free to leave the place to join the fairy cavalcade. This makes her recovery even more of a challenge than retrieving her from the court of Alexander or Constantine would, for 'there' escapes clear temporal and spatial, or even logical, approximations.

Whether the queen was taken with the palace tree or transported to under another tree is a very literal question that is difficult to avoid, even if no answer can fully satisfy the curiosity of the reader. What can be ascertained about it is that the *ympe-tre* acts as a portal that links the two worlds, similarly to the huge rocky portal that Orfeo discovers following the cavalcade. Unlike the other gateway, however, it is not always open and the difficulty in getting to the other side does not lie in establishing its location, which is clearly well known, for it lies in the homely palace grounds. Its liminal character is only activated by the 'vndrentide' (l. 65), the noontime that sees Heurodis repose under the boughs, as well as the queen's sleep, a condition in which she finds herself halfway between life and death.[57] It also seems very likely that, in the first place, it is made possible by the grafting, the coexistence of two organisms within one bark mirroring the simultaneous presence of the tree in the two worlds. The combination of these factors allows the tree to function as a portal and explains the fairy king's command for the queen to return to the tree at noon on the following day.[58] In line with both the folk and literary fairy tradition, the gateway to Faerie remains easily available yet closed until various liminalities — spatial, temporal and ontological — overlap and force it open, taking Heurodis completely unawares.

Orfeo and his wife may also be seen as liminal figures themselves, though admittedly this is more of a consequence of their interactions with fairies than the original trigger of the encounter. Insanity, or rather the readers' possible interpretation of both the king and queen's behaviour as insane, is the vehicle which the narrative uses to endow the royal couple with liminality. In fact, what at first glance appears to be the queen's fit of madness prompted by the terror of the abduction can also be read in quite a different way.[59] One may wonder what

---

[56] Anne Marie D'Arcy, 'The Faerie King's *Kunstkammer*: Imperial Discourse and the Wondrous in *Sir Orfeo*', *Review of English Studies*, 58/233 (2007), 10–33 (p. 21).

[57] *Vndrentide*, or *vnder-tide*, could refer either to noon or to 'tierce, the third hour of the canonical day, which ends at nine o'clock in the morning' (*Old English Dictionary* quoted in Jirsa, p. 141). Jirsa suggests that the text invokes the former meaning, as indicated by the phrase 'hot vnder-tides' in line 282 (p. 142).

[58] The queen does not mention the fairy king specifying the exact time, but the text features the time of *vnder-tide* again in its description of the knights' preparations on the following day and of their anticipation of the abduction attempt.

[59] For an informed reading of the tale which not only identifies the queen's affliction as madness but also points to its schizophrenic quality, see A. C. Spearing, 'Madness and Gender', in *The Spirit of Medieval English Popular Romance*, ed. by Ad Putter and Jane Gilbert (Harlow: Longman, 2000), pp. 258–72. See also Derek Pearsall, 'Madness in *Sir Orfeo*', in *Romance Reading on the Book: Essays on Medieval Narrative Presented to Maldwyn Mills*, ed. Jennifer Fellows and others (Cardiff: University of Wales Press, 1996), pp. 51–63. My approach does

the fairy king actually wants from Heurodis. Keeble observes that, unlike in other Breton lays, 'no specifically amorous motive is attributed to the fairy', but at the same time acknowledges the importance of the spring setting

> when miri & hot is þe day,
> & o-way beþ winter-schours,
> & eueri feld is ful of flours. (ll. 58–60)[60]

It is in the 'comessing of May' (l. 57) that Heurodis reposes under the tree, and so, although no direct motivation for the abduction is given, the informed readers of medieval romances, familiar with the convention, are likely to assume that this is yet another case of a fairy looking for a lover. The same interpretation of the setting may also easily be ascribed to Heurodis, for as a representative of the human plane of reality in the tale, she belongs to a world the medieval readers would likely identify with and be a part of.

When John Block Friedman noted the curious omission of the motive for the abduction in *Sir Orfeo*, he found this particularly puzzling given the overall level of detail in the story.[61] If this omission is indeed meaningful, then its meaning actually forecloses any attempt to determine the exact nature of the fairy king's true intentions and the rationale (or its lack, that is madness) behind the reaction of Heurodis. On the one hand, the intention of the fairy king seems rather obvious, for the notion of fairy lovers, or even rapists, who set upon mortals was widespread. One may mention here the story of *Sir Degaré* or Chaucer's ironic treatment of the theme in the Wife of Bath's tale, where friars seem to have supplanted fairies in being the ones who act as 'incubi' towards women.[62] On the other hand, the fairy king in no way consummates the relationship, and when Orfeo visits his castle he seems preoccupied with other business than taking advantage of Heurodis. The motive for the abduction thus remains both essentially obvious and inherently enigmatic. This ambiguity as to the reason behind the abduction, in turn, has a bearing on the interpretation of the condition of Heurodis.

As Katherine Briggs notes, the belief in mortals serving as fairy wives or husbands has been one of the most widespread and characteristic elements of fairy lore.[63] This initial assumption may have been strong enough to prompt the queen to disfigure herself in order to discourage the fairy king from acting on what she may have believed to be at least partly desire.[64] Caldwell argues that 'Heurodis's self-mutilation [...] connects her to a tradition of holy and chaste women in the early Middle Ages' who used 'deliberate disfigurement . . . to prevent their being raped by invaders. The preferable form of mutilation was something highly visible and easily accomplished', which Heurodis's 'crached visage' (l. 80) clearly conforms to.[65] From the reader's hermeneutical perspective, the queen's intentions hover between madness and

---

not in any way contradict readings that acknowledge the madness of Heurodis or construct coherent readings of the poem around it. Instead, it points to the fact that whatever arguments one brings into the discussion to posit madness as a key notion in the lay, the text never allows one to settle the matter for good.

[60] N. H. Keeble, 'The Narrative Achievement of Sir Orfeo', *English Studies*, 56 (1975), 193–206 (pp. 195–96).

[61] Friedman, p. 22. Friedman notes that passages about Orfeo growing a beard in the woods serve an important structural function, as the beard allows him to enter his castle *incognito* upon his return.

[62] 'In every bussh or under every tree / There is noon oother incubus but he': Geoffrey Chaucer, *The Complete Works of Geoffrey Chaucer*, ed. by F. N. Robinson (Oxford: Oxford University Press, 1985), p. 84 (ll. 879–80 of Fragment III). Note the reference to assaulting women under a tree. For a comprehensive treatment of the subject, see Saunders, *Rape and Ravishment*.

[63] Briggs, pp. 146–54.

[64] Caldwell, pp. 291–92.

[65] Caldwell, pp. 291, 295.

clever forethought, and it is impossible to establish beyond any doubt whether what Heurodis does upon awakening amounts to a case of total mental collapse or is merely a symptom of a premeditated, though self-injurious and ultimately ineffective, defence strategy. In effect, neither the fairy king's, nor the queen's intentions seem clear.

With Orfeo and his sojourns in the wood, the readers face the same kind of interpretive hesitation. The problem here is not so much the king's decision to live the life of a beggar as the fact that many a time he chances upon the fairy hunt:

> He miȝt se him bisides
> (Oft in hot vnder-tides)
> Þe king o fairy wiþ his rout
> Com to hunt him al about
> Wiþ dim cri & bloweing,
> & houndes also wiþ him berking;
> Ac no best þai no nome,
> No neuer he nist whider þai bi-come. (ll. 281–88)

Knapp is right in pointing out that 'the text provides no evidence whatsoever that this fairy world is a creation of Orfeo's disturbed mind' and the concreteness of this experience is further strengthened by the fact that it is by following the fairies that Orfeo reaches their world.[66] There is nothing, however, that would thoroughly dismiss D. M. Hill's interpretation that 'the passage constitutes a representation of the threat of madness: an objectifying of a mental state',[67] and that we can 'see the hunt as part of a pictorial representation of the threat of insanity in the form of hallucination'.[68] After all, the text makes it clear that the visions of the fairy cavalcade come to Orfeo 'in hot vnder-tides', and the readers may reasonably attempt to dismiss the experience as post-traumatic hallucinations or visions induced by sunstroke. Curiously enough, if they do so, they run into the paradox of having to account for Orfeo's discovery of the rocky gateway upon following the hunt and have little choice but to resign to the realization that the case is hermeneutically irresolvable; on the other hand, if they take the visions at face value, they accept the significance of the temporal liminality of midday which apparently prompts the experience. Just like Heurodis's self-mutilation, which lies half-way between madness and pragmatism, Orfeo's woodland visions are liminal — somewhere between dream and reality. And in an analogous fashion, the rhetorical structure of the tale leaves its readers no choice but to face and accept the liminal on one level or another.

There is more to be said about Orfeo's journey into the wilderness, but the presence of this kind of an interpretive trap set for the readers calls for a closer look at *Sir Orfeo* from a metaliterary perspective. For the transgression from one domain to the other is at the root of not just the plot of this poem, but also of its generic self-identification as a Breton lay. Keeble observes that 'the first twenty-four lines of the poem [...] constitute the fullest Middle English account we have of the Breton lays'.[69] They are indeed laden with information about the lays, providing something of a working definition of the genre. The text describes the lays as tales of magic and adventure, both serious and humorous, but in most cases indebted to fairy lore in one way or another:

---

[66] Knapp, p. 265.
[67] Cited in Knapp, p. 264.
[68] Cited in Knapp, p. 265.
[69] Keeble, p. 194.

> Layes þat ben in harping
> Ben y-founde of ferli þing:
> Sum beþe of wer & sum of wo,
> & sum of ioie & mirþe al-so,
> & sum of trecherie & of gile,
> Of old auentours that fel while,
> & sum of bourdes & ribaudy,
> & mani þer beþ of fairy;
> [...]
> In Breteyne þis layes were wrouȝt,
> [First y-founde & forth y-brouȝt,
> Of auentours þat fel bi dayes,
> Wher-of Bretouns maked her layes.] (ll. 3–10, 13–16)

One is struck by the contrast between the repetitive 'sum' and the insistence that within this hotchpotch of themes '*mani þer beþ* of fairy'. Keeble believes, however, that 'we need to notice that the point that the poet is making' by ascribing authorship of the tale to others, Bretons in this case, 'is a Medieval commonplace'.[70]

While medieval literature abounds in such references to sources, true or fictional, the remark in *Sir Orfeo* curiously positions the text halfway between Brittany and England. At the same time, the plot itself merges the ancient and the medieval, situating the action neither fully in the Roman province of Thrace nor medieval England. Instead, Orfeo reigns over Inglond from his kingly seat in Traciens, identified by the text as Winchester (ll. 49–50). Conflation and confusion of sources may be common among medieval authors, but *Sir Orfeo* is quite unique in this respect in the way the poet does this. A look at the opening lines of *Sir Gawain and the Green Knight* suffices to emphasise the difference:

> Hit was Ennias the athel and his highe kynde
> That sithen depreced provinces, and patrounes bicome
> Welneghe of al the wele in the West Iles:
> Fro riche Romulus to Rome ricchis hym swythe,
> With gret bobbaunce that burghe he biges upon fyrst,
> And nevenes hit his aune nome, as hit now hat;
> Ticius to Tuskan, and teldes bigynnes;
> Langaberde in Lumbardie lyftes up homes;
> And fer over the French flod Felix Brutus
> On mony bonkkes ful brode Bretayn he settes
> wyth wynne. (ll. 5–15)[71]

The basic idea here is one of progeny and the transfer of culture to far-off regions, which forges links between them and their distant points of origin. Such was the official ideological foundation of Ancient Rome, as attested by Virgil's *Aeneid*, which saw Aeneas, mentioned here by the *Gawain*-Poet, flee Troy to settle upon the Tiber. This conventional kind of linkage is evident in the tale of King Orfeo in the way the text posits itself stretched across the English Channel, fusing the Breton tradition of lays with the still developing Middle English poetics.

The curious mixture of ancient Thrace with the capital of Wessex, however, strikes a somewhat different note, as the two do not merely maintain a connection over a large distance,

---

[70] Keeble, p. 194.
[71] *Sir Gawain and the Green Knight*, in *Pearl, Cleanness, Patience, Sir Gawain and the Green Knight*, ed. by A. C.

as Troy and Rome would, but actually merge in this tale, though without losing their own identity. Traciens is still Thrace and Winchester remains a city in Inglond, but the text allows them to coexist on one plane of reality. This move, fundamentally alien to both the *Gawain*-poet and Virgil, is at the core of the poem and structures it on all levels. The mortal world and Faerie coexist within the fabric of the tale just like the ancient and medieval threads from which the fabric was woven.

To uncover more of the tale's indebtedness to liminality, one may also invoke the more theoretical, or anthropological, formulations of the notion associated with rites of passage. It is never explained in the poem why Orfeo abdicates, leaving his kingdom in the hands of the steward, and removes himself to the woods. It has been argued that the loss of Heurodis and the loss of kingly power may be connected, one triggering the other.[72] This may be read as an expression of the integrity of the whole experience of the fairy intervention, with the abduction of Heurodis effectively enforcing a liminal state upon Orfeo and pushing him away from his royal duties, the society and all the categories that had thitherto defined his existence. Deep in the heart of darkness, not just that of the forest but also of his inner self, he has to shape himself anew out of the raw elemental energies that the text so strongly emphasizes in its descriptions of his lying 'on hard hethe' (l. 243), or on the moss with 'wilde wormes' (l. 252), from which, in his unkempt condition, he seems hardly differentiated. And it is in the woods that he rediscovers his talent for the harp, which gives him a different identity, that of a minstrel, and the powers to outsmart the fairy king and regain both his wife and, eventually, the throne. He never sheds off this identity, ushering himself into his long-abandoned palace to the accompaniment of his own harp, and as he reclaims the crown and undergoes ritualistic ablution and ceremonial hair-cutting — as they 'baþed him, & schaued his berd' (l. 585) — the text leaves the readers with the image of an enthroned minstrel-king, this reincorporation of Orfeo with the now-altered identity into the social and administrative structure of the court concluding his rite of passage.

One other theoretically-oriented approach to *Sir Orfeo* has been to invoke the notion of abjection. James Wade refers to this idea in his discussion of the numerous mutilated bodies arrested in their motion in the fairy castle.[73] He reads the arbitrariness of the fairy king's whim in 'keeping such abjections'[74] as the key to the interpretation of this scene, but one may also wonder about the actual nature of abjection itself, which, as Wade puts it, is 'a physical manifestation of the ambiguous, of that which disturbs identity, system, order' and 'traumatically shows us our own death'.[75] One of the original examples of the abject given by Julia Kristeva in *Powers of Horror* is indeed the dead body,[76] but the mechanics of the particular feeling of horror which Kristeva termed abjection are better revealed through the study of the way the human mind fails to make sense of bodily integrity and separation. Kristeva's example is that of nausea and vomit,[77] wherein the expulsion of matter from one's digestive system does not effect a proper 'othering' and separation but amounts to expelling what remains part of oneself, producing a horrifying blurring of boundaries that momentarily

---

Cawley and J. J. Anderson (London: Dent, 1976), pp. 157–254.

[72] For more on this connection, see Oren Falk, 'The Son of Orfeo: Kingship and Compromise in a Middle English Romance', *Journal of Medieval and Early Modern Studies*, 30 (2000), 247–74.
[73] James Wade, *Fairies in Medieval Romance* (Basingstoke: Palgrave Macmillan, 2011), pp. 76–80.
[74] Wade, p. 80.
[75] Wade, p. 80.
[76] Julia Kristeva, *Powers of Horror*, trans. by Leon S. Roudiez (New York: Columbia University Press, 1982), p. 3.
[77] Kristeva, pp. 2–3.

renders the categories of self and other, familiar and unfamiliar, or those of inside and outside, invalid.

Kristeva's psychoanalytic inclinations strongly suggest one more example, perhaps the true origin of the abject as such — the separation of mother and child, where the categories of 'I' and 'other' also falter. In *Sir Orfeo*, the abject understood in this way merges with the liminal, showing that the two notions approximate in their meaning the same phenomenon. Diane Purkiss rightly points out that the vision of bodies in the fairy castle is 'a collective spectacle of horror, but it is also a portrait of those whose deaths have come through a violent assault on the body's integrity, whether from within or without, by another'.[78] This is indeed what connects people 'with-outen hade' (l. 391), or those who 'þurth þe bodi hadde wounde' (l. 393), with 'wives [...] on child-bedde' (l. 399). All these people, liminally positioned between life and death but no longer subject to either of the two, are at the same time pure abjections, not only because they are corpses in the eyes of Orfeo and may induce in him, or the readers, this particular feeling of horror,[79] but also because their condition reflects the underlying principles of abjection — the confusion of self and other, and the violation done to the stability of bodily integrity. One cannot help but agree with Wade that whatever really happened to Heurodis, she was subjected to 'a kind of psychological ravishing',[80] which the violated bodies of the fairy king's victims, the queen among them, metaphorically imply.

It is also possible to connect this conflux of liminality and abjection with a very common trope in fairy beliefs, namely the notion of bodily contamination. The idea that eating fairy food somehow conditions the perpetual entrapment of the foolish mortal is well known,[81] but, as Purkiss argues, it may also manifest itself through the prohibition of speaking:

> To speak is to give something of yourself away, and there are powers eager to make use of what you have. To speak is also to open the body. Just as one must not eat the fairy food, so one must close one's mouth on words.[82]

> Like eating the fairy food, speaking opens the mouth and allows change to become permanent; once the boundaries of the body have been breached, magic can be done.[83]

This may help explain the speechless gazes of Orfeo and Heurodis upon their encounter in the woods (ll. 323–24); while the lack of words between the two may easily be read psychologically, it might also reflect their instinctive recalcitrance towards further enslavement by fairies.

The impression left by the story is, in the end, essentially optimistic, despite the rather pessimistic vision of human life subject to the whims of fortune. The boundary between possession and loss in an individual's life may be traversed at any moment, even within the palace grounds which, of all places, ought to be a safe haven for the royal couple, and until Orfeo and Heurodis complete their rite of passage, events move in one direction only, which is symbolically mirrored by the *ympe-tre* portal, which too only works one way. The entropy

---

[78] Purkiss, p. 77.
[79] D'Arcy (p. 11) is right to note that 'the narrator does not register horror on the part of Orfeo, even after he sees [Heurodis], but rather a sense of strangely detached wonder' (ll. 405–6, 409–10). My argument is therefore that abjection has more to do here with the violation of bodily integrity than any immediate emotion of fear or disgust.
[80] Wade, p. 77.
[81] Carole G. Silver, 'Tabu: Eating and Drinking, Motifs C200–C299', in *Archetypes and Motifs in Folklore and Literature: A Handbook*, ed. by Jane Garry and Hasan El-Shamy (Armonk, New York: Sharpe, 2005), pp. 103–7.
[82] Purkiss, p. 57.
[83] Purkiss, p. 112.

of the world seems invulnerable to resistance on man's part, and yet King Orfeo manages to regain what was lost. Conscious efforts and kingly might amount to nothing, but the power of his inner strength, his music, and his love for Heurodis are enough to supply a denouement that for once overcomes the liminal and contingent nature of man's existence. Yet the fairies of *Sir Orfeo* are definitely more than just embodiments of fate or fortune. They are the pure figures of liminality, and alongside unsettling the lives of Orfeo and his wife, their presence in the narrative undermines the solidity of basic conceptual categories such as the self and the other, or the familiar and the alien. Beneath the story of King Orfeo weeping for his beloved wife lies the horror of the maddening blurring of categories and the dread of the disintegration of one's identity.

What this article has shown is that liminality is more than just a major theme underlying the narrative of *Sir Orfeo*. It is also, hauntingly so, a dynamic principle underlying the structuring of the tale's hermeneutic reception, shaping the readers' experience of the text. Their grasp of what they are exposed to is as confused as that of Orfeo or Heurodis, and they struggle as much as the tale's human protagonists in trying to discover the fairy king's true intentions or to ascertain his moral alignment. Fairies produce a change in the life of Orfeo just as much as they affect the hermeneutic process of the tale's interpretation. In an analogous fashion to Orfeo being pushed against his will into a liminal state from which he has to re-emerge, the readers of the romance are made to piece together a number of overlapping liminalities in an attempt to produce a coherent understanding of the text. Their experience is one that brings them face to face with the terror of the threshold embodied by the fairies.

Þjalar-Jóns saga

Philip Lavender[1]

Introduction and Genre

Þjalar-Jóns saga is an entertaining tale, written in Iceland, suffering from something of an identity crisis. This introduction to the saga contains spoilers as regards its plot. Some may prefer to read the translation first and treat the introduction as an afterword.

There is one medieval manuscript of the saga (on which see below), dated to around 1400, and other than this we know very little about its early history. Stefán Einarsson claimed that it was written at Reykhólar on Breiðafjörður, but provides no rationale for such an identification.[2] He had also claimed at an earlier date that

> the Icelandic *lygi sögur* derive both from the Norwegian school of Abbot Robert's translated romances and from the native *fornaldar sögur* from the last quarter of the thirteenth century. The strand of the genre which derives from the *fornaldar sögur* is easily discernible from the first to the last. Here belong, in the period 1300–50, *Vilmundar saga viðutan*, *Þjalar-Jóns saga*, *Hrings saga ok Tryggva*, and *Sigurðar saga fóts*; in the period 1400–1500, *Álaflekks saga*, *Sigurgarðs saga frækna*, *Valdimars saga*, and *Jóns saga leiksveins*. The influence of chivalrous romance on these sagas is slight for their chief characteristics are native motifs and native style.[3]

Thus we are apparently dealing with a *lygisaga* ('lying saga'), written between 1300 and 1350, which displays little influence from translated Old Norse romances, themselves particularly associated with the court of Hákon Hákonarsson of Norway (r. 1217–63). The somewhat pejorative term *lygisaga*, extremely sporadically attested in medieval writings, is not widely used today, having been dropped in preference of *native*, *original* or *indigenous riddarasögur*. If we accept the latter term then it is clear that *Þjalar-Jóns saga* has been considered to tend more to the 'indigenous' end of the scale than the *riddarasaga* end, an opinion also held by Einar Ól. Sveinsson, who said that its style 'has little in common with that of the romances, and as regards its matter it may with as much justification be called a Heroic saga as a romance'.[4]

---

[1] I wish to thank the anonymous peer-reviewers whose feedback has greatly improved this translation and the introduction. Any errors that remain are, however, purely my own.
[2] Stefán Einarsson, 'Heimili (skólar) fornaldarsagna og riddarasagna', *Skírnir*, 140 (1966), 272.
[3] Stefán Einarsson, *A History of Icelandic Literature* (New York: John Hopkins Press, 1957), pp. 163–64.
[4] Einar Ól. Sveinsson, 'Viktors saga ok Blávus: Sources and Characteristics', in *Viktors saga ok Blávus*, ed. by Jónas

In spite of these statements, however, *Þjalar-Jóns saga* has never been included in any of the collected editions of the *fornaldarsögur*, such as Rafn's (1829–30) or Bjarni Vilhjálmsson and Guðni Jónsson's (1943–44).[5] Yet having not made the cut for the latter collection, it is also notably absent from Bjarni Vilhjálmsson's collection of *riddarasögur* (1963). He explains in the overall introduction to that collected edition, referring to the various volumes, that 'er þeim ætlað að vera sýnishorn' ('they are intended to be a selection'), yet two of the other *fornaldarsaga*-style sagas mentioned by Stefán Einarsson *are* included.[6] *Þjalar-Jóns saga* could be said to take place prior to the settlement of Iceland (it is hard to tell since other than a 'viking' ethos, there is little overtly historical detail to grasp on to), but it definitely does not take place in Scandinavia, a requisite for inclusion among the *fornaldarsögur*.[7] Rather, the focus of action is northern France and Russia, both areas which, while not Scandinavian *per se*, did see intense settlement from Scandinavia in the early medieval period.[8] The Mediterranean, African and Asian climes which are so common in other indigenous *riddarasögur* remain on the periphery, as do Saracen threats, learned and fiercely defensive maiden-kings, and extended motifs adopted from the works of Chrétien de Troyes.[9] It is only relatively recently that certain scholars have fished this saga out of the gap to which it had been consigned and taken a decisive decision on its generic status. Marianne E. Kalinke and P. M Mitchell included it in their *Bibliography of Old Norse-Icelandic Romances*.[10] Conversely, the 'Stories for All Time: The Icelandic Fornaldarsögur' website and online bibliography include the saga among its legendary pre-Icelandic settlement texts.[11] It remains to be seen whether either of the designations will stick.

Sources and Motifs

The ostracism which *Þjalar-Jóns saga* has been subjected to has mostly been expressed in negative terms: what the saga does not contain. But there is a great deal that the saga does contain which can nuance our approach to it. In brief, the saga tells of Eiríkur, a prince in France, who becomes the companion of a mysterious stranger named Gestur. This stranger

---

Kristjánsson, Riddarasögur, 2 (Reykjavík: Handritastofnun Íslands, 1964), pp. cix-ccxii (p. cxxxiii).

[5] *Fornaldar sögur Norðurlanda*, ed. by Carl Christian Rafn, 3 vols (Copenhagen: Popp, 1829–30); *Fornaldarsögur Norðurlanda*, ed. by Bjarni Vilhjálmsson and Guðni Jónsson, 3 vols (Reykjavík: Bókaútgáfan Forni, 1943–44).

[6] Bjarni Vilhjálmsson, 'Formáli' in *Riddarasögur*, ed. by Bjarni Vilhjálmsson, 7 vols (Haukadalur: Íslendingasagnaútgáfan, 1963), I, xvii. Incidentally, 9 of the 11 sagas in the oldest manuscript containing *Þjalar Jóns saga* are included in Bjarni Vilhjálmsson's collection. The *fornaldarsaga*-style sagas which are also present are *Vilmundar saga viðutan* and *Sigurðar saga fóts*. These, along with *Hrings saga ok Tryggva*, although not *Þjalar-Jóns saga*, make it into *Late Medieval Romances*, ed. by Agnete Loth, Editiones Arnamagaeanae, series B, 20–24, 5 vols (Copenhagen: Munksgaard, 1962–65).

[7] On these requisites see Philip Lavender, 'The Secret Prehistory of the *Fornaldarsögur*', JEGP, 114 (2015), 526–51 (p. 535).

[8] Horst Zettel, 'France, Norse in' and Haakon Stang, 'Russia, Norse in', in *Medieval Scandinavia: An Encyclopedia*, ed. by Phillip Pulsiano (New York: Garland, 1993), pp. 219–20 and 556–58 respectively.

[9] On these genre features see, for example, Jürg Glauser, *Isländische Märchensagas: Studien zur Prosaliteratur im spätmittelalterlichen Island*, Beiträge zür nordischen Philologie, 12 (Basel: Helbing & Lichtenhahn, 1983); Marianne E. Kalinke, *Bridal-Quest Romance in Medieval Iceland*, Islandica, 46 (Ithaca, N.Y.: Cornell University Press, 1990).

[10] Marianne E. Kalinke and P. M. Mitchell, *Bibliography of Old Norse–Icelandic Romances*, Islandica, 44 (Ithaca: Cornell University Press, 1985), pp. 132–34. Glauser, Isländische Märchensagas, pp. 315–17, also includes the saga under the genre alluded to in the title of the work.

[11] Compiled principally by Matthew Driscoll and Silvia Hufnagel (http://fasnl.ku.dk).

turns out to be the eponymous Jón, a wondrously skilled craftsman and engineer, who has been ousted from his homeland after his father, the king, was defeated and killed by the usurper Roðbert. Together they travel to Jón's homeland where, through deception, ingenuity and prowess on the battlefield, they recuperate the lost patrimony. The saga ends with both men getting married to the women of their choice and having their kingdoms consolidated.

A clear link to the *fornaldarsögur* can be found in chapters 12 and 13, when in a flashback the young Jón, sentenced to death by the evil Roðbert, is left locked in some stocks in a dangerously exposed area outside of the fortress walls. When night falls and Jón is attacked by a monstrous she-wolf, he is able to save himself. He does so thanks to his mother, who has managed to send her maid to him with a knife and honey, the latter of which, smeared on his face and in his mouth, tricks the she-wolf into poking her tongue between his teeth so that he can bite down on it and restrain her while he attacks. The scene should be instantly recognisable to anyone familiar with *Völsunga saga*. It is reproduced in full here:

> Signy learned that her father had been killed and her brothers taken prisoner and sentenced to death. She calls King Siggeir aside and said, 'I want to ask you not to have my brothers executed so swiftly, but have them put in stocks instead, for the old saying "happy the eye that gazes its fill" expresses my feelings well. I won't ask for a longer stay of execution for them, for I expect that my request would fall on deaf ears."
>
> Siggeir replies, 'You must be completely out of your mind. You ask for worse treatment than beheading for your brothers. But your wish shall be granted. The greater their suffering before they die, the better I like it.'
>
> He now gives orders to do as she asked. A huge pair of stocks were fastened over the legs of the ten brothers somewhere out in the forest. They are left sitting there all that day and into the night. But in the middle of the night an old she-wolf came to them out of the forest as they sat trapped in the stocks. This large and ferocious-looking beast bites one of them to death, devoured the entire body, and then made off.
>
> In the morning Signy sent the man she trusted most to her brothers to find out how they were. Upon returning, he tells her that one of them is dead. It grieved her to think that the same might happen to all the others, but she was at a loss for a way to help them.
>
> To make a long story short, the same she-wolf came at midnight nine nights in a row, killing and eating one of the brothers each night until only Sigmund remains alive. But before the tenth night arrives, Signy sends her trusted messenger to her brother Sigmund. She gave the man some honey and instructed him to smear it on Sigmund's face, putting some of it into his mouth. The messenger now goes to Sigmund, does as he was told, and then returned home.
>
> During the following night, the she-wolf comes as usual. She intended to bite Sigmund to death as she had done to his brothers, but she catches the scent of the honey that had been smeared on him; she licked his face all over and then sticks her tongue into his mouth. Afraid of nothing, he bit into the wolf's tongue. She gives a violent start and pulls back, pressing so hard with her paws against the stocks that they split apart. Sigmund held on so tightly with his teeth that the she-wolf's tongue was torn out by the roots, leaving her dead. Some say that this beast was the mother of King Siggeir and that she resorted to foul witchcraft to take on this guise.[12]

Völsunga saga is generally believed to date to the thirteenth century, so it would seem more likely that the borrowing is into *Þjalar-Jóns saga*, and not in the reverse direction. There are

---

[12] *Völsunga saga — The Saga of the Volsungs: The Icelandic Text According to MS Nks 1824 b, 4o*, ed. and trans.

two further reasons to believe this is the case. The first is *Völsunga saga*'s repeated references to wolves and lycanthropy, as a result of which the she-wolf's attack fits fairly seamlessly in, as opposed to in *Þjalar-Jóns saga* where it is a somewhat unconnected anomaly. The second is the slightly clunky use of the motif in *Þjalar-Jóns saga*. The whole point of the honey is to enable Sigmund to maim the she-wolf without access to a weapon, but in *Þjalar-Jóns saga* he has a knife as well, making the honey more or less superfluous.

Nevertheless, the scene as it stands serves to emphasise Jón's prowess. He is no ordinary man, but a prodigious hero, capable of taking down fearsome monsters. Grimstad suggests that Sigmund's ripping out of the she-wolf's tongue in *Völsunga saga* is 'a feat evocative of the mythological slaying of Fenrir' (p. 33), and this idea of a divine pagan overlay could be extended to *Þjalar-Jóns saga*. Jón first turns up disguised as Gestur, a popular Odinic pseudonym in Old Norse tales, and one of his superlative possessions is the self-replicating ring, Gáinn, a parallel to Óðinn's Draupnir.[13] He is in many ways a legendary hero of a kind with Örvar-Oddur and Göngu-Hrólfur.[14]

Despite these heroic and mythic overtones, an even more thoroughgoing connection can be seen with one of the *riddarasögur*. As noted by Jürg Glauser, there is a clear connection between *Konráðs saga keisarasonar* and *Þjalar-Jóns saga*.[15] The argument in favour of this special relationship is bolstered by the codicological evidence of them being 'frequent friends'. Of the many manuscripts containing *Þjalar-Jóns saga*, 13 contain the two sagas in immediate succession and there are a further 5 in which the two appear non-consecutively. Such a close pairing is a fairly rare occurrence.

Konráðs saga keisarasonar tells the story of Konráður, the prince of the Land of the Saxons, and his sworn brother Roðbert.[16] They travel to Miklagarður (Constantinople), where Konráður's inability to speak the language puts him at the mercy of Roðbert, who turns out to be a treacherous scoundrel. Roðbert's machinations (he pretends that he is the prince and Konráður his servant) put Konráður in danger and come close to preventing him from achieving his goal, marriage to the beautiful and wise princess Mathilda. Luckily Mathilda is also a polyglot and manages to communicate with Konráður and expose Roðbert's treachery. Surprisingly, considering the genre, Roðbert does not get his comeuppance and die at the end of the saga, but lives to fight another day. It is this Roðbert who seems to be the main antagonist of *Þjalar-Jóns saga*. That this is not just a coincidence or an example of conventional naming patterns for villains is borne out by the details of the saga: when Roðbert is introduced in chapter VII he is said to be 'svo fróður at hann talar allar tungur' ('so wise that he speaks all languages'), and at the end of the saga Jón and Eiríkur visit Konráður as part of the celebratory parade around Europe.[17]

Early audiences seem to have been well aware of these intertextual strands. Árni Magnússon (1663–1730), for example, on f. 21r of AM 576 b 4to discusses how the two

---

by Karen Grimstad, Bibliotheca Germanica Series Nova, 3 (Saarbrücken: AQ-Verlag, 2000), pp. 89, 91.

[13] See Rudolf Simek, *Dictionary of Northern Mythology*, trans. by Angela Hall (Cambridge: Brewer, 1993), pp. 65–66.

[14] *Fornaldar sögur Norðurlanda*, ed. by Guðni Jónsson, 4 vols (Reykjavík: Íslendingasagnaútgáfan, 1954), II, 199–363 (*Örvar-Odds saga*); III, 161–280 (*Göngu-Hrólfs saga*).

[15] Jürg Glauser, 'Þjalar-Jóns saga', in *Medieval Scandinavia: An Encyclopedia*, ed. by Phillip Pulsiano (New York: Garland, 1993), pp. 664–65. On this connection, see also Kalinke, *Bridal-Quest Romance*, pp. 179–85.

[16] Otto J. Zitzelsberger, *Konráðs saga keisarasonar*, American University Studies, Series I: Germanic Languages and Literature, 63 (New York: Lang, 1987).

[17] *Þjalar-Jóns saga; Dámusta saga*, ed. by Louisa Fredrika Tan-Haverhorst (Haarlem: H. D. Tjeenk Willink & Zoon,

sagas in question share one and the same villain. At the start of the twentieth century (1902) a postscript to *Jarlmanns saga ok Hermanns* on pp. 64–65 in Lbs 2497 8vo expresses in similar terms the character interaction even beyond the two named sagas:

> Eins og endir þessarrar sögu ber með sér, þá er hún inngangr að Konráðssögu Keisarasonar, er fór til Ormalands. En framhald Konráðssögu er Þjalar-Jóns saga, því Roðbert sonarsonur Jallmanns er [...] Konráð mat það meira er hann lagði eigi þyngdi refsingu á hann fyrir svík hans, en hann gerði. Þessar 3 sögur eru því eiginlega ein sögu að vissu leiti: 1. Hermanns og Jallmanns, 2. Konráðs keisarasonar og Roðbert svíkara, 3. Þjalar-Jóns og Eiríks forvitna.

> (Just as is implied by the end of this saga, it is an introduction to the saga of Konráður keisarason, who travelled to the country of serpents. And the continuation of *Konráðs saga* is *Þjalar-Jóns saga*, since Roðbert is the grandson of Jarlmann [...] Konráður considered that to be important when he did not punish Roðbert more severely than he did for his deception. These three sagas are thus in some way a single saga: 1. *Jarlmanns saga ok Hermanns*, 2. *Konráðs saga keisarasonar*, 3. *Þjalar-Jóns saga ok Eiríks forvitna.*)[18]

Not only do we follow different generations of the same families through these three sagas, but similar concerns also arise time and again. Trust and treachery are key concerns: Jarlmann does not trust Hermann in his saga, but apparently without justification; Konráður trusts Roðbert in his saga, but certainly should not; Jón and Eiríkur start off uncertainly in *Þjalar-Jóns saga*, but following on from this tentative beginning come to be something of a dream team and can use their solid relationship to challenge the suspicious and deceitful Roðbert and ultimately defeat him. Two personality traits which are also emphasised and interact with the already-mentioned themes are curiosity and ingenuity. Geraldine Barnes has recently shown how in *indigenous riddarasögur* the misapplication of curiosity (or *forvitni*) can have just as negative effects as the appropriate use of it can have positive ones.[19] Jarlmann in *Jarlmanns saga ok Hermanns* is not curious enough about the *kuflungar*, and Konráður in *Konráðs saga keisarasonar* should have been a bit more curious about what Roðbert was saying. Yet curiosity can also get one involved in tricky situations, as is the case when Eiríkur incessantly questions Gestur/Jón (compare also Barnes' example of Dínus drambláti). This risky trait is ultimately counterbalanced, however, by Gestur's boundless ingenuity.

If there is one thing which really sets *Þjalar-Jóns saga* apart from its peers, it is the way the tale revels in architectural complexity and artesanal ingenuity (the title itself and Jón's cognomen refer to the *þél* or 'file', a great tool used by a great craftsman). From the construction of a road across an impenetrable plateau (unparalleled in medieval Icelandic literature) to the detailed description of underground tunnels into hidden cellars or Roðbert's fortifications, the text shows an extreme sensitivity to topography and manmade interventions

---

1939), p. 12 (normalised). Hereafter just ÞJs.

[18] Paul Bibire has also commented on the connection between *Konráðs saga keisarasonar* and *Jarlmanns saga ok Hermanns*: 'As mentioned above, there are clear, intentional and explicit relationships between *Clari saga* and *Nitida saga*, and between *Konráðs saga keisarasonar* and *Jarlmanns saga ok Hermanns*. In both cases, the second saga takes the same situation and examines it from an opposed viewpoint, as if to provide a commentary upon the first saga': Paul Bibire, 'From *Riddarasaga* to *Lygisaga*: The Norse Response to Romance', in *Les Sagas de Chevaliers (Riddarasögur): Actes de la Ve Conférence Internationale sur les Sagas Présentés par Régis Boyer (Toulon. Juillet 1982)*, ed. by Régis Boyer, Serie Civilisations, 10 (Toulon: Presses de l'Université Paris-Sorbonne, 1985), pp. 55–74 (p. 70).

[19] Geraldine Barnes, *The Bookish Riddarasögur: Writing Romance in Late Medieval Iceland* (Odense: University Press of Southern Denmark, 2014), p. 58.

upon it. In this sense it bears comparison with yet another saga, namely the 'post-classical' *Íslendingasaga*, *Króka-Refs saga*.

Króka-Refur is characterised by his ingenuity, and in one of the most memorable scenes of the saga his wilderness fortress in Greenland is besieged. An attempt is made to burn the structure down, but this fails due to Refur's having constructed a system of hydraulics which pumps water through pipes and into the walls which are being assailed. A Norwegian merchant named Barður gets involved and receives advice from King Haraldur Sigurðarson in Norway, who tells him to find and block off the pipes. Once Barður has helped to incapacitate the defences, the next wondrous event occurs when one of the fortress walls comes tumbling down, and out rolls a ship on wheels. With Refur and company aboard it hurtles down to the water and sails away:

> fellr sa virkishlutrinn, er fram horfde at siónum; þar var svo gegnt til ætlad, at virkid fell i skurdinn á framan-verdann sævarbackann; þad var suo slétt sem ein fiol. Enn i þui er virkid fell, rann þar epter fram skip á huelum og þegar fram á sióinn. Þeir Refr draga þegar segl vpp.[20]

> (That section of the fortress which faced the sea fell down. It was made with a plan in mind, so that the section fell into the trench pointing out down the beach to the sea. It was as smooth as a plank. And as soon as the fortress wall fell, a ship on wheels rolled out and immediately down towards the sea. Refur and his people raise the sails.)

The similarities with chapters 17–19 of *Þjalar-Jóns saga* are clear (and all the more so since comparable features appear nowhere else in Old Norse literature): a hydraulic system used to control the flow of water into a confined space and a dramatic exit from said confined space on a wheeled ship through a collapsing wall. The specificity of these features makes them almost certainly related, and yet the differences are also significant. In *Króka-Refs saga* the hydraulic system is put in place as a defence against attacks made with fire; in *Þjalar-Jóns saga* it appears mostly to be employed as a weapon (neither Roðbert nor his men are even aware that there is anything going on inside the mountain). The water dammed up by Jón does not put out a fire, but is an army-flattening deluge.

Based on the dating of the two sagas, it is reasonable to assume that *Þjalar-Jóns saga* borrowed the motif from *Króka-Refs saga*. Moreover, the content of the sagas backs up such a conclusion. The details of these contraptions are highly reminiscent of various accounts of Continental siege warfare, and it is only in *Króka-Refs saga* that these features are integrated into a 'siege' of sorts, and King Haraldur Sigurðarson, frequently associated with tales of siege-breaking during his Mediterranean odyssey (for example in *Heimskringla*),[21] is consulted in order to break the stalemate.[22] Yet there may be traces of various other sources of knowledge and traditions in this scene. Glacial floods in Iceland and medieval field irrigation systems in Greenland could have been real-world inspirations.[23] Life inside a mountain and construction of fabulous ships link neatly with the representation of dwarves in the *Prose Edda*, such as

---

[20] *Króka-Refs saga og Króka-Refs rímur*, ed. by Pálmi Pálsson (Copenhagen: Møller, 1883), p. 29.

[21] *Heimskringla: Nóregs konunga sǫgur*, ed. by Finnur Jónsson, STUAGNL 23, 3 vols (Copenhagen: Møller, 1893–1900), III, pp. 80–91. See also the translation in *King Harald's saga*, trans. Magnús Magnússon and Hermann Pálsson (Harmondsworth: Penguin, 1966; repr. 1977).

[22] No actual source can be found among the stories told of King Haraldur Sigurðarsson: it may be from a lost narrative or simply have been inspired by such narratives. It should be mentioned that at a later point in *Þjalar-Jóns saga* an actual siege takes place, when Jón and Eiríkur attack Roðbert's fortress.

[23] I am grateful to Reinhard Hennig for suggesting glacial outburst floods as a possible inspiration for the episode.

those who created Skíðblaðnir (and let us not forget that Jón is fostered by dwarves after the death of his father and his escape from Roðbert). The close juxtaposition of the construction of a wondrous ship by a prolific craftsman and the unleashing of a deadly torrent may also bring to mind biblical and apocryphal stories of Noah. Whatever the elements which came together to make the scene as it stands in *Þjalar-Jóns saga*, the outcome and impression it leaves is 'epic', and the imaginative and detailed combination of elements can remain fresh and exciting to readers even today.

It should also be emphasised that chapter 3 in particular, despite having mostly gone unnoticed, stands out in the corpus of saga literature. The presence of both skaldic verse and a riddle, apparently in an eddic metre, is surely unique among *fornaldarsögur* and *riddarasögur*.[24] The stanzas are very corrupt and the riddle is fragmentary and of uncertain origin, but in many ways this simply heightens their esoteric appeal.

Manuscripts and Editions

The website for the 'Stories for All Time: The Icelandic Fornaldarsögur' project lists 46 manuscripts of *Þjalar-Jóns saga*, and since its compiling yet another manuscript (Lbs 4813 8vo) has come to light after being catalogued at Landsbókasafn, bringing the total to 47. The list includes both complete and partial texts: in fact two of the 'defective' items listed, AM 582 4to and AM 537 4to, were originally one manuscript (AM 582 4to contains just the final leaf, the vast majority of the preceding text being preserved in AM 537 4to). Three other of the items listed, AM 576 b 4to, AM 576 c 4to and NKS 1144 fol., do not contain the saga as such, but rather excerpts and summaries.[25] Papp. fol. nr 98 contains a Swedish translation. That leaves 42 complete or partial Old Norse texts of the saga.

Louisa Fredrika Tan-Haverhorst considers 33 manuscripts in the text-critical introduction to her edition, of which 30 are complete or partial texts in Old Norse. That means that there remain 12 texts, several in private or North American collections, for which, as yet, there are no theories as to where they might fit into a stemma. They are the following:

> Arnamagnaean Collection, Reykjavík: SÁM 6
> Harvard University, Houghton Library, Cambridge, MA: Icel. MS. 32
> Johns Hopkins University, Baltimore: Nikulás Ottenson 9
> Landsbókasafn Íslands, Reykjavík: Lbs 3625 4to
> Landsbókasafn Íslands, Reykjavík: Lbs 2497 8vo
> Landsbókasafn Íslands, Reykjavík: Lbs 4370 8vo
> Landsbókasafn Íslands, Reykjavík: Lbs 4492 8vo
> Landsbókasafn Íslands, Reykjavík: Lbs 4813 8vo
> Private collections: Böðvar Kvaran 11 4to
> Riksarkivet, Stockholm: Säfstaholmssamlingen I Papp. 3
> Byggðasafnið á Skógum: Skógar (no shelfmark)
> University Library, Yale, New Haven, CT: MS Z 113.81

The stemma which can be drawn up on the basis of Tan-Haverhorst's findings regarding the 30 studied texts is as shown in figures 1 and 2 overleaf.

---

[24] An edition of the skaldic stanzas will be include in the ongoing project and series Skaldic Poetry of the Scandinavian Middle Ages; 'Stanzas from *Þjalar-Jóns saga*', ed. by Philip Lavender, in vol. VII, *Poetry in Fornaldarsögur* (forthcoming 2017).

[25] In the Royal Library in Stockholm there is another manuscript containing an excerpt, Papp. fol. nr. 96., which is

Þjalar-Jóns saga

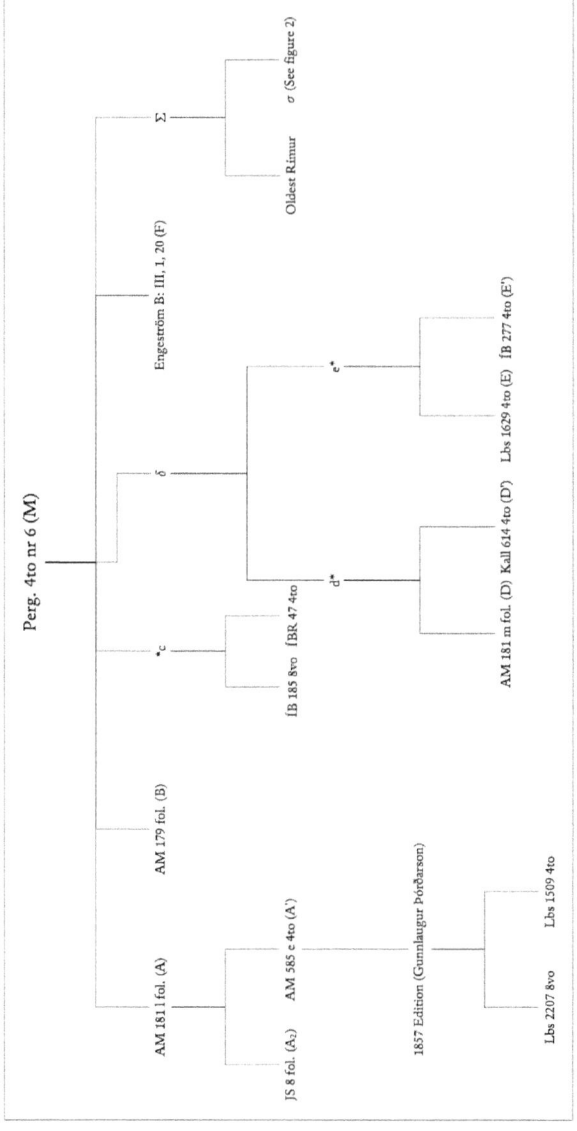

Figure 1: Stemma showing the main subgroups of texts of *Þjalar-Jóns saga*, as determined in the introduction to Louisa Fredrika Tan-Haverhorst's edition. For the manuscripts in the σ-group see figure 2. Connecting lines do not rule out the possibility of intermediate, non-extant, manuscripts. (NB. No chronology is implied by vertical positioning). The relationship of the texts as shown here is somewhat simplified: for example, Tan-Haverhorst suggests that AM 585 c 4to may have been influenced by a c-group text (p.xvi), and Kall 614 4to shows influence from either a σ-group text or the oldest *rímur* (p.xxxi). Asterisks and Greek letters represent hypothesized non-extant texts.

There have been two editions of the text to date. Gunnlaugur Þórðarson's 1857 edition is based on three seventeenth-century Arnamagnæan manuscripts, principally AM 585 e 4to (called A; Tan-Haverhorst calls it A'), with lacunae filled out with and alternative readings supplied from AM 181 l fol. (B; Tan-Haverhorst calls it A) and AM 537 a 4to (C; Tan-Haverhorst calls it S'). Louisa Fredrika Tan-Haverhorst's 1939 edition reproduces the text from Perg. 4to nr 6 (there given the siglum M) up to the point where it breaks off (two sentences into chapter 14), and the continuation is taken from AM 181 l fol. (as already stated, there given the siglum A: see figure 3). Various snippets missing from the fourteen chapters of text in Perg. 4to nr 6 are also filled out from AM 181 l fol.,[26] and in the later part of the text Tan-Haverhorst judiciously includes a small selection of improvements which are well-testified in other manuscripts. Thus the edition, and hence this translation, which is based on Tan-Haverhorst's edition, presents a somewhat hybrid text.

There are good reasons why such a composite text might be of interest. In the first place, Tan-Haverhorst's study of the various texts is by far the most thorough to date. She presents Perg. 4to nr 6 presumably because it is the oldest manuscript by a long way (c.1400, following which there are 10 or so manuscripts from the seventeenth century). Yet presenting a translation of it alone would be frustrating for a reader seeking narrative closure. AM 181 l fol., from which the denouement is drawn, is said by Tan-Haverhorst to be 'ongetwijfeld een afschrift van' ('without doubt a copy of') Perg. 4to nr 6.[27] Thus the ending provided is as close to how we may imagine that the original ending in Perg. 4to nr 6 to could have been before it was damaged.

It is also worth mentioning that five separate sets of *rímur* (late- and post-medieval narrative poetry) are known to be based on the prose saga.[28] The earliest of these are from the sixteenth century (found in two manuscripts: AM 143 8vo, ÍB 634 8vo), and the author is unidentified. The other four sets, all from the eighteenth and nineteenth centuries, are composed by séra Hjörleifur Þórðarson, Guðmundur Jónsson í Hrútshúsum, Árni Þorklesson and Guðmundur Jónsson í Grímsey (in collaboration), and Guðlaugur Magnússon. Little will be known about their treatment of the narrative content until somebody takes up the challenge of carrying out a study of them.

Note on the Translation

No translation of this saga has previously been published in any language.[29] The chapter numbers here are included following Tan-Haverhorst's edition. Perg. 4to nr 6 has no chapter numbers, but rather large initials at the start of new sections. In the later manuscripts, such as AM 181 l fol., chapter numbers are included in place of those initials, and Tan-Haverhorst based her numbering on these later exemplars.[30] The translation stays close to the text, reproducing the mixture of tenses as they stand in the prose. This can sometimes be slightly

---

not currently listed in the online bibliography.

[26] On a couple of occasions, where AM 181 l fol. also has a lacuna, the lacunae from Perg. 4to nr 6 are filled out from other manuscripts, such as AM 181 m fol. (which Tan-Haverhorst gives the siglum D).

[27] ÞJs, p. v.

[28] Finnur Sigmundsson, *Rímnatal*, 2 vols (Reykjavík: Rímnafélagið, 1966), I, 507–9; ÞJs, pp. lxix–lxxxi.

[29] While this translation was being prepared for publication, it came to my attention that an MA-thesis had been submitted at Háskoli Íslands which also contained a translation of the saga (September, 2015). The author is Cecilia White, but I have unfortunately not been able to take her findings into consideration here.

[30] It should be noted that the number 'XX' appears to have been accidentally duplicated, thus appearing at the start

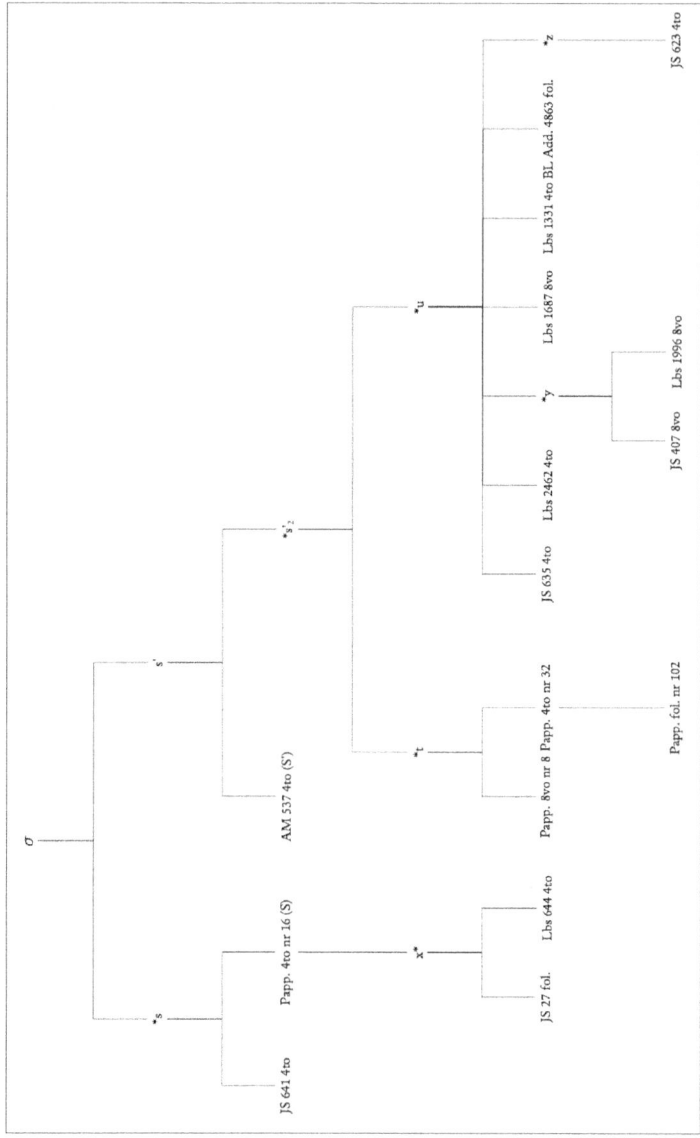

Figure 2: Stemma showing the manuscripts from the σ subgroup of texts of *Þjalar-Jóns saga*, as determined in the introduction to Louisa Fredrika Tan-Haverhorst's edition. Manuscripts which contain only excerpts (such as Papp. fol. nr 96) or translations (such as Papp. fol. nr/ 98, as Swedish translation) are not included here.)

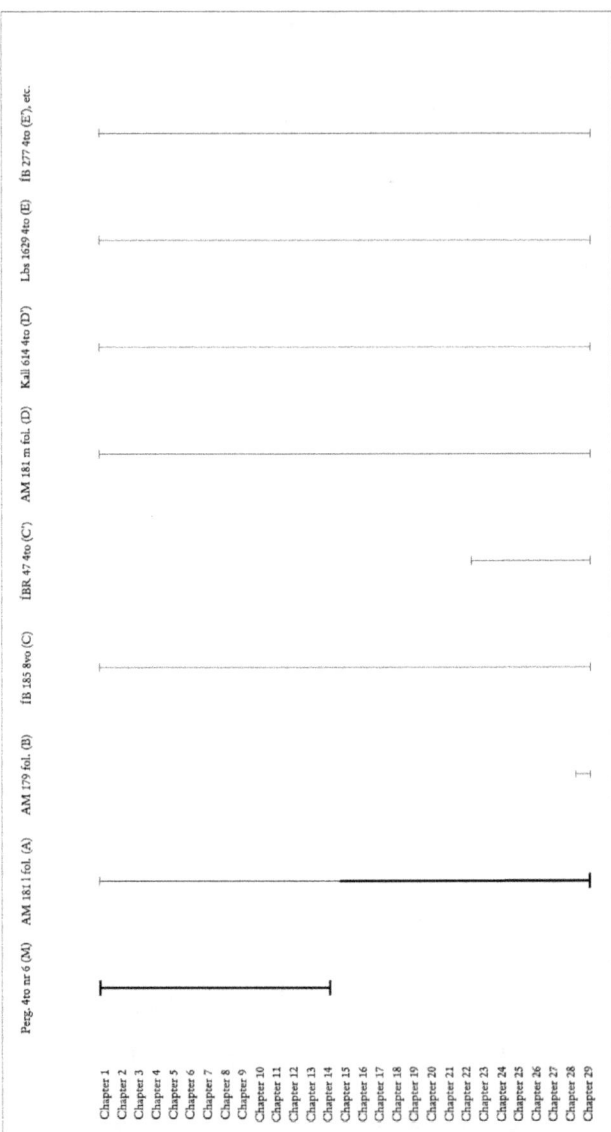

Figure 3: Diagram showing the proportion of the text of the saga represented in a selection of the oldest witnesses. As is clear, the majority of the manuscripts represented here contain the full 29 chapters, with only three presenting a defective text. The bold line represents the text which is used as the base of Louisa Fredrika Tan-Haverhorst's edition as well as this translation.

disorienting for a modern reader, but its retention can also help us engage with some of the dynamics of the story-telling as it would previously have been experienced, at once distant and then suddenly in the thick of the action. On some occasions it has been necessary to be somewhat freer with the translation in order not to sacrifice comprehensibility. One particular example is the frequent use of many personal pronouns in passages in the Old Norse, where the abundance of *hann* and *honum* ('he' and 'him') ends up sounding very clunky in a translation. On a few such occasions some liberties have been taken to make the referents more transparent with qualifiers.

The names of characters are normalized to an approximation of their Modern Icelandic forms (e.g. *Hlöðver* instead of *Hlöðvér*). This is most obvious in the presence of an epenthetic '-u-' in names ending in '-r' (i.e. *Eiríkur* instead of *Eiríkr*). This treatment is chosen partly because the resulting form may appear more approachable to English-speakers wishing to pronounce them, but also because the vast majority of the manuscripts of the saga are from a time period in which the linguistic change which led to the insertion of the vowel had already occurred. Place names present a particular problem in the saga. Where possible the Old Norse terms are translated with their geographical equivalents in English, but as with many other similar sagas, we must accept that the geographical and political make-up may be anachronistic (from a rigorous historical perspective) if not completely illogical (non-contiguous countries/regions are described as if they share borders). It must, however, also be borne in mind that the purpose of mentioning these various countries was not to provide an accurate historical and geographical treatise, but to create a cosmopolitan sense of wonder.

---

of two consecutive chapters in AM 181 I fol. This means that all of the subsequent chapters, 22–29, are also in that manuscript numbered one less than they actually are. Tan-Haverhorst corrects this error.

Þjalar-Jóns saga

Here begins the saga of Jón, son of Svipdagur, and of Eiríkur the Curious.

[I]

There was a king named Vilhjálmur who ruled over Gaul.[31] He was a powerful and excellent king, wise and benevolent. His royal seat was at Rouen in Gaul, because in the past Rouen was the principal city in that land. He was married to Elínborg, the daughter of King Hlöðver of the Land of the Franks. They had one son, who was named Eiríkur. He was the most handsome of men, large in stature and well-proportioned, able in all those pursuits which are befitting of an educated man. He knew many of those languages which were common in the neighbouring countries.

When Eiríkur was fifteen years old, his father procured for him five well-manned and -provisioned warships for his entertainment. He went raiding with them, and it was certainly profitable. And in the autumn he had ten ships and set course with them back to Gaul and spent the winter there with his father. And in the spring he has these ten ships prepared and went raiding in the East over the summer. He was victorious and had the upper hand wherever he fought. And in the autumn he had fifteen ships, loaded with wealth, and set course for home once more in the autumn and stayed with his father over the winter. And since this enterprise had gone well for Eiríkur, he went raiding a third summer with these fifteen ships and thus becomes renowned on his raiding expedition in the East, to such an extent that no warrior-king was thought to be greater than him. He never plundered merchants or peaceful men; and kings and nobles, if they heard of his journeys and raiding expeditions, along with his lineage and moral conduct, received him with feasts and invitations of hospitality, going to meet him with all pomp and a warm reception, and moreover on parting giving him great, costly gifts of invaluable treasures and jewels. Thus he had refuge in each and every kingdom. The fourth summer his voyage was prepared with twenty ships, and when he is ready, the king himself, his father, and Queen Elínborg, his mother, and all the people accompanied him out to his ships and wished him a good journey and that he return safe and sound.

[II]

King Vilhjálmur remains behind in Rouen in Gaul. At that time it was a large and densely populated city. It was also the case that south-east of the city was a high mountainous area, so great, broad and long that it was a cause for great sorrow that no supplies could reach them except by a longer route. The mountainous area was completely encircled with crags and precipices, so that nothing could get up there except for birds capable of flight. There, there were neither male nor female reindeer, nor any four-footed beasts. No man had set foot

---

[31] Valland, Frakkland, Saxland, Flæmingjaland, Hólmgarður and Miklagarður are some of the important places visited. *Valland* is often used to refer to France in a vague sense, although it originally seems to have been the designation for Celtic Gaul. Since Frakkland, the Land of the Franks, is also mentioned, Gaul is the more appropriate designation for Valland in this narrative (to have France and the Land of the Franks existing simultaneously would be awkward), and that term will be used. We also, however, find Flæmingjaland, that is Flanders, which was certainly not a political entity while Gaul still existed. See the 'Note on the Translation'.

up there, and nobody knew what it might be like up there. Just in front of and at the foot of the mountainous region were wide level plains, fair meadows with babbling brooks.

The king greatly enjoyed ball games and jousting. It is said that one fine day the king summons his knights out of the city to a joust on the level plains which were previously mentioned. The king himself leaves the city and a chair is provided for him to sit on. And when he has been sitting for a while, it becomes apparent that he is not quite himself on that day as compared to how he usually is. He looks up towards the mountain and does not take his eyes off it. The king had two advisors, one named Amon and the other Abmon. They were brothers and had been with the king for a long time.

Amon approaches the king and spoke: 'Lord, why do you stare so intently at the mountain, so that you pay no heed to the games?'

The king answers: 'Something is different up there on the mountain, similar to when a cloud of dust is kicked up where a great many men ride. I suspect that somebody must be moving around on the mountain, where it must be quite challenging to get access to. For that reason it is unlikely that I would know of any creature having its abode there.'

And towards the end of the day they see that a man walks down from the mountain, a turn of events at which they marvelled greatly, because they see that neither ravines nor crags could impede him. He bore on his shoulders something that could best be described as a satchel or pack of some sort. He seemed rather large to them. He makes at once for where the king sits, with his retinue performing their games in front of him, and lays down his load and goes into the circle. It can be said that nobody greets him, but then he does not greet anyone either.

He goes before the king and addresses him in this manner: 'May you sit there, most blessed of all kings, in honour and high esteem, peace and happiness.'

The king took this well and asks who he might be.

He replies: 'Call me Gestur Gunnólfsson, but I cannot tell you of my lineage or native land. And "a beggar's errands brook no delay".[32] Lord, I request lodgings from you for the winter.'

The king answers: 'I seem to be placed in rather a difficult position, as regards offering you lodgings for the winter, since you will neither state your lineage nor native land. I have moreover not made it a habit to take in men like you. I have the feeling that you will be difficult to provide for. You will have to seek elsewhere.'

Gestur answers: 'I think that I have never heard any king say such things. I won't wait a long time for that which won't be granted. May you live as the most infirm and wretched of all kings! I shall also bear word of your avarice and misery until I find another more wretched than you.' He then went briskly out of the circle of men, without directing a word to anyone.

The king is left behind and covers his face with his hands and spoke to his advisor: 'Go to this Gestur and tell him to come to me and that I want to talk to him.' He does so. Gestur then comes before the king and asks what he wants from him.

The king spoke: 'How was it that you came across this mountain, the same one which no man remembers anyone to have traversed?'

Gestur answers: 'I went across the mountain on my own two feet and I have cleared a path so broad that two wagons may drive along it side by side, and cleared away the shale and boulders into the ravines and crevices in the earth, so that they are now no more uneven than a highway.

---

[32] In other words, when one is asking a favour, it is better to get straight to the point.

The king spoke: 'That is quite some feat that you have performed. But what have you had besides your hands?'

Gestur answers: 'I dragged a kind of sledge made of tree trunks with rope around either end along the ground — if not the outcome would have been otherwise — and by this means shoved the larged rocks out of the way. But those rocks which wouldn't budge I struck with a rock hammer and smoothed the remains over with this thing which I have here in my hand, and I worked on that for two months.'

The king looked at his hand-tool: there was a single shaft with iron tubes on the ends, and jutting out a piece of iron four ells in length and similar in form to a file or a chisel carved out of tusk. The king said that winter lodgings were at Gestur's disposal and said that he had well earned it.

'I will accept the lodgings,' he said, 'and this route across the mountains is shorter than you might imagine, since a lot of effort has been expended in clearing it, and nevertheless I would like for you to give a name to the route, since it will be traversed by many.'

The king did so and called it the 'File Road', and the name stuck, even to the present day. It is no more than a morning's journey to those districts which it previously took many days to get to. Now Gestur asked for a house to sleep in and a seat for him alone, one which nobody else would sit in. The king had that arranged, getting for him a malt-barn and a seat on the upper bench near to his retainers. Gestur made himself very comfortable in that house. He discretely fetches his belongings from the mountain, where he had hidden them. Gestur was always taciturn and had little to do with the other men.

[III]

In the autumn Eiríkur is seen sailing to land with thirty ships. The warship which he captained was fitted with tents made of costly cloths, and his fleet was quite magnificent. The king and the queen and all the people went to meet him. Now that Eiríkur has arrived home, he is soon told what this great Gestur has achieved in terms of road construction in Gaul. Many people thought that he must be a troll or a highwayman. But some entertained other suspicions. Eiríkur asked his men to stay away from that man. Gestur always ate and drank modestly, and treated the other men decently. He was, however, jovial with his bench-companions if they spoke to him. He was a large man and strong. The vast majority of the time he wore a cowl and a fur cloak, and it was hard to make out how strapping he was.

There was a man named Rauður, who was in charge of fitting out expeditions for the king. He was envious and deceitful by nature, strong and most likely a shapeshifter.

He speaks thus to the king: 'What could happen, even if I were to sit in Gestur's seat?'

The king said there was no need for that and that he would not have any part in it, should Gestur be displeased.

Rauður made good on his threat, and at that moment Gestur walked into the hall and asked him to go away.

Rauður answers: 'I think that this seat is not more poorly occupied than previously.'

Gestur then gripped him by the thigh and drags him out of the seat and sets him down on the hall floor so roughly so that the bones inside him broke. From that time forth he was never the same, and he was carried away. But the king did not blame Gestur for this. All men marvelled at his strength and exchanged glances.

On another occasion, Gestur was late to take his seat. Prince Eiríkur sat in the seat. The king asked him not to sit there, but he remained seated.

A little later Gestur walked into the hall and comes before Eiríkur and stood there a little while and spoke: 'You must think that it is a good idea to sit here.' And he walked away afterwards and out to his house. Eiríkur followed him out, and before Gestur had closed the door, Eiríkur arrived and asked him to let him in. Gestur did so, but was not all that quick about it. Eiríkur enters and sees that inside there has been hung such a fine wall-hanging that he has never seen anything comparable. It was embroidered with gold thread in many places and made with the utmost skill. Blankets had been laid on the floor, interwoven with silk in many places. There was a bed fit for a single person in the house, and the costly woven cloth on the bed was trimmed with fur, as was also the case with the pillow cover. Hanging over the bed was a single large gold ring. The prince took the ring down and saw that it was made out of thirteen sections,[33] and some parts were made of white gold, and others of red gold. He thought that he had never seen such a fine treasure.

He spoke to Gestur: 'Will you give me this ring?'

'I won't,' said Gestur. 'Do you think we are really so very different when it comes to generosity? When you came back from raiding you brought with you costly goods and coloured cloth and fine treasures, and I never asked you for anything, but then you didn't offer me anything. You sat in my seat, and I could see that you weren't keen on me staying for the winter.'

The prince answers: 'I wanted to put your nature to the test, Gestur, and for that reason I sat in your chair. So what's the ring called?'

Gestur answers: 'From iron-slag and gilt thread Sægrímir was made. So what is it?'[34]

The prince answers: 'The hardest of iron-slags is that which plays upon the heart of a man, in other words great sorrow. Gilt thread is red gold, and Sægrímir is white gold. And the ring has been made as a memento for the man who has experienced great sorrow, so that he shall often think upon his sorrows when he looks at it, and I name it Gáinn.'

'You are a wise man, prince, because that man was greatly distressed when the ring was made.'

The prince saw where three chests stood in the house. He asked Gestur to get the keys for him in order to open up the chests. Gestur got two keys for him, although somewhat reluctantly, and sat down on the third chest. The prince opens up the chests and sees that they are empty and thought that the wall-hangings and Gestur's bedclothes must have been in them. Eiríkur asked him to fetch him the third key in order to open up the chest which he was sitting on. Gestur said that that would not happen, unless they put each other to the test, 'but it may be the case that you will think your worst suspicions about me have been proved if I give you a run for your money.' He spoke this verse:

---

[33] The information given here can be compared with what is stated later in Chapter 13, where we are told that the ring was originally made of thirteen pieces, but then later divided into four.

[34] The name *Sægrímir* is reminiscent of *Sæhrímnir*, mentioned by Óðinn in *Grímnismál* as being a boar which is roasted and eaten every night but magically reconstituted in the morning. See Rudolf Simek, *Dictionary of Northern Mythology*, p. 273. Gestur's riddling answer concerning the name of the ring, with its alliteration, can be construed as being in an eddic metre: 'Af sindri ok seimi | var Sægrímir gjör | eða hvat er þetta?'. Such a riddle, spoken by a mysterious stranger under the pseudonym 'Gestur', raises clear associations with the 'Gátur Gestumblinda' section of *Hervarar saga*, where Óðinn adopts the disguise of a man named Gestur inn blindi in order to challenge King Heiðrekur in a test of wits. See *The Saga of King Heidrek the Wise*, ed. and trans. by Christopher Tolkien (London: Nelson, 1960), pp. 32–44.

> The possessors of the shield (= warriors) will never hinder the maple tree of spears (= warrior); I lie awake early on account of that pain caused by the props of drink (= women). The launchers of the quarrel of arrows (= launchers of battle = warriors) will still be quick with words about me, such that I should not be completely safe, if I now quail.[35]

Eiríkur became even more curious now to see inside the chest, when Gestur spoke thus, and asked him to open up. Gestur asked him not to blame him if he should come to feel worse off than before. Eiríkur promised sincerely not to. Gestur then fetched him the key and stood up from the chest, and Eiríkur unlocked it and found there in the end chest many smith's tools, exceptionally well wrought. And in the chest a wooden partition was fitted. Beneath it was a cloth or bundle of coloured fabric wrapped up in linen cloth. And when he unfolded it there was a velveteen cloth inside, and after that a silk cloth, and inside the cloth there was an effigy in the form of a maiden, dressed in fine-woven velvet and beautiful and lifelike, so that he would have thought, had it given off heat or spoken, that it was alive.

Eiríkur then spoke: 'She must be amazingly beautiful, the girl whom this effigy is modelled on, and I make this vow that I shall marry that maid, if she is untouched, and no other, assuming she is alive, and I shall not take a drink at home in Rouen at Yule until this is settled.'

Gestur smiled and spoke: 'You will never settle this matter if you rely on your judgement alone, and I will call you Eiríkur the Curious.'

'Then you must give me the ring as a naming-gift,' said Eiríkur.

'Far from it,' says Gestur, 'if I know what I'm doing.'

Eiríkur asked whether he knew how to make things with all those tools which were gathered together there and would fulfil the requirements of any kind of smith. Gestur said that he needed all of them. Then the prince asked whether he had made the ring and the effigy. And Gestur spoke this verse:

> My mind laughs when appeasers of the seagulls of battle (= appeasers of ravens/eagles = warriors) bring your woman before me; I desire the Gefn (= goddess) of the headdress (= woman). I praise the beautiful Syn (= goddess) of the sea-day (goddess of the gold = woman) herself; the ground of buried silver (= woman) causes me suffering. The wolf knows what he had eaten.[36]

'The Fenris Wolf knew what he was chewing on when he bit the hand off Týr, the son of Óðinn. I also know all too well where I have looked away from.[37] I have sculpted this lifelike effigy. You would also be greatly impressed if you should come to see in the flesh the maid whom it was based upon.'

Then Gestur did not want to speak any more.

---

[35] Gestur's verse suggests a conflict and concern for certain women. Eiríkur, through his somewhat impertinent questioning, may be aligned with the warriors 'quick with words' (i.e. slanderers, accusers, taunters). Not responding to such taunts could be seen as a sign of weakness, and thus place Gestur (and the women he pines for) in danger.

[36] The first part of this verse is extremely corrupt and the translation is highly conjectural. One of the main problems is that the expression of longing for a woman seems much more appropriate for Eiríkur at this particular point, where he has just seen the effigy. Love would seem to be equated with a wolf devouring its prey, i.e. an instinctual imperative which disregards consequences or the violence of the action, although they are apparent. The prose that immediately follows presents a further nuancing of this interpretation.

[37] The meaning here is somewhat obscure. It could be a contemplation on revenge and hopeless inevitability: Fenrir knew that biting Týr's hand off would not do him any good, but bit anyway as payback for the betrayal. Gestur seems to state that he too knows all to well the wrongs done to him, as well as being reminded by the effigy, and thus also seeks revenge.

[IV]

The prince now walks out of the house, and his men stood around it and did not want to go in and interrupt their conversation. Eiríkur then goes to the royal hall and declares publicly what he has vowed along with the whole conversation that he had shared with Gestur. But the king and the queen and all the people became quiet upon hearing that and say that Gestur's machinations had caused all this misfortune.

And when spring arrives, the king asks his son what course of action he intends to take. Eiríkur said that he intended to set out from that land with thirty ships and seek his potential wife. The king asked him to try to convince Gestur to go on the expedition with him, but Eiríkur says that he can hardly ask for anything in this case. But they go to his quarters nevertheless.

Gestur stood up to meet them and greets the king warmly, 'and it is a rare occurrence to see you here! Is there some matter which you wish to tell me of?'

The king answers: 'I greatly desire that you go on this journey with my son and share your advice with him so that he may fulfill his vow, because it seems to me that you are somewhat responsible for all this.'

Gestur spoke: 'I was not the cause of your son's enquiries, although I would not use force to prevent him from seeing my possessions or lock them away from him so that he should have had to forcefully get access to them. Now I will travel with him if he agrees to give me the final word on what our troop, the two of us included, does for the duration of our trip.'

Eiríkur agreed to that then, and Gestur asked him to stop with his preparation of the ships. And as time passed, with a lot of the summer already behind them, Eiríkur came to speak with Gestur and asked how long he intended to wait, but he said it was not too late yet.

[V]

Gestur now asked Eiríkur to get eighty knights ready, those whom he knew to be most skilful and valiant with weapons, as well as twenty squires and cooks to carry out menial tasks. And when this host was fully assembled, Gestur says that they will ride along the 'File Road' and take the land route. The king accompanies his son on his way. The queen and the other people were deeply moved on saying goodbye to Eiríkur.

They now ride along the wide road, up to the point where the crags had been smashed and the 'File Road' cleared. There was a smooth road there so wide that two or three wagons could drive along it side by side, and there were walls on both sides so that nothing could be seen over them except for the bright sky. Every ravine and chasm in that place had been filled with rubble, and a gateway, which one had to ride through in order to find a resting place, had been broken through the wall of rocks.

Now they arrive at such a place and dismount from their horses. Gestur then brought out the ring Gáinn from under his cloak and spoke: 'Here is that ring which I know to be the most precious, because whosoever has it on his person may not be harmed by fire or sea, neither water nor venomous beast. Are you at all tempted, Lord, to receive it in exchange for your offer of winter lodgings?'

The king looked at the ring and spoke: 'This is a great treasure, but it seems to me that you are going to have more need of it now, and I would like for you to hold onto it.'

Gestur spoke: 'I was just curious, king, because I won't give this to anybody right now, if I have any sense. But I wanted to know whether you valued more highly your own greed or the outcome of your son's journey. Now I shall truly reward him for these words of yours, if I have the chance.'

They then sat down and drank, having fun listening to Gestur, and they said that he had fully earned his winter lodgings by clearing this route, which they had now seen, and it was more the work of a troll than a man.

Gestur smiled and said: 'He does not go alone to the forest, who accompanies another.'

After that the king and Eiríkur part ways, and the king wishes them well. And when Eiríkur and his men come down from the mountain to a flat plain, he and Gestur ride behind, because Eiríkur sees that Gestur is so weary that he cannot ride and is acting strangely. In front of a bank of earth Gestur took out of his sleeve a bundle of furs.

Gestur spoke: 'You will be a fitting accoutrement to very few people.'

He flung down the ring and rode on his way to where the others were. But Eiríkur turned his horse back and took the ring. And when he returned Gestur asked him why he had dawdled, and Eiríkur told him.

'You did well,' said Gestur, 'I want to tell you that at times such dark thoughts play upon this ring that I cannot hold onto it. And for that reason I put it down in an easily recognisable place, because I thought it more likely that I would find it there if I should resolve to turn back once the oppressive thoughts had passed away from me. And for that reason I rode behind, because I didn't want other people to notice this odd behaviour.' Eiríkur said that it would be thus.

[VI]

It is not said how long they rode along that route, but what is mentioned is that they come to a level plain at the foot of a mountain. On that plain there were large stones and beautiful rocky outcrops. Gestur went up to the stone which was largest and knocked on it with his hand. Immediately a door appeared there. Gestur went into the stone and came out a little later, and with him both a male and a female dwarf. They were short and the point on their bodies where their torsos divided into two legs was very low down. They were squat-faced and broad-nosed. They greet Prince Eiríkur, and he asked them their names.

The dwarf answers: 'I am called Svammur, and my wife is called Svama.'

Then Gestur spoke: 'I have asked this dwarf, who has been my foster-father, if he will loan you a sea-going vessel, in order to sail to those lands which I want to travel to, but he has expressed reluctance.

Eiríkur asks what remuneration he will accept.

The dwarf says: 'If you will be mindful of your duty and proceed according to the instructions of this Gestur, who calls me his foster-father, it will then be tolerably sufficient, fate permitting, but not otherwise.'

Eiríkur said that he had agreed to that.

Now they go to their men (because Gestur had planned in advance that the dwarf should not be seen by any other men). They now sleep through the night. Eiríkur and Gestur arranged for a lot of meat and butter to be taken secretly to the stone during the night. And when they woke up, the two of them went to the stone, and the male dwarf and the female dwarf were outside, cheerful and animated, and they greeted them warmly and offered them thanks for the large amount of delightful food which they had given to them. The dwarf then went up to a large boulder and knocked on its rocky wall, and the boulder split down the middle so that a door appeared. Inside was a quite splendid ship which was fully rigged, such that Eiríkur thought that he had never seen anything like it.

Svammur spoke then: 'You shall have the benefit of this, Eiríkur, because I and my wife and my children have come into your land and are your subjects; and secondly because you intend to go on a mission upon whose success I think a lot is riding; thirdly, and this is decisive, because my foster-son has every intention of accompanying you. Here then is the ship which I will lend to you, and I can say in its favour that space for another man will always be found when another berth is assigned, and there will always be a favourable wind when you want to sail somewhere. In addition I will assign my own and my wife's good fortune to you so that you may be successful.'

After that they kissed Gestur and wept loudly and went into their stone, and it closed behind them. And they went to their men and told them to get dressed and accompany them and see a quite splendid ship which was fully rigged in a cave. They launched it on the sea, and that was very easy for them. Gestur ordered them then to go aboard. They asked what to do about some of their group. Gestur said that it would all work out otherwise than they expected. And as the number of people increased, there was always found an extra berth when another one was assigned. And when they had loaded the ship as they wanted to, there was neither a surplus of men at the tables or in the sleeping quarters. Then a strong wind came, and they sailed out to sea, and that wind held up until they see a beautiful land and a large fortress with graceful towers approaching.

[VII]

Now it must be said that as soon as they see that land, Eiríkur asks Gestur if he knows anything about which land that might be.

Gestur answers: 'I think that I recognise this land, and it is called Hólmgarður.[38] And east of this land is Galizia, and to the north is Kænugarður and Russia, Kirjalaland, the Land of the Giants, Kvenland, the Land of the One-Footed Men, the Land of the Tiny People and many other lesser countries, and many kings rule over these kingdoms. This is called the Kingdom of Hólmgarður as far as it stretches, but some call it the Kingdom of the Tatars. All of the minor kings are liege lords of the King of Hólmgarður himself. Now we have arrived at Hólmgarður, from which place Kænugarður lies to the north, and to that fortress which is called Kastella. It is the fortress closest to the capital, and the town[39] just beyond the fortress is called Aspis. An earl by the name of Roðbert rules here over this fortress and that kingdom here which is part of Hólmgarður and Kænugarðar. He is so wise that he speaks all of those languages which I have been told are to be found in the world. He is also so intelligent that he is familiar with nearly all decisions. Very little which could be harmful to him takes him unawares. I would not

---

[38] Hólmgarður is Novgorod, but, as with other toponyms in this saga (see footnote 31), the place names here are used in such a loose way that it is difficult to see them as representing any geographical reality and are probably better understood merely as exotic eastern names. The region of Galizia (in modern-day Poland and Ukraine), for example, is south-west of Novgorod, not north, and Kænugarður (or Kiev) is certainly not north, but rather south.

[39] Aspis is actually called a *kaupstaður*, that is 'a place where goods are bought and sold'. In a general sense this is just any settlement of sufficient size for it to become a centre of trade, hence the translation here, 'town'.

say that he is good at giving advice, because as far as that is concerned I would consider him to be lacking. And yet you must visit this earl. He will offer you hospitality, because he knows that you are the son of a distinguished man and have come a long way. He will ask where you plan to sail to. You must say that you plan to sail out across the sea. He will say that it is late in the summer and he will offer you and your men winter lodgings in the fortress, since there are not so many of you. You must accept and ask him to provide a separate drinking hall and sleeping quarters with lodgings for you and your men, so that you will be comfortable. Say that your men are light sleepers and bad-tempered when they drink, and don't settle for anything less. And the earl will not then be able to retract his offer. He will inquire directly how many men accompanied you, and you must say that you have eighty knights and twenty servants. The earl will say that somebody else must have travelled with you across the sea. You and all the others must completely deny this, since your life depends on it. Say also that no living being has travelled with you. Start conversations often with the earl, because you will learn a lot from him. And we must go our separate ways for the time being.'

He dives off the ship now, and Eiríkur sails to the shore. The earl's men saw the ship and told the earl that they had not seen a more magnificent ship, and that it was completely painted above the waterline, and the carvings which were on the prows were inlaid with gold. There was also costly fabric used for the sails and tenting. And they said that they thought somebody important must be the captain of that ship. The earl then calls his advisor and asks him to invite the ship's captain back there, if he should be noble. He does as he has been commanded, goes before Eiríkur and greets him, because he had been told that he was the captain. He inquires after his name and lineage, and Eiríkur tells him. And when the messenger has carried out his mission, he goes to the earl and tells him. And when he hears that Eiríkur has come to visit him, he goes to meet him with his men and greets him most joyfully and invites him to a feast, and Eiríkur accepts. The earl asks him where he is going with such a small party, and he says that he plans to sail out over the Greek Sea and make the acquaintance of foreign chieftains and thus learn the customs of good men. And at that time such was deemed to be an honourable pursuit among wealthy men. And when the earl heard that Eiríkur planned to visit wealthy chieftains, he thought that his repute would be carried all that much further, the greater the honour that he showed to him. He asked Eiríkur and all his men to stay with him for the winter. Eiríkur gladly accepted that offer and asked him to provide a drinking hall and individual sleeping quarters and other lodgings. He said that his men were bad drinkers and intractable if they should take offence. And although the earl raised some objections to this, he wouldn't retract his offer to Eiríkur. He then asked precisely how many there were in Eiríkur's party. He said that he had eighty chosen men and twenty serving men.

'And one more,' said the earl.

'No,' said Eiríkur, 'nobody else came with us to this country.'

'Then it must have been,' says the earl, 'a horse or a hawk, a cockerel or some kind of creature, since I thought I caught a glimpse of something like that on your ship, when you were within sight of land.'

Eiríkur asked the earl not to imagine that he would lie to him over such a thing, which was of no consequence, and the matter was dropped. And Eiríkur received great hospitality from the earl.

[VIII]

It has been said that at some point before Yule, in the night, three boards sprang out of place from the wooden panelling around Eiríkur's bed. Gestur appeared and asked him to get up and come with him if he wanted to see the maiden whom he had sworn to make his own. Eiríkur got dressed up in his fur tunic and bound a piece of golden lace around his forehead. He picked up his sword. Then Eiríkur went out through the panels, and Gestur put the boards back in place, so that nothing out of the ordinary could be seen. They went down into the earth until they came to an outhouse, and in the cellar there was a pond, and one could walk along some of the walls, but in certain other places the water passed under one of the walls.[40]

Gestur spoke then: 'Earl Roðbert has had this cellar constructed and this wall placed over the water, because he thought it would be his salvation, if men came to know of the cellar and waited in ambush for him, if he could leap into the water and dive under the wall.' Gestur proceeded now until he had flung open three doors. They were then in a living area. Inside were two women so beautiful that Eiríkur thought that he had never seen their like. He thought that he recognised the younger of the two women, since he had seen the effigy based upon her. The women embraced Gestur, and a joyful reunion between them ensued, and they sat him between them and called him Jón.

[IX]

And when they had been sitting there for a long time, Gestur speaks to Eiríkur: 'You have accompanied me out of your country on account of your curiosity, and now I will illuminate some things for you by means of a story. And it starts like this, that there was an earl named Svipdagur who ruled the fortress Kastella and this kingdom, which is subject to it, and Kiev and all of those fortified towns and farms and all the kingdoms which are subject to it. His father was Dagur the Strong, and Dagur's father was called Jón. The whole line of their ancestors had ruled over these kingdoms. Svipdagur had a queen, whose named was Likoridis. She was the daughter of Philippus, the King of Flanders. They had two children. The son's name was Jón, and the daughter's Marsilia. The three of us are now here, mother and children.

'And when I was eight years old, and Marsilia two, Roðbert came here with many ships and an overwhelming army, and he was freshly arrived from Serkland and was accompanied by vikings and black-men[41] and many unpleasant types. He had also been raiding in the East and had acquired there three treasures which were so excellent that their like will not be found. One is the ring Gáinn, and every nine nights gold drips from it, such that one can live most comfortably on that wealth. The second is a sword, which he calls Sigurvandil, and he who

---

[40] The architecture is somewhat difficult to follow here, but it seems to be the case that Eiríkur and Gestur enter the cellar of a separate building through Gestur's underground tunnel. The pond which is in the cellar of this building also conceals a secret entrance and exit, allowing one to swim under the wall and make a speedy exit in case of an ambush. There is, presumably, also the normal entrance (stairs?), which is not explicitly mentioned, as well as the doors which lead into the subsequent chambers of the cellar, ending with the one where Eiríkur and Gestur meet the women.

[41] In different contexts this word can be used loosely to refer to Africans, Ethiopians or, perhaps, berserks (*blá-* can be translated as 'black' and 'blue'). The conceptualization of the ethnic groups alluded to is hazy and involves a pejorative and problematic association of exotic otherness with antisocial and antagonistic behaviour. See, for example, Richard Cole, 'Racial Thinking in Old Norse Literature: The Case of the *Blámaðr*', *Saga-Book*, 39 (2015), 21–40 (pp. 36–37).

carries it will always be triumphant. The third treasure is a helmet, which is called Ægir. There is no man so insignificant that if he has it upon his head he does not seem awe-inspiring. These treasures come with this enchantment and fortune that the man who has them with him cannot be harmed by sea or lakes, poison or fire, or venomous animals or sword edges.

'Now when Roðbert arrived in this country, he immediately sent men to the earl with these terms: to decide whether he wanted to fight on the following day or flee the country with his queen on account of him. Earl Svipdagur was a great warrior, and his luck had never failed. He said that he would rather fight than flee his country, and so he immediately had the war-arrow sent out, as might well be done when faced with Roðbert's hostilities, and he himself prepared his army for battle. And when Roðbert was told of the earl's choice, he worked himself up for battle that same day. And the earl left the fortress, and there was a hard battle, although not a long one due to the day being nearly over. Roðbert had a much larger army, and when he saw that he did not make a dent on account of the valour of the earl and the men of the fortress, he had the peace-shield raised and rested that night.

[X]

'Such a great number of men, both from the town of Aspis[42] and from other nearby fortresses and farms, came to the earl that night that he now had only a slightly smaller army than Roðbert. And when Roðbert sees that, he accompanied his army to where there was higher ground and a good vantage point. He now cast himself headlong into fierce battle. The earl was on a horse and had a large mounted retinue with him, but he himself was the doughtiest warrior, and he attacked so fiercely that Earl Roðbert's army retreated from the high ground. Now he urges on the army, because he had equipped his selected warriors well with weapons and armour, and he himself was steadfast in chivalry and leadership of armies. A large part of his host was on horseback, and that was much to the detriment of the earl's men.[43]

'For a long time there was no way to tell who would have the victory. But as the day wore on the army pressed forward against the earl and there were more deaths on Roðbert's side. He sees now that he will not be victorious on that day. He then has the peace-shield thrown up. And as night fell, and the charms which proceeded from Roðbert's weapons (which meant that Roðbert might not fail to be victorious) diminished, the earl thought that he would defeat Roðbert early the next day.[44]

'The earl now rides with his host to the fortress and lets his guard down, because they were called truce-breakers who pounced on others at night, from the time when the white shield

---

[42] Aspis, already referred to, is here called *Aspide* (though I have maintained the original name in the translation). The same variation is witnessed when the mountain is referred to, yet the text specifically states that the mountain was named after the town. The different forms are most likely a sign that the name was taken from a Latin source (Aspis/Aspidis, Aspide the ablative form). A scribe or author may have retained the Latin endings, rather than adapting it to a Norse paradigm, in order to retain a sense of the exotic nature of the locale.

[43] At this point both of the key players are at times referred to as 'the earl' or just 'he', leading to a certain amount of ambiguity as regards who is responsible for which actions. I have not attempted to clear up this ambiguity, which, although perhaps the result of scribal imprecision, neatly gives a sense of the chaos of battle, and its blurring of boundaries.

[44] Presumably Earl Svipdagr has noticed Roðbert's marvellous weapons, but does not know that they make him impervious (the comment in parentheses is directed at the audience as a reminder, not intended to be a statement of what Earl Svipdagr himself thinks). The fact that their efficacy decreases at night adds to Svipdagr's failure to recognize their significance. Otherwise he might be less sanguine about the possibility of victory the following day.

was raised until the red shield was borne aloft in the morning or the war-trumpet was blown at the start of hostilities.

[XI]

'Now when Roðbert comes to the ships, he lets his men drink themselves into good spirits. After that he surreptitiously calls the armies together and begins to speak: "You are well aware that this earl is so difficult to deal with that he has nearly put us to flight, and that would have come to pass, had we not raised the peace-shield. Rush upon him and his host now from all directions! I do not intend to risk our necks in further encounters where the risk to our lives is equally great. You must now get kitted out as quickly as possible and use the element of surprise, force your way into the fortress and enter yelling and urging each other on."

'They did just that. And although a great host had been gathered, most of them became alarmed and panicked and woke to the sound of war-cries and the clash of weapons. The situation was the same in the place which Roðbert was shown to, where the earl rested. They surrounded the sleeping quarters and broke in. The earl leapt up in his underclothes and defended himself boldly. Roðbert pressed the attack so hard that the earl fell. He then ordered most of the men who had been close friends of the earl killed. Nobody put up any opposition. Most people then submitted to him because he seemed so terrible in the helm of Ægir. But since it was the custom of bellicose types to depose kings from their kingdoms and take possession of their wealth and lands, many foolish men said that it must be these possessions which he sought. Roðbert then had himself named earl. He came to find out that I was Earl Svipdagur's son. He then had me arrested, and all people praised my stature and appearance. The earl drew his sword and wanted to strike me down by the hall wall, but at that moment the queen, my mother, stepped forth and pleaded for my life.

'The earl refused that, but then said: "Since I intend to take you as my queen, I will not kill him in your presence."

'The earl ordered his men to drown me on the high seas far from land and stab me there and bring my blood to him. The men were not keen on doing this, because they thought that vengeance might be taken. Two retainers are mentioned, one named Hringur and the other Eilífur. They had been with my father for a long time and served him faithfully. They offered to carry out this deed, and a boat was acquired for us. They rowed with me away from land.

'Then Hringur spoke: "We two brothers wish to grant you your life, though we know it will be the death of us."

'They took blood from me and collected it in a bowl and covered it over. They then took me to an island by the name of Ilmarhólm, so called because in that place there is no shortage of herbs and apples which one can live off.[45] Then they rowed back to land and said to the earl that they had killed me and cast the body overboard. The earl asked to see the blood. They reached forth the bowl, and the earl dipped his finger in the blood and lifted it to his mouth and spoke: "This is the blood of a living man, and you have deceived me and allowed Jón the son of the earl to live. Now you shall give your lives in his place." Then he had Hringur and Eilífur taken and placed between two fires, because they wouldn't reveal anything about Jón, and they both burned to death there. After that the earl puts a bounty on my head, twelve

---

[45] 'Ilmur' means 'sweet smell' or 'perfume', and thus Ilmarhólm is the 'Island of Perfume'. Such fragrant and fruitful locations evoke associations of the earthly paradise.

marks of silver, if anyone should be able to tell him something about me. And since most people are predisposed to be scoundrels, should the chance arise, the following happened to me.

[XII]

'There was a man named Haki, a farmer, and he frequently went out fishing. One day, when he rowed past the island, he saw that there was a man in the forest up in the branches playing around. It occurred to him that I must be there and how much money the earl had placed on my head. He thinks that he will get no mean compensation and rows back to land and goes hastily to meet the earl and tells him that he has seen a young and handsome man on Ilmarhólm and says that he thinks it must be Jón. The earl ordered his men to go to the island. Haki went with them.

'They came to the island, then the men searched and could not find me. They surrounded the forest and thus searched for me. Haki led the way, but I took hold of a bird-hunting spear and aimed it at his eye, and it came out the back of his neck, and he fell down dead. The earl then became angry once more. But I did not have any weapons except for the bird-hunting spear, which I hunted with in order to get food, and they were barely wounded by it. Ultimately, I fell before the earl and laid my head on his knees and placed myself in his power. The earl ordered me tied up and taken back to land and from there to a forest, and all the retinue and Earl Roðbert accompanied me. All people grieved on my behalf. And just as I was ready to be tied to the oak trees, and they were bent together,[46] my lady mother came forth and pleaded for my life, because she hadn't known that I had been found, because the earl concealed it from her. She pleaded her case insistently and said that she would betray him at the first opportunity if I should die that day before her eyes. It ended with the earl ordering that I should be placed in stocks on the barren land beyond the confines of the fortress. And no living thing which found itself outside of the fortress at night could hope to survive, neither man nor cattle, on account of the she-wolf who lived in the forest, as well as the other venomous beasts, and the situation is likewise in many places in the land when the sun sets. Then I was fastened into the stocks, and a thick iron girdle was placed around my waist and locked into place on the stocks. I was also fastened down with many other bonds across my limbs. The earl declared vehemently that if someone should help me, he would lose his life. After carrying this out, all the men rode home and locked the gates to the fortress, and everyone thought that I was sure to die.

[XIII]

'When the men come home in the evening, my lady mother is aggrieved and racked with sorrow. She tries to figure out the best way for her to help me. Then she sends her maidservant with two pots of honey and, when nobody was looking, placed a gold ring on her finger. That

---

[46] The idea of some form of execution involving being tied to an oak tree is not well documented, although this is said to be the preferred form of torture of Rothi, a Ruthenian pirate mentioned in Book VII of Saxo Grammaticus's *Gesta Danorum*. Another example which helps explain The idea of some form of execution which helps explain its origin can be found in one of the texts of *Göngu-Hrólfs saga*: 'Anis var fangaður í orrustunni og lét Hrólfur eikurspretta honum í sundur. Og lauk svo hans æfi' ('Anis was captured in the battle, and Hrólfur had him torn apart by horses [?]. And that was how he died'. (Chapter 34 in AM 589 f 4to, my own normalised transcription.)

ring had belonged to my mother's kinsmen and had many innate qualities, so that any man who had it could not die.

'The maiden went on her way until she found me, where I sat fastened to the stocks. She spattered honey around the stocks and on them. Next she gave me food and smeared all the honey over me and placed the thick crystallised honey in my mouth. She placed the gold ring on my finger. She cut the straps from my hands and feet and spread her cloak over me. Then she went away. The weather was cold, and I began to freeze. And when a third of the night had passed, I heard such a great disturbance in the forest that each oak-tree smashed to pieces against the others. Then a she-wolf, so large that she reached up only a little lower than the branches on the oaks, came forth. She was short-legged, stout, long-tailed and big-headed. Even if a hundred knights were to come up against her, they would all end up dead at her hands. And I saw certain death lying ahead for me.

'A conviction then occurred to me, when the writing was on the wall, that the being who had shaped heaven and earth and all creatures must be great. I made the firm decision that, should I come out of this unharmed, I would follow that faith. The she-wolf circled licking the grass around the stocks when she recognised the smell of honey. She licked me from my heels to my nape. My mother had sent me a knife and a belt, and I held onto the knife. And when she had licked me, the she-wolf reached her tongue into my mouth, because she recognised the smell of honey. I bit into the tongue and stabbed her from above, and held the blade in place, and with my other hand I reached into the mouth of the she-wolf and cut her tongue out at the root, and she flailed about so violently that the whole stocks were lifted off the ground and were smashed to pieces. I was then free. I had the she-wolf's tongue, but she lay in her death throes until she died. And so I was protected by that belief which I had held firm to in my heart, so that the she-wolf did not lay a tooth nor a claw on me, any more than if I had been a red-hot iron.

'I then put my cloak on and ran away from that place until I came below a large stone. I couldn't keep going from there on account of the cold, because my wounds were stiffening in the cold and I passed out. But when I woke, I was being carried by some being, and it ran incredibly fast and put me down upon a stone. This was the male dwarf and the female dwarf. They removed the iron girdle from me and cleaned my wounds in a washing-tub. They placed me in a comfortable bed and strove to fetch me everything.

'And when my wounds had healed, the dwarf spoke: "We can't stay here much longer now because of the magic and the troubles which will afflict your life if he gets his hands on you."

'After that they moved their home into King Vilhjálmur's kingdom, to that plain where they are now. Then the dwarf speaks to me and says that I should make the most of my father's legacy and make use of those good things which he made for him. He then hands me the ring, Gáinn, and says that he has taken it from Earl Roðbert while he was sleeping. And the ring had seemed to be in one piece, but was put together of thirteen pieces which had previously been one. He called it Gáinn as a reminder that I should be heedful of the wrongs done to me by Earl Roðbert, if I should get the chance to do something in that regard.[47] He also said that the earl had focussed his thought so much on this ring that its power was equal to that of two minds, which would affect whether I should be able to keep it in my possession. And for that reason we divided the ring into four parts in order that he should never get hold of it.

One of these scribes or authors has apparently, at some point, mixed up *eykur* 'draught animal, horse' for *eik* 'oak' and thus created a new method of execution.

[47] The verb *gá* in Old Norse means 'to pay heed to'.

'I learnt many pursuits and skills from the dwarf. He also frequently told me of Earl Roðbert's doings. He wanted to go ahead and marry the queen, but she asked that he wait three years until she had had time to recover from her grief. And since the earl has many enemies in the land, and the queen's words held a lot of weight, he let himself be convinced. And once that period had passed, the earl brought up this promise and her betrothal. She then asked that he should wait for five years for Marsilia, her daughter, "and that match is much more fitting for you, since she is young, and I am old, and she doesn't remember her father's murder." The earl was talked into it, and fixed his hopes on this.

'I was then sixteen years old, at the time when I cleared the File-Way along with these dwarves. I planned to make a big dust-cloud on the mountain by filing each crag into two with the marvellous tools which the dwarf had made. Then we also designed the effigy of Marsilia, which you saw back home in Gaul. She is now ten years old, and I am eighteen. I have now reminded you of your oath. You must now choose whether you will be free of your declarations regarding Marsilia, or try to get her from the earl.'

Eiríkur answers: 'I shall fulfill what I said I would, to have this maiden or no other.' They affirmed their promise now. Then Jón spoke: 'Now we must go away, and we have sat here too long, because the thoughts of the earl are now upon this place.'

[XIV]

Now they go away, and when they come out of the living quarters, the earl walks in the other end of the cellar with two men, one named Rogerus and the other Rodgeir. They had been with Earl Svipdagur, and the earl had forced them into his service. He had on his head the helmet Ægir and was girded with the sword Sigurvandil.

Jón then speaks to Eiríkur: 'We cannot harm the earl because he has his weapons. There is now no option other than to dive into the water and swim out under the wall.' And that is what they did.

The earl speaks: 'What was that lurking in the shadows in the cellar?'

Rogerus said: 'A bird flew in through the window and swooped around the room and then flew out again.'

'That's a strange bird I glimpsed,' said the earl.[48]

He launched the spear which he was holding onto into the building. It struck Eiríkur in the thigh above the knee, and by that point he had made it into the water. Eiríkur pulled the spear out of the wound and dried the blood off with the lap of his kirtle. Then they dived out under the cellar wall. There was an opening on the outer side of the wall and it led to the passage under the cellar wall. Earl Roðbert dried off the spear and looked at it and says: 'It seems as if there are drops of blood on the socket of the spearhead.'

Then Rodgeir said: 'That is red water-clay.' The earl didn't say much more.

But Eiríkur and Jón got out of the water.

Then Jón says: 'There is no doubt now that the earl will have suspicions about how you were wounded, and if you conceal it from him, he will take that as proof that he was the one who wounded you, and that will be the death of you. Now you know that there have been two Norwegian merchants here over the winter. One of them is named Þrandur and the other

---

[48] There could be a pun here in the Old Norse 'undarlegur fuglssvipur' (literally 'a strange bird-swoop'): a *svipur* is both a fleeting image of something and a 'swoop' (as in the movement of a bird).

Árni. You have entered into conversation with Ingibjörg, their sister, and Þrandur has let on that he is extremely angry with you because of this. Now it is my advice that you discuss this with Þrandur, and you agree on a plan, so that the wound is attributed to him.' And once he has told Eiríkur how he should proceed, they part ways for the time being.

[XV]

Now Eiríkur goes to the sleeping quarters, and they were locked, but he opens every lock, without the use of a key, and went over to the bed quietly and woke up his squire and asked him to go to Þrandur the Norwegian and tell him how he should act. He did so. Eiríkur remained behind and bound his wounds. Then he woke two of his faithful companions, and they went to Ingibjörg's bower. Eiríkur sat down in conversation with Ingibjörg, as he was accustomed to do. And when the squire came to the quarters where Þrandur was sleeping, he knocked on the door. The other man asked who was there. The squire answered that that was irrelevant, 'but I have business with you, which you will be curious to hear of.' Þrandur opened the door and showed him into the quarters, and the squire struck up a conversation and told him of Eiríkur's request and how everything should play out and in addition he gave him a purse of money, which Eiríkur had sent to him. It was a lot of money in gold and silver.[49] Þrandur was pleased with the purse of money and said that he would do as had been asked of him. The squire explained how things stood to Eiríkur, and Þrandur woke Árni, his brother, and told him of Eiríkur's message and shows him the money. The brothers saw eye-to-eye on this.

Þrandur now walks into the lodgings where his shipmates slept and woke them up and asked them to accompany him. Then he went to Ingibjörg's bower. Eiríkur sat on the edge of the bed, but Ingibjörg lay in the bed. He was dressed thus, in underwear with an under-kirtle and long cape over the top. Under the cape he had the patch of his kirtle which he had bled upon. Þrandur came to the bedroom where Eiríkur was and leapt at the door so hard that it was flung open. He lowered his spear at Eiríkur and aimed it at his waist. But he swerved so that the spear landed between Eiríkur's legs. He then rubbed the patch of his kirtle on the spearhead, so that a rent was formed. Then the spearshaft was bloody and likewise the spearhead. He then tore the bandage off his wound and bled a great deal, and secreted it under his belt. Eiríkur then leapt up, and Þrandur ran out, and at that moment Árni, Þrandur's brother, walked in and asked Eiríkur to declare his own terms of compensation for that heinous deed. This whole ploy was carried out in such a sly manner that nobody suspected otherwise than that Þrandur had wounded Eiríkur. They said that it was bound to happen sooner or later.

[XVI]

The news that Þrandur had wounded Eiríkur spread like wildfire. Eiríkur sends for Earl Roðbert and has him informed that he is wounded. The earl came quickly and tended to Eiríkur's wound. He now wanted to know whether it was the same blood which Þrandur had on his spear and dipped his tongue in it and now realised that it was one and the same blood and it came from Eiríkur. The earl then discreetly asked those men who had been present

---

[49] The text reads 'fé frítt í gulli og silfri', which makes little sense since payment is either in kind ('frítt') or in money ('í gulli og silfri'). Perhaps the text originally read that he paid him in both money and kind.

about the wound, and all of them said that Eiríkur had been wounded by Þrandur, because nobody knew otherwise.

Eiríkur's wound healed quickly, and he was back to full strength in no time. He often talked with the earl and learnt from him many entertaining things and various languages. The earl often had his knights perform in jousts for entertainment, and Eiríkur proved to be extremely skilled in all forms of chivalry and accomplishments. Men praised him greatly. The earl said it would certainly be justifiable if his leg-wound had been avenged. The earl thought that Eiríkur would have avenged himself if Þrandur had been the one to wound him, assuming there had been no trickery. On account of these words of the earl, Eiríkur came to speak with Þrandur and Árni and said that the earl accused him of fear and cowardice, since he did not avenge himself, and thus he was suspicious about whether he had wounded him.

'Now the time has come when it is safe for the ships to sail, and it is my suggestion that you sail away from this place.'

Eiríkur gave fine gifts to the brothers and to Ingibjörg fine clothes and many great treasures. They parted on the best of terms, and they sailed north to the countries there and were thought to be the best of merchants, and they are now out of this story. Now the rumour circulated that the brothers left so quickly because Þrandur feared vengeance would be taken. Now most of the earl's suspicions were soothed. Eiríkur was esteemed by all men for his cheerfulness and humility and generous gifts. He was also a wise man, and many sought to confide in him in order to receive wise counsel.

[XVII]

It is said that once when Eiríkur lay resting, Jón came to him and asked him to get up and go with him. He did so. They took exactly the same route as before, when Jón had dug out the undergound tunnel leading to Eiríkur's sleeping quarters. They came to that chamber where the mother and daughter were. They greeted them warmly. Then they sat down, and Jón speaks to Eiríkur.

'Now I shall tell you my scheme, which I have devised over the winter. I have carved out a doorway in Mount Aspis and fitted a door into it with huge wooden beams and turf laid over the top. The mountain is full of water. I have ready and waiting there a ship and eighty men, those who are the most worthy and noblest in this country. I have ensured their loyalty to me with gifts of money. I have also fitted out your ship, and it is on the water there ready by the coast. Now I want you to ask the earl to call a meeting on the plains which are just outside of the fortress. There are flat expanses there up to the mountain and lying in from the sea. The ship is floating there at the foot of the plain. All of your men should board it there. And above the plain is that doorway which I have cut out of the mountain. Now I want to know whether you have kept the ring Gáinn safe since you placed it on your hand.'

Eiríkur said that he certainly had kept it safe.

Jón said: 'I knew that you would take on that responsibility, and I wanted to test your sagacity. But if the earl arranges the meeting, you must go unarmed before him with excellent treasures and the ring in your hand. The earl will recognise the ring and assume that you want to give it to him. He will then take his helmet, Ægir, and sword, Sigurvandil, off. You must then take the helmet and the sword and make a run for it and see whether you can make it to your ship. Your life and fate depends upon you getting hold of those treasures, because then you will be taking the earl's good luck with you. But he won't, however, die on the spot. And at the same moment that you do this, I will be up above releasing the water out of the mountain down onto the earl's army. Along with it will come the ship on wheels. I shall make sure that my mother and sister are on it, Rogerus and Rodgeir too. We shall then sail to Gaul. And if you get hold of the treasures, you must mind not to look back. And you must have the meeting arranged for three days from now.'

After that they part from the ladies feeling most happy. And when they came out of the living quarters, the earl walked in the other end of the cellar. Jón quickly removed the two loose boards in the wall-panelling of the cellar, went into the narrow tunnel, and replaced the boards.

The earl says: 'What crashed there in the dark?'

Rodgeir says: 'The door slammed.'

They all then continue on their way. Jón and Eiríkur parted with the plan laid out as described.

[XVIII]

In the morning after breakfast Eiríkur came to speak with the earl. 'You are aware that you have hosted us here over the winter both well and nobly. Now I ask of you that you have the people of this fortress summoned to a meeting on those plains which lie outside of the fortress, your assembly place, so that they can see there the gifts which I want to give to you.'

The earl said that he showed his distinction in such behaviour and hurries off.

Yet as a result of Eiríkur's persuasiveness all the people were summoned out of the fortress. The earl himself accompanied them out onto the plains which lay at the foot of Mount Aspis. On the outer edge of the plains was the town, which the mountain took its name from, and many men came from there. The plains were laid out in such a way that there were slopes on either side, and each side was bordered by a lake, but the sea lay at the foot of them. There by the coast was moored the ship which Jón had prepared. There was a quay jutting out from the land, and all of Eiríkur's men waited there.

Now Eiríkur proceeds before the earl with many excellent treasures and the ring Gáinn. And when the earl sees the ring Gáinn, he removes his helmet and lays his sword down on the ground, because he thought that Eiríkur would give him the ring, and he became wide-eyed at this sight. And it is the custom of noble men to lay aside their weapons when they receive gifts from distinguished men.

Eiríkur takes the helmet and places it on his head, and he slides the ring Gáinn up to his elbow. He takes up the sword, Sigurvandil, and draws it, and then most people are not eager to be in his way. He then breaks into a sprint, and men were scrambling over each other. Most of them were heading away, because they did not think it would be a good thing to stand before him. Earl Roðbert calls out loudly and ordered his men to apprehend him. Men then leapt up, and there was no shortage of the clanging or clashing of weapons, din and shouting. But since the earl's retinue, the knights and the noblemen, were positioned nearest to him, it was not possible for them to get hold of Eiríkur, because by that point he was way beyond the chosen warriors, and the slaves and villagers were not very courageous in attacking. It was also one of the qualities of the helmet Ægir that men fell down on all sides when they looked him in the face.

And when he had his hands full, and the earl's retinue was close by and sought him out, then all the men heard a great and powerful crash in the mountain. Immediately after they saw a large sward of turf, a wall made out of beams of timber, all fixed together, embedded in a doorframe and locked into place with large iron bars. It was all made with so much skill, that many small rivers were dammed up, with the effect that the narrow waterway behind was powerfully swollen with water. Men had wondered throughout the winter about the drying up of the rivers. Many large wooden beams, which had been put in place to strengthen the wall, were employed in this construction. Along with the great crash and outpouring of water from the mountain there came a great 'dragon' or ship. It was all painted above the waterline, and the dragonhead on the ship was golden. It ran on wheels and went in a straight and level path and headed directly out towards the sea. There was a man holding onto each rope, and they supported the ship so that it would not tip over. The ship now rolls in the powerful torrent as fast as a bird flies. Jón had built this ship over the winter with the help of seven craftsmen. First he had had a wooden platform constructed, on which he built the ship, so wide that it touched both sides of the mountain. He also made the doors in the mountain and the section covering the doors. Towards it he directed the large river which had previously flowed out on the side away from the fortress. There were smaller settlements there, and he thought that they would be slower to get suspicious. On account of this channeling of the water, the lakes on the mountain dried up. There were many crags and peaks on the mountain which one might now access without getting one's feet wet, and yet ships below. There were flaming torches there night and day so that no corner was in shadow. And when half a month remained until he intended to launch the ship, he blocked all of the waterways which led out of the mountain. The dragonboat then rose up, so that the dragon-head was on a level with the doorway on the same day as the meeting was arranged. This plan was so cunningly devised that the waters might be made to recede or augmented, because some of the waters rose more rapidly than others, but could then be gradually diverted. There is hardly another plan which can be deemed so ingenious or feat so daring that has ever been carried out in that land.

[XIX]

Now the story must be picked up again at the point where Earl Roðbert and his men see this great wonder, and they become terrified and panicked, and each of them wants to save his own neck. But that is not possible, because there were lakes on both sides of them and the deep blue sea lay ahead of them. But Eiríkur sprints as fast as he can and never looked back until he reaches his ship. He benefitted from the fact that he was always the fleetest of foot and swiftest in all things. They then set sail, because a fair wind was blowing out to sea. And it was at the very same moment as the men of that country arrived on the quay, that their enemies came together, and 'the fox saw the dog, but the dog was oblivious'.[50]

Now it should be told how the earl was up on the plains with his retinue of knights and the men of his country. At that time there were also black-men with him and many other unsavoury types as well as all those people who had not died with Earl Svipdagur and outlived him. He now understands the whole ruse. And faced with this marvel, which the people saw,

---

[50] The most reasonable interpretation of this would seem to be that the 'fox', i.e. the one being chased, is Eiríkur, who is reunited with his men on the boat just as the men pursuing him arrive on the quay. Those men are the 'dogs' so intent upon their pursuit that they do not see the great danger that lies behind them, i.e. the torrent of water.

that the big wooden beams and the large ship come rushing down with the powerful torrents, and realising that the people who were in the way stood no chance of surviving, some of them leapt into the lakes, but the vast majority of the assembled people were caught in the way of those big wooden beams and the large warship. Nearly all of them drowned there, except those ones alone who were brave enough to fling themselves into the lakes.

The big warship comes all the way to the sea with all on board safe and sound, and at such a pace that it is quickly very far from land. Jón Svipdagsson is aboard with eighty men. Rogerus and Rodgeir, who had been Earl Roðbert's servants, were there, because he thought that nevertheless he might be able to count on their loyalty, because they received great distinctions from Earl Svipdagur. Jón also had Likoridis with him, who was the mother of his mother and the daughter of King Philippus of Flanders.[51] It had happened on one occasion during the winter that, when Eiríkur passed an attic room, he had seen an old, feeble lady. She was worn with age, as tends to be the case with old people. She had white hair. And when Eiríkur saw Elínborg and Marsilia her daughter, Jón had asked him whether he had seen any woman like that. And he explained how that had come to pass. Jón said that she was called Likoridis and was the mother of his own mother, Elínborg. From such things one may note what a wise and perceptive man Eiríkur was. A large group of other noblemen also accompanied them, though they are not named here. Jón also had the sons of many noble men on his side and their loyalty, though they themselves did not travel with him.

[XX]

Now we should tell how Roðbert and many other men are carried along by the water. There were also many who were carried out to sea, and a great number of men drowned there. But the earl started swimming, as did those men who were most capable, and headed for land. The earl also saved the lives of a great many men, and they all praised his courage.

And when all those whose lives could be saved had made it back to land, they headed back to the fortress. Many people who had seen the marvellous events came to meet them. The earl said that the men should hurry to the ships and sail after them. Everyone who can then hastens to the fleet which the earl had assembled for raiding. So many people came together that the earl had ten ships. They hoisted the sails and rowed off. But when they had come a short way from land, they suddenly saw that the ships were filling with sea-water below them. They then wanted to take in the sails, but that was not possible because there were strong gales. So they were carried a long way out to sea. The earl was then so raging and furious that he ordered them incessantly to keep up the chase, and it ended with the ships completely filling up, before they cut the stays and brought down the sails. And as a result of that some of the ships were capsized, because the sails got tangled up over the edge of the boat, but those which remained upright were destroyed due to the fact that it was impossible to bail all the sea-water out, and the inclement weather was so extreme blowing out from the coast that nobody could make it back against the weather.

Those ten ships were lost there, so that no man made it back to shore alive, except for Earl Roðbert. He dived under each breaker and headed back to land. Many men were waiting on the

---

[51] The text seems to be confused here. We have already been told (in chapter IX) that Jón's mother is named Likoridis, but here we are told that Likoridis is his grandmother, and his mother's name is Elínborg. Elínborg is the name of Eiríkur's mother, first mentioned in chapter I.

coast, and they all praised his courage, that he had made it alive out of that peril. The earl was very unhappy with how things had turned out: he had lost a great deal of manpower and was himself greatly weakened. Jón and Eiríkur's ships had also been lost from sight. Earl Roðbert now went home to the fortress and ordered his men to eat and drink and told them all to come to him in the morning in the fortress. That was done, but because the earl seemed angry to the people, and because it wasn't possible to know what he would do or how it would turn out, people were not quick to come and meet with the earl. He then has the people summoned all together in the fortress and asked good men to give him wise counsel about how to solve his predicament, 'and I have considered summoning all the people from the town, Aspis, because you have kinsmen, friends and relatives there who are yet to be seen.'

Everybody said that this was advisable, and moreover that the fortress would be at its strongest if it could count on the strength of the town, and a memorable loss of life would be the outcome for the party which was slow to take advantage of it. It was now agreed upon that a meeting would be called in the town.

[XXI]

Roðbert now has the people summoned to an assembly in the town, and a great many people are gathered. He called upon many people who lived nearby, and they had to travel over the big lakes which had poured out of the mountain, and it was late in the day before all of his troops managed to get anywhere, because all the ships which were moored at the fortress were damaged. Some people got hold of small boats or rafts and conveyed themselves to that place in such manner and navigated the currents around the strait on skiffs. Roðbert helped in whatever way he could, but it took a long time. The day was nearly over by the time the meeting was convened, but it was well-attended, because some people had to check on family members, and others on friends. But those men who had sworn loyalty to Jón were forbidden by him to attend the earl's assembly and came to no harm as a result, while the others, the townsmen and people from the countryside who had not been warned off, suffered greatly.

Now Roðbert stands up and says the following: 'Everybody is aware of the loss of life, livestock and wealth that we have been subjected to by the evil traitor named Eiríkur and the many people who have been accomplices in his plans. Nor is it unknown to you how I treated him well, and how he deceived me and said he wanted to give me gifts and proceeded with many fair and treacherous words, which were later laid bare when he took those two treasures from me, the likes of which have never been possessed. One of them was the helmet Ægir, and the other the sword Sigurvandil. Nothing could withstand its blow, and whoever wielded it was always assured of victory. But you cannot be told of all the characteristics of the helmet. He also had in his possession a treasure which was stolen from me ten years ago, the ring Gáinn, and that man who wears it can never be taken unawares.

'Then he made the waters come crashing down on us from the mountain, and along with them the ship upon which was the beautiful Marsilia. And I saw her clearly where she was sitting on the canopied deck as well as Elínborg, her mother. I also saw there a man who I believed to be dead. He has moreover been the cause of all of this treachery and has been the brains behind it. You are also aware that they drowned all of those people who had assembled there, so that only a few escaped with me. And when we made it to dry land, we took ten ships and sailed after them, but didn't notice that they were damaged on account of our great anger. And every last man drowned there, but I alone made it back to land. Now there is no seaworthy ship anchored at the fortress. I was made to feel the loss of my companion instead, since the beautiful and noble Marsilia was gone, and you all have lost kinsmen and friends and untold wealth. I will never know happiness until I get her back. And yet though I have suffered greatly, you have lost even more: kinsmen and friends, wives and children and all kinds of treasures. You will not soon forget this sorrowful parting—and tell me, what man has wrought greater evil in this land? But now I ask of you all—soldiers, townsmen and all my countrymen—since we are in a most difficult position, that you all grant me your trust and support to avenge this insult and wrong which has been commited upon us. I now ask all of you that you give me good advice in this, but I will be your leader in such matters. Were it my decision, we would immediately go and raid Gaul and burn and torch everything, because I stake my life on it that this shall be avenged.'

His speech was well-received by all the people. They said that it was necessary to avenge the wrongs that had been done to them and all the destruction that had been wrought on that land, but they said that there were no warships ready in that place, and all the others which they knew of were nothing but cogs and merchant vessels, not appropriate for making war. It could be discerned by their words that the men of the town wanted to dissuade the attempt to go raiding that summer by listing the difficulties associated with it, and they considered them to be significant. Then the common people stood up and everyone else with them and ruled out the possibility of making an expedition abroad that summer. They said that this revenge would have been appropriate to carry out, were it not for the fact that it would be even more harshly repaid. They all guessed that Jón must be alive and that he had been the cause of these deeds. They remembered then all of the good will that Earl Svipdagur had shown to them. They also said that he had no hope of support that summer. That having been said many of the men of the fortress went away. The people were much less eager to give Earl Roðbert any help at that time.

Now the earl sees that the people of that land have turned away from him. He now discusses with his friends what he should do. They come to the agreement that he should carry out the expedition the following summer and win friends to his cause over the whole country by means of costly gifts. Earl Roðbert now sees that people will not be subservient to him in other lands, if he travels with a small host, when they deny him support in his own kingdom. The assembly is now broken up, with the expedition planned for the following summer. The waters from the mountains had by that time receded so much that it was possible to traverse that place on horseback. Let us now leave Earl Roðbert to sit and scheme.

[XXII]

Now we must tell how Eiríkur and Jón had fair winds. They came with their ships to Gaul and come to rest in the royal anchorage. Nothing was covered in cloths that weren't furs, nor were there any sails but silk ones. Their arrival was quite magnificent, because the weather was calm, and the sun shone on the dragon-head. Everything was covered in gold, and the ships were painted in a tasteful manner above the sea-line. The poop-deck on the warship was draped in white fur.

Now King Vilhjálmur is told that his son, Eiríkur, has arrived back in the country. He then had all the people summoned together out of the fortress to meet him. A very joyful reunion ensued, and the king invited them home to a lavish feast and to stay with him, along with all their men, as long as they wanted. They accepted that offer. The king himself and Queen Elínborg went to meet Marsilia and her mother. All men marvelled at her beauty and attractiveness and excellent courtly manners, because nobody thought they had seen her like. The king placed them in the high-seats beside him, and there was no lack of fine dainties or varied entertainments. Eiríkur then announced his proposal, and asked for Marsilia's hand in marriage. Jón and his mother responded favourably to his request and said that it would be fitting, since he had put his life in jeopardy on account of their tribulations. An agreement was reached that Marsilia should be married to Eiríkur on the condition that he should go raiding to Jón's inherited lands with him and get together an army for that purpose and not leave until Roðbert had been killed.

The feast was then prepared, with no expense spared, and there was no person who was not invited. There was no shortage of the finest men, whom Eiríkur invited from all over the land, all earls and noblemen, who were thought to be the most distinguished. Jón was also accompanied by many men who had been the most respected at his father's court in the kingdom of Hólmgarður. And there was no lack of provisions. And when the guests were sitting there enjoying themselves, Jón had a seat fetched and sat down on it and told the whole story about how Earl Roðbert toppled his father from the kingdom and how he wanted to kill him and what help had been forthcoming and which bay he had rowed out into to find him. He brought forth the sword, the helmet and the ring, and explained their characteristics, and everybody praised them and spoke well of the feast and of the good fortune that they had been able to escape from their hardships. At the feast Jón gave all the possessions, which Roðbert had taken from them, back to Rodgeir and Rogerus and all the noblemen, if they should accept him as the sole leader over the country. He and Eiríkur gave impressive gifts to all the men, and they promised to give him their support. The wedding lasted half a month, and nobody remembered having been witness to such a feast. No men were now considered worthy of such high renown as the foster-brothers.

[XXIII]

Summer now passes by, as does winter, and spring arrives. Jón comes to speak with Eiríkur and asked him whether he wanted to make good on his promise, 'because it seems to me that you have thought very little about it, but instead embrace your wife joyfully and light-heartedly.'

Eiríkur says that sixty fully-prepared ships were moored off the coast, but said that he intended to get another sixty from a levy. Jón thanked him for his support and said that it would be sufficient if they had sixty ships. He said that most of the people of that land would be turned to his cause. Eiríkur said that he had heard rumours that Earl Roðbert wanted to send out a levy and said that he would prefer to have a greater force at his command than the people of that country. They had one hundred and twenty ships. Accompanying them on the expedition was Marsilia the beautiful and all those men who had left Hólmgarður with Jón. But King Vilhjálmur and his queen remained behind and they parted with Jón with much affection.

Now we should tell how Earl Roðbert had a rampart and moat built around the fortress Kastella, so great that they could not be crossed, and he filled the moat with water. He also had improvements made to the fortress walls, where they were broken. Then he had each of the gateways into the fortress sealed with iron doors. Then he had supplies of water channelled into the fortress so that he could be not conquered by means of fire or weapons. He then also had an extremely strong tower constructed out of the hardest bricks. It was so high that from it one might see across the whole of the land and far out to sea, if enemies were attacking. Earl Roðbert had had that tower built for the eventuality that if the fortress was taken, he might defend himself from the tower. This tower was made with such great craftsmanship, that no man could devise how it might be taken. Men say that the stone wall was sixty fathoms high and eighty fathoms from one side to the other and ten fathoms thick. Up on the stone rampart a marvellous tower was to be found with polished glass windows adorned all over with gold and silver, as much as was deemed tasteful, carved and engraved both outside and in with marvellous artesanry. Up on the tower was a weathervane, and attached to it a flag of gold-woven fur with a coat-of-arms upon it. The tower was circular inside and had wooden steps curled up it like a sea-snail shell, and that was how one came up. Earl Roðbert slept there each night with one hundred men. He had had work begun on these constructions as soon as spring came, while Jón and Eiríkur were away, and proceeded with it throughout the summer and the winter to arrive at this point. He did it because he did not want to rest everything on the men of that country, because he thought they would be unreliable if Jón were to arrive. They were now three nights away from all of Earl Roðbert's troops arriving in the fortress Kastella, those who were expected to respond to the levy. That troop was better inclined to Jón, son of Svipdagur, than to Earl Roðbert.

[XXIV]

Now we must turn to Eiríkur and Jón. They had favourable winds, and nobody spied them en route. They are now one night's sailing away from Hólmgarður, three nights before Earl Roðbert's army is supposed to enter the fortress, Kastella. Then Jón asked Eiríkur whether he preferred to besiege the fortress and risk having Earl Roðbert fight against them, or take the town, so that the earl should have no hope of support from that direction, 'because people will be wary of us after having suffered so greatly on our account'.

Eiríkur chose to besiege the fortress, 'but I think that our advantage in numbers, should the earl choose to fight, will not be too great.'

They now separate their forces. Jón rushed into the town with his troop. The men of the town had arrayed themselves in battle ranks and armed themselves, and there was some resistance. But since Jón had a fine and large troop, things quickly went badly for the men of the town. Jón pushed ahead and struck out on both sides, and all fell back before him. It ended up with everyone submitting to Jón and pledging themselves to him. It is said that that night Earl Roðbert had gone to the toilet. He had seen out from the window that a fleet of ships had arrived in that land and a large army was approaching the fortress and the battle in the town. He then ordered that the people of the fortress be woken up and told all men to arm themselves, since 'we are not so superior in might compared to this group of people who have come here. Let's prepare ourselves boldly, and let's turn the tables before the town has been won, and they come to their support.' And now Earl Roðbert rides out of the fortress with all of his troops.

[XXV]

Now Eiríkur sees that the earl, the king with his troops, wants to fight. Fierce battle now breaks out. Earl Roðbert had a greater army, and he himself was right in the vanguard: he now urges his men on. Eiríkur fought and was particularly brave. He lashed out in all directions, revealing his valour. And it ended with the earl's ranks falling back behind the fortress wall. Earl Roðbert also now sees where Jón rides with his large troop and recognises him clearly — he had the helmet Ægir on his head and the sword Sigurvandil in his hand — and he is pretty sure now that the town has been won. He calls out now with a booming voice that the men should flee into the fortress and defend their lives. It ended with him and his troop making it into the fortress in spite of tough opposition. The gates of the fortress were then locked behind them. Eiríkur had pressed such a fierce attack that some of the men of the fortress had retreated into the moats which had been excavated around the fortress, and had drowned in them.

They now pitch their war-tents on the level plains around the fortress. They attack the fortress for three days, but make no headway. Nor can any man come up with a way to take the fortress, be it with catapults or other war-machines. Jón then seeks the advice of his men on how the fortress should be taken, but nobody could provide a solution.

Jón then speaks: 'It is my advice that every man should take a bundle of wood from the forest, because that will not arouse suspicions among the men of the fortress, and take it to his tent. Half of our army shall do that, while the other half shall attack the fortress. They will think that it is our firewood. There are now only three nights until Earl Roðbert will have summoned all of the men of the land to this place, and then we will be outnumbered.'[52]

The day passes and evening comes. The peace-shield was then raised. And when Jón's men had eaten and drunk, Eiríkur told them to put on their armour. Once they were convinced that the people of the fortress were asleep, they took out their bundles of wood and carry them to the moat. The army then crossed over this bridge. Jón now arrives at the gates of the fortress and hews the lock off with the sword, Sigurvandil. And while he does this, Eiríkur brings down the drawbridges, which had been constructed across the moat. The army then proceeded across. These bridges were down during the day, when men needed to ride across or transport other items to the fortress, but they were hoisted up in the evening, and then no being had access to the fortress. The men of the fortress thought that such precautions would suffice, as they had on the previous nights, and so most of those who had been posted as lookouts went to sleep.

The men had a rude awakening to find that Jón had arrived there with his entire army. He placed Rogerus and Rodgeir in the vanguard, in case the men of the fortress should arm themselves. And he and Eiríkur now went with one thousand men to the quarters where Earl Roðbert had recently been sleeping, because Jón had gotten hold of wise men, who had been with the earl a short time previously in the fortress, and were familiar with all his tricks and the layout of his rooms. They found a passageway and went down it until they came into the tower and proceeded without making a sound. The tower was fitted with spiralling wooden platforms inside, and they walked on until they came to a wooden ceiling. A trapdoor was fitted into it, and it had a strong lock. Jón broke it open, and there were the sleeping quarters of Earl

---

[52] Again, there seems to be some confusion. When Jón and Eiríkur arrived there were apparently three nights until the reinforcements arrived. We have just been told that the fortress was attacked for three nights, which should mean that the reinforcements are now about to arrive. It may be that Jón's plan is supposed to have been devised in the meantime. In any case, the point is that there is a pressing need for a solution to be found.

Roðbert and his retainers. Jón ordered them all to be apprehended. He himself proceeded up the tower and into the upper part and went around all the sleeping chambers and could not find the earl. They then walked up to a room which had an iron door fixed into a marble wall, and it was locked also. Jón bashes the lock open and breaks the latches. The door then springs open. That chamber was completely draped in gold-embroidered woven fabrics. The earl was resting there and two lads beside him. Roðbert heard the crash when Jón smashed in the lock and woke from his sleep and grabbed his weapons. Immediately on entering the chamber, Jón and his men took hold of Earl Roðbert, because he did not have any sneaky escape plans, because he thought that none of his enemies would be able to get at him there. He did put up, however, a valiant defence, before he was apprehended, but it ended just as people say, that no one person can stand against the many.

[XXVI][53]

Now Eiríkur and Jón come down from the tower and have the earl, all tied up, with them as well as many other men. They came out into the streets, and there they found a large group of men from the fortress, because Rodgeir and Rogerus had arranged it thus with the men. And when they see Jón with the excellent helmet, Ægir, his size and beauty, and all the people serving him, and Roðbert tied up and defeated, as was fitting on account of his treachery, all the men of the fortress are won over to accepting Jón's authority, and many were very keen to do so, having previously served his father. And what Jón had achieved was considered to be quite something for a single night's work. The morning after he had everybody summoned to a huge assembly, and discusses there with his friends how Roðbert should meet his end, but an agreement could not be reached on that.

Jón then speaks: 'It is fitting that Roðbert should meet the same end that he dealt to Hringur and Eilífur as punishment for not killing me.'

They then had two fires made, and they tie Roðbert up in between them, and there he ended his life. Many people said that was a fitting end for him because of his treachery, and many people are of the opinion that there has never been a traitor equal to Roðbert. All the people from the whole country now submitted to Jón, including the army which had been intended to support Roðbert. Everybody was delighted with Jón, and people thought that he had been whisked out of the clutches of death, escaping from the many trials and mortal perils which he had found himself in and the many trials which he had been subjected to. Most men loved him dearly, especially those men who had served his father. And when it was thought that his power was perfectly assured, he discharges all of Eiríkur's troops, except for five ships, and gives marvellous gifts to all the chieftains in return for their support. On account of such things he became extremely popular, and all people wished him well.

On one occasion Jón comes to talk with Eiríkur and said that he wanted to travel across the sea to Greece and fulfill his promise to seek out the Holy Land. Eiríkur said that that was a good plan. They now had the journey prepared in most elegant style, both with ships and weapons, and Rodgeir and Rogerus would be in charge of the defence of the land in the meantime. They now head first to Miklagarður, because they thought it was the most opulent

---

[53] In this chapter, although Konráður and Roðbert, according to *Konráðs saga keisarasonar*, are childhood friends, it seems strange that Konráður would be angry on account of Roðbert's death considering all the betrayals that he was subjected to at Roðbert's hands. Perhaps the sworn brotherhood that united them prevents him from openly revelling in his enemy's downfall.

place to visit. King Konráður, son of Emperor Ríkarður, was there. The king welcomes them with joy and affection and sent them on their way with excellent gifts, because the emperor, his father, had written to him so that he would not be angry with them about the killing of Earl Roðbert, given the necessity that drove them to avenge the wrongs done to them.

[XXVII]

Now Jón and Eiríkur sail to the Land of the Saxons, and Jón captained the warship which he had built inside the mountain, and Eiríkur the other warship which he had had made, which was the greatest of treasures. Marsilia the beautiful accompanied them on the journey, and their convoy was exquisitely decked out. They came to land exactly where they would have chosen to. Konráður was at that time also in the Land of the Saxons, having come to have his son, Vilhjálmur, crowned as the emperor of the Land of the Saxons. And when the father and son came to know that there were ships moored there, they guess that some noble and renowned men must have arrived in the country and they go to meet them with peaceful and hospitable intent, inviting them again to their home for a sumptuous feast. Jón and his companions remained there until the consecration of the emperor took place. Then Jón and Eiríkur and Marsilia received baptism and the true faith, along with all of their men. And all men praised their good fortune. They recognised then that Jón and Eiríkur were from the most noble families. And after the feast they went to the kings and thanked them for their nobility with fine words and said that they intended to visit King Hlöðver, Eiríkur's paternal grandfather. And King Konráður and his son, the emperor, happily gave them leave and in addition excellent gifts and their friendship.

Then they sailed to France and met King Hlöðver. He welcomes Eiríkur, his kinsman, with pomp and distinction, and does likewise with all the others. The king and everyone else think that they are paragons among men, on account of their strength, wisdom, beauty and all their accomplishments. King Hlöðver was always organising jousts, throwing and swimming contests and other sports. Eiríkur always proved himself to be the best knight and excelled in all sports. Jón, however, could not contend against another man on account of his strength and manliness. He thus easily took the victory in all sports, throwing and swimming contests, tournaments and all the other pursuits which were customarily enjoyed there.

[XXVIII]

It is not mentioned how long they were there, but what is mentioned is that they were sent on their way with noble gifts and pomp. From there they sailed to Flanders. They were received most warmly there. Jón learned that King Philippus, his maternal grandfather, was dead, and his son had taken on the rule of the kingdom. But this young king had not heard news about Jón from the kingdom of Hólmgarður for a long time, and when Jón told him everything that had happened to him, and how it had ended, there was a joyful reunion between them. And he thought that Jón had providence on his side, given that he had been able to extricate himself from as grave and as many sufferings as he had been subjected to. They stayed there for the winter enjoying great hospitality. And when summer came they asked to return home and were sent on their way with many excellent gifts and great words of praise, and they part ways the best of friends.

They now set sail, and nothing is said of their journey before they arrive in the kingdom of Hólmgarður. Men now see their fleet approaching from the fortress, before they arrive at their anchorage. Nothing was draped with cloth other than fur and silk and gold-woven fabric, and all the warships were painted above the sea-line in a most tasteful way. And when the people of the country knew that the foster-brothers had arrived, they hurried to welcome them with all the worthiness and honour which they could muster. And when Jón had been home only a short while, he sends out a message to the whole kingdom that every man capable of riding a horse and able to take his drink shall come to meet him in a month's time. In addition he sends Rogerus and Rodgeir to the supreme king in Hólmgarður and asks for his daughter's hand in marriage for Jón. Time passes until the stipulated month, leading up to the assembly, has passed, and the appointed day arrives. Many common people and huge crowds come to the fortress, Kastella, in droves. And at the same time Jón's messengers return bearing the message that the foster-brothers should attend Jón's wedding with all their noble vassals in the capital city. And after receiving this news they go to the assembly, where Jón is made chieftain over all of that kingdom which his father had ruled. Once that was done Jón asked all the lords and chieftains and governors within the kingdom and all the common people to abide by Christian law and worship God. And at the foster-brothers' beseeching, everybody agreed to submit themselves to that faith and the rule of those laws, as Jón so desired it to be arranged, and thus the meeting was adjourned.

[XXIX]

Then Jón once more calls all the noble people of the kingdom to him and announces to them once again that he will attend his wedding, and invites all the nobles to accompany him. They then prepare for the journey, five hundred men strong, and all of them equipped with fine weapons and clothes and horses. They proceed without stopping until they come to the kingdom of Hólmgarður, where they are welcomed with all the honour and hospitality which it is conceivable to show in this world, since they receive an invitation from the supreme king and are taken to the most sumptuous hall which there was in the city, and so began an excellent feast. Jón then restates his proposal, and asks for the princess' hand in marriage, which was not difficult for him to attain, because all men can see what a paragon among men Jón is, and thus perceived and understood his magnanimity, him being all the wiser on account of his abundance of refined senses. Jón was then united in marriage with the princess accordingly as established by the laws and just process of the land. The feast was then extended, and Jón made toasts in response to his wedding to the princess with much honour and distinction. On the second day of the feast the king has people summoned to an assembly in the city, and at that meeting he gives a long and wise speech, thanks all his most loyal men, who had stood by him throughout his whole reign, and said that he was now bent over with age and had one daughter as his heir, who stood to inherit his legacy and wealth, and she was married to the man whom he knew to be most noble in that land, 'and so now I will give,' said the king, 'the kingdom to Jón, and he shall be called king, and I entreat one and all, the rich and the poor, to be loyal and faithful to him, subservient and good-willed, like brave lords to a true king.' The king ended his speech with everybody pledging their full allegiance to Jón. Kings and dukes, barons and earls, submitted to Jón and swore loyalty to him, and afterwards knights and nobles, and last all of the common people. And thus the assembly ended. But the wedding feast continued for half a month, and once it was over King Jón gave excellent gifts to everybody as befitted their rank. King Jón then gave Rodgeir and Rogerus the earldom which he had inherited from his father, and Jón was now the supreme king over the entire kingdom of Hólmgarður and had many children with his queen, and all those who were descended from him became the most distinguished men. And as far as Eiríkur is concerned it can be told that he heads home to Gaul, sent on his way by King Jón with excellent treasures befitting of royalty, and when he arrives home his father, the king, and the queen are overjoyed. And a little later King Vilhjálmur dies. Eiríkur then takes over the rule of the kingdom, and all men said that he was the most fitting person to do so in those lands, both on account of his lineage and prowess and great authority. He and Marsilia had two sons, the one named Vilhjálmur after his father, and the other Svipdagur after the earl, who was her own and Jón's father. And thus we end the story of Jón, son of Svipdagur, and Eiríkur the Curious.

REVIEWS

Geraldine Barnes, *The Bookish Riddarasögur: Writing Romance in Late Mediaeval Iceland*. The Viking Collection 21. Odense: University Press of Southern Denmark, 2014. 211 pp. ISBN 978-87-7674-791-6.

A new English-language monograph on the literary merits of medieval Icelandic romance is long overdue. It is not since Marianne Kalinke's *Bridal-Quest Romance in Medieval Iceland* (1990) that a substantial group of these texts has been discussed at length. Now, eighty years after the publication of Margaret Schlauch's pioneering study *Romance in Iceland* (1934), this new book by Geraldine Barnes is a welcome addition to the still small — but growing — body of work on the genre. Promising to provide 'readings of a group of *riddarasögur* which, in their debts to encyclopaedic writings and historical thought can [...] be called "bookish" ' (27–28), the monograph focuses on the romances written in medieval Iceland for Icelanders — the so-called indigenous *riddarasögur*, in contrast to those translated from other medieval European languages. The book's introduction offers a brief historiography of these non-translated *riddarasögur* as a whole, and alerts the reader to the various types of learned material that the romance authors drew on in their composition, from the early encyclopaedic work of Isidore of Seville, to the Old Testament history written in *Stjórn*, to the widely disseminated *Speculum Historiale* of Vincent de Beauvais.

Barnes's study comprises five chapters, which discuss a group of *riddarasögur*, each text in its turn, from different thematic perspectives. The first of these, 'Mapping and Measuring the World', considers *Nitida saga*, *Victors saga ok Blávus*, and *Vilhjálms saga sjóðs*, and reveals ways in which these three romances draw on encyclopaedic material to demonstrate different understandings of world geography. The three medieval continents of Asia, Africa, and Europe, and the four cardinal directions, feature as organising principles in these romances, but the way in which each manifests this is different. Barnes shows how *Nitida saga* takes the conventional medieval understanding of the three parts of the world and upends it into a 'counter cosmography' (p. 35) that makes the author's northern homeland central, and likewise, how in *Victors saga ok Blávus* the three regions of the world represented by the romance's three main characters — Victor (Europe), Blávus (Africa), and the maiden-king Fulgida (Asia) — are used in a text that ultimately comprises 'a northern framework and a northern centre', playing on the popular *translatio studii et imperii* topos (p. 45). In the chapter's final section, the fastidious and chiefly geographical facts and measurements described throughout *Vilhjálms saga sjóðs* are shown to form an important part of its dual framework of learned material and other *riddarasögur*; the text arguably assumes that its audience is 'well positioned to appreciate [its] comic intertextuality' (p. 52).

Chapter 2, 'The Boundaries of Knowledge', takes *Dínus saga dramblát*a, *Kirialax saga*, and *Clári saga* as its focus, showcasing discussion of the use and abuse of learning and knowledge in each case. Barnes shows how in *Dínus saga dramblát*a a guide for the appropriate use of worldly knowledge and curiosity, rooted in patristic theology (p. 58), is ignored by the rival protagonists Dínus and Philotemia, who in their desire to outwit each other suffer the unfavourable consequences of what is depicted as unnatural curiosity and prideful vanity. Contrasting with this are then discussions of *Kirialax saga*, which takes a licit desire for knowledge and understanding of creation as the basis for the protagonist's quest (pp. 66ff.), and *Clári saga*, which, while showing its characters to be learned yet curious, does not make this a feature of the romance (p. 75). Barnes reads *Dínus saga dramblát*a and *Clári saga* (notable as one of the earliest *riddarasögur*) against each other in particular, and argues that they may 'be considered in the context of the development of late medieval Icelandic romance as two ends of a broad compositional spectrum — from relatively straightforward exemplum in [*Clári saga* ...], to the structural and ethical complexity' on display in *Dínus saga dramblát*a (p. 76).

Chapter 3, 'The March of History', centres on *Saulus saga ok Nikanors*, *Ectors saga*, *Vilhjálms saga sjóðs*, and *Adonias saga* to show how both an awareness of and a concern for world history and written historical sources is evident in many Icelandic romances. Barnes begins by discussing how some *riddarasögur* use the motif of inscriptions, especially on walls, as an important means of transmitting history, as a notable feature among the romances that claim such ancient inscriptions as verifiable sources for the stories they tell. Similarly, we are shown in a brief section called 'ekphrasis and memory' how the legend of Troy also features prominently in many *riddarasögur*, as a part of this desire to acknowledge and build upon the past. In the individual discussions of the four romances featured in this chapter we see the role that Troy plays in each, as part of the 'images of the past, as both word and picture, [which] serve as inspiration for the present' authors and readers in medieval Iceland (p. 111).

Chapter 4, 'Defending Christendom', looks at five romances: *Jarlmanns saga ok Hermanns*, *Kirialax saga*, *Saulus saga ok Nikanors*, *Sigurðar saga þögla*, and *Rémundar saga keisarasonar*. The chapter considers how images of crusading, the Christian knight, and conversion appear in many *riddarasögur*, and particular attention is paid to *Rémundar saga keisarasonar*, in which, Barnes shows, 'a model of crusader knighthood is explicitly articulated' (p. 145). We see how this longest of all *riddarasögur* draws on an array of learned material and other sources not only incidentally to enhance the story it tells (as some other romances seem to do), but to present a detailed picture of a Christian understanding of the world and the place of the questing crusader knight within it. Discussions of the other four texts in this chapter similarly illuminate the different ways in which each romance incorporates religious aspects into its setting, characters, and plot: we see how *Jarlmanns saga ok Hermanns* and *Saulus saga ok Nikanors* can be seen as a pair with similar themes, and how an episode in *Kirialax saga* draws on a 'typical [...] Christian-heathen engagement [from the genre of the] chanson de geste' (p. 124).

Chapter 5, 'Sailing to Byzantium', focuses on six romances, three of which were not already discussed in earlier chapters: *Dámusta saga*, *Bærings saga*, and *Sigrgarðs saga ok Valbrands*. Barnes discusses the history of the negative understanding of Constantinople and the Byzantine Empire in western European medieval romance due largely to the schism of

1054, failed crusades, and the sack of Constantinople in 1204 (pp. 147–51); contrasting with this, we are then shown the largely positive understanding of the same people and places in medieval Scandinavian thought, through earlier Old Norse sagas and historical or encyclopaedic works (pp. 151–58). In the section 'Constantinople in the *riddarasögur*' Barnes draws on examples from a range of late medieval Icelandic romances to show how they 'serve the common purpose of extolling the magnificence of Constantinople' (p. 158). The chapter ends with separate sections dedicated to *Sigrgarðs saga ok Valbrands* (pp. 171–76) and *Kirialax saga* (pp. 176–81), which both provide particularly illuminating and celebratory depictions of the Byzantine Empire.

The book ends with a brief conclusion, 'Profiling the Audience', which considers the afterlife of the *riddarasögur* through the genre's (chiefly post-Reformation) manuscript tradition. Beginning with an overview of the types of medieval audiences that may have enjoyed these romances at the time of their composition, Barnes argues that the authors of the late medieval Icelandic romances may have been 'a coterie of writers, familiar with each other's work and likely to be writing as much for their peers as for their anonymous patrons' (p. 183). Barnes then considers post-Reformation audiences, for which there is far more evidence due to the continued tradition of manuscript production. The manuscript evidence of *Dínus saga drambláta* with its three redactions is considered, as a largely representative case study on the audiences and enduring popularity of an Icelandic romance into the centuries after the end of the Middle Ages. The bibliography, separated into editions, translations, and dictionaries on the one hand, and secondary sources on the other, covers most of the bases, though Barnes modestly omits references to any of her own work, of which there is much relevant material. The volume unfortunately lacks an index; however, a listing of sagas in each chapter title, along with running headings indicating the saga under discussion on each page, attempt to compensate for this shortcoming. Overall, this is an important new work that can provide the basis for many future discussions of medieval Icelandic romance. The range of *riddarasögur* covered is impressive, although this does sometimes leave the reader wanting more in the way of discussion and analysis at the end of certain sections on individual texts. While in some cases the depth of analysis may have been sacrificed for its breadth, this leaves the book an excellent starting point for more detailed work by others; indeed, Barnes gladly acknowledges that she has here 'barely touched the surface of a group of sagas only just beginning to come under close scrutiny as individual works of literary narrative' (p. 191). Particularly as a study in English, *The Bookish Riddarasögur: Writing Romance in Late Mediaeval Iceland* opens up the genre to a wide audience, and perhaps especially to students, and experts from related fields, who may not be able to read these still largely untranslated romances for themselves.

SHERYL McDONALD WERRONEN UNIVERSITY OF COPENHAGEN

Carolyn P. Collette, *Rethinking Chaucer's 'Legend of Good Women'*. York: York Medieval Press, 2014. 184 pp. ISBN 9781903153499.

In *Rethinking Chaucer's 'Legend of Good Women'*, Carolyn Collette, Emeritus Professor of English Language and Literature at Mount Holyoke College and a research associate at the University of York's Centre for Medieval Studies, considers how to approach a poem that has 'seemed to annoy or bore' present-day readers. She argues that, in order to view the *Legend* as more than an anomalous 'puzzle' that struggles to find its place within the broader corpus of Chaucer's work, it is necessary to change fundamentally the methodologies used to analyse it. Rather than examining its sources or reception, Collette sees the poem as part of the broader literary, philosophical, and ethical culture of fourteenth-century Europe in order to argue that the *Legend* deserves recognition as an essential step in the development of Chaucer's poetic corpus.

The book is divided into five main sections, each of which aims to situate the *Legend* within both Chaucer's œuvre and their broader cultural context. The first chapter focuses on the importance of books to the early humanism of Edward III's court and how such 'bibliophilia' may have influenced Chaucer's own creative approach to existing texts. The second explores retellings of tales of 'exemplary women' and argues that Chaucer's heroines in the *Legend* appear more 'radical' than their counterparts in the work of Gower, Boccaccio, and Christine de Pizan. The third section delves deeper into the Aristotelian ideas circulating in fourteenth-century Europe and how such concepts appear in the *Legend*. The fourth chapter compares the *Legend*'s portrayal of women's love with that of *Troilus and Criseyde*. The fifth and final section examines women who appear in the *Canterbury Tales* and argues that *Troilus*, the *Legend*, and the *Tales* constitute a progression from the tragic to the comic. Collette's argument thus both encompasses and moves beyond the *Legend* in its exploration of Chaucer's work as the product of a specific cultural milieu.

Collette's monograph provides an important and refreshing new perspective on one of Chaucer's less studied poetic works. She employs literary, linguistic, and historical analyses of a wide variety of texts in order to shed light on the *Legend* itself. Particularly interesting is the examination of Aristotelian ideas on love and moderation in relation to the *Legend* and other contemporary works. A thorough but accessible overview of these ideas as they appear in Nicole Oresme's fourteenth-century translations of the *Politics* and *Ethics* forms the basis for a convincing account of how Chaucer builds upon the works in the *Legend*. The comparison of the *Legend*'s presentation of Aristotelian concepts with that of *Troilus and Criseyde* strengthens this point further through demonstrating that the *Legend*, far from being an isolated work, is central to understanding Chaucer's innovations within a specific literary and philosophical tradition.

Despite the book's generally clear and concise arguments, some stylistic factors occasionally make points hard to follow. While most longer quotations in French and Latin are translated into English, some are not, presenting a potential challenge for those unfamiliar with either language. Additionally, at times quotations from Chaucer's work seem overly long, with little close analysis given over to many of the lines. That said, most of the examples used are judiciously chosen and contribute to the book's overall argument.

Rethinking Chaucer's Legend of Good Women provides a welcome opportunity to consider Chaucer's poem — and his other poetic works — in a seldom-discussed way. Accessible and relatively short, it paves the way for further work on Chaucer's less 'popular' works as innovative products of their time.

PELIA WERTH   UNIVERSITY OF LEEDS

Reviews

Reconsidering Gender, Time and Memory in Medieval Culture, ed. by Elizabeth Cox, Liz Herbert McAvoy and Roberta Magnani. Gender in the Middle Ages 10. Cambridge: Brewer, 2015. xii + 203 pp. ISBN 978-1-843-84403-7.

The book under review is a collection of ten essays (plus an introduction) that sets out explicitly to reconsider what might be identified as three of the most popular (and perhaps also most controversial) subjects in contemporary Medieval Studies. In her introduction (pp. 1–12), '*In principio*: The Queer Matrix of Gender, Time and Memory in the Middle Ages', Liz Herbert McAvoy offers a brief methodological reassessment of the relationship(s) between gender, time and memory — the book's three designated focal areas — that invokes, and in some regards revisits, prominent cornerstones of established scholarship. With regard to gender and time (as well as space), Herbert McAvoy centres her discussion around the works of Carolyn Dinshaw, Judith Halberstam and Luce Irigaray, as well as canonical texts such as Michel Foucault's 'Des Espaces Autres'. Turning to memory, she provides a (re-)reading of Augustine's famous passage on the 'past-ness' of memory (*Confessions* IX.14) that draws upon the seminal work of Mary Carruthers in order to 'challenge the absolute homogeneity of identities as generated alchemically through the interplay of gender, time and memory' (p. 7). This questioning of traditional notions of homogeneity also sets the stage (and tone) for the book's subsequent chapters, which are deliberately organised, not chronologically, but in terms of the human (female) life-cycle.

Amongst the book's ten chapters, particularly outstanding are those by Patricia Skinner and Anne E. Bailey. The fact that I concentrate on these two here should, however, by no means be taken as an indication of negativity towards the other contributions, since it is only due to lack of space that I do not consider them all in turn. Skinner (Chapter 1, pp. 13–28) opens 'The Pitfalls of Linear Time: Using the Medieval Female Life-Cycle as an Organizing Strategy' by presenting compelling evidence to support her key argument that linearity is an idealised illusion with regard to how medieval people experienced their own lifetime. Rather, she contends, we should perceive of medieval lives (and women's lives in particular) as cyclical experiences, which, in turn, generated cyclical memory media. Whilst this suggestion is not unprecedented, Skinner's contribution offers new and important evidence. Her nuanced reflection on a wide range of relevant sources, ranging from the ninth to the fifteenth centuries, lends additional credibility and substance to the argument, whilst also advocating terminological flexibility and interdisciplinary negotiation. Bailey's 'Gendered Discourses of Time and Memory in the Cult and Hagiography of William of Norwich' (Chapter 7, pp. 111–26) offers a case study on the cult and hagiography of William of Norwich, which claims additional significance by adding examples of Latin hagiography (and arguably history) to a volume of essays that concerns itself, first and foremost, with works of vernacular literature. Through an analysis of these Latin texts (namely *The Life and Miracles of St William of Norwich* by Thomas of Monmouth) in the light of concepts and terminologies such as those developed by Sherry Ortner, Caroline Walker Bynum and Claude Lévi-Strauss, Bailey demonstrates that medieval memories of the dead were constructed and consumed differently by men and women, thus pointing to distinct and gender-specific narrative strategies.

Overall, this is an accomplished book that engages with a wide range of perspectives and sources, literary texts in particular, including works written in Old and Middle English, Old French and to some extent Latin. In putting together the list of chapters and contributors, the editors deserve additional credit for achieving a healthy balance between established academics and early-career researchers, thereby providing the volume with originality and momentum. There can be no doubt that the book was inspired by interdisciplinarity and dialogue between different academic fields. Yet one might wish for a somewhat more consistent effort to combine literary and historical studies (the latter being represented mainly by Bailey, Skinner, and Fiona Harris-Stoertz's contribution 'Remembering Birth in Thirteenth- and Fourteenth-Century England'). All in all, however, this is a fine volume that delivers on its promise by encouraging the reader to reconsider his/her conceptions of gender, time and memory in the Middle Ages.

    BENJAMIN POHL   UNIVERSITY OF BRISTOL

Also published by *Leeds Studies in English* is the occasional series:

LEEDS TEXTS AND MONOGRAPHS

(ISSN 0075-8574)

Recent volumes include:

Approaches to the Metres of Alliterative Verse, edited by Judith Jefferson and Ad Putter (2009), iii + 311 pp.

The Heege Manuscript: a facsimile of NLS MS Advocates 19.3.1, introduced by Phillipa Hardman (2000), 60 + 432pp.

The Old English Life of St Nicholas with the Old English Life of St Giles, edited by E. M. Treharne (1997) viii + 218pp.

Concepts of National Identity in the Middle Ages, edited by Simon Forde, Lesley Johnson and Alan V. Murray (1995) viii + 213pp.

A Study and Edition of Selected Middle English Sermons, by V. M. O'Mara (1994) xi + 245pp.

Notes on 'Beowulf', by P. J. Cosijn, introduced, translated and annotated by Rolf H. Bremmer Jr, Jan van den Berg and David F. Johnson (1991) xxxvi + 120pp.

Úr Dölum til Dala: Guðbrandur Vigfússon Centenary Essays, edited by Rory McTurk and Andrew Wawn (1989) x + 327pp.

Staging the Chester Cycle, edited by David Mills (1985) vii + 123pp.

The Gawain Country: Essays on the Topography of Middle English Poetry, by R. W. V. Elliot (1984) 165pp.

For full details of this series, and to purchase volumes, or past numbers of *Leeds Studies in English*, please go to <http://www.leeds.ac.uk/lse>.

www.ingramcontent.com/pod-product-compliance
Lightning Source LLC
Chambersburg PA
CBHW080940300426
44115CB00017B/2893